The Art of Fulfilling Your Nature

The Art of Fulfilling Your Nature

AN ANTHOLOGY

Justin O'Brien, PhD
(Swami Jaidev Bharati)

The Art of Fulfilling Your Nature

For permission requests email the publisher, The Wanderer's Journey
thewanderersjourney108@gmail.com

Library of Congress Control Number: 2022908955

ISBN: 979-8-9865022-1-2 Paper
ISBN: 979-8-9865022-0-5 Hardcover
ISBN: 979-8-9865022-2-9 e-book

Editors and proofreaders: Nandini Avery and Katie Sheehan
Cover design, interior layout, and typesetting by Paul Nylander | Illustrada
Front cover photo by Brad Armstrong
Back cover photo by Nandini of Swami Jaidev hiking in the Himalayas

Published by The Wanderer's Journey
Saint Paul, Minnesota

"When you are in the world, be in the world. You love to be in your head, your contemplation. No, I want you in the world. Get in here thoroughly. Find out what it's all about so that you become fearless in there and deal with all the unpredictability."

Then he added the icing, "When you understand the world for what it is, what it's all about, you will have the freedom that most people will never know exists."

— As told to Justin
by Swami Rama

Contents

Contents

Preface

THE FLASH

Suddenly, for a moment, it shown. A kind of illumina-
tion, all of society forged as a surreal bureaucracy. At
first, it both repelled and fascinated me. What occurred
was not random, entertaining metaphors but the
incredible, connected range of cultural institutions, civil,
federal, and religious, especially with their multiple,
coercive resources, military bodies, policies, laws,
ordinances, celebrations, social rules, and penalties that
are projected upon citizens, all united together.

It wasn't any particular fact or any evaluation of them
as good or bad, right or wrong, that aroused my enthrall-
ment. It was the simplicity of the compelling way these
bureaucratic segments govern our lives with such preten-
tious formality that issues into nothing less than domi-
nation. At the same time, the insight expanded into how
society accedes, in an uncritical, surreal co-dependency
rally, to the status quo.

A VAST SCENE IN ALASKA

A mountain range and lowlands . . . it startled me by its attractiveness . . . I was drawn into seeing it . . . even compelled . . . did not want the experience to end . . . felt completely enthralled . . . strangely pleasant . . . and a feeling of lightness . . . time and my bodily feelings slightly slowed down . . . no other desires . . . I just wanted to behold the beauty as a whole and in its individual features as my eyes slowly surveyed the terrain . . . from the start a gentle sense of increased, supple, vitality . . . flashes of spontaneous questions arose: could I endure this for long times . . . would I want to pull back from it . . . does it get more expansive, richer, whatever that means . . . could I bear this kind of reality, not in memory, but somehow as a cognitive background, as it were, without any loss, in my aware-ness, and still engage daily life . . . could I remain in its presence forever . . . could this be a prelude to even more astonishing visions?"

— Justin O'Brien

The two experiences above, as recounted by Justin, show that it is possible to be unapologetically discerning of—and utterly awestruck by—the world in which we abide. Use this book as a guide to fulfill your human potential.

Nandini Avery
Katie Sheehan
Editors

Introduction

Swami Jaidev Bharati (Justin O'Brien, PhD, 1932–2021) was an exceptional man. He was a theologian college professor who left a university career to follow his Gurudev, Swami Rama of the Himalayas, and dedicate his life to discovering and teaching. I was one of the fortunate students that crossed his path. This book collects a sampling of poems, papers, talks, and lectures from throughout his life. His other well-known published works include *Walking with a Himalayan Master*, *Meeting of Mystic Paths*, and *The Wellness Tree*. He founded and served as spiritual director of the Institute of the Himalayan Tradition in St. Paul, Minnesota, although he taught and lectured globally on spirituality, holistic wellness, comparative religions, and the philosophy of consciousness.

His first-hand experience of growing to be a master (swami) in the Himalayan Tradition guided his writings and teaching. Perhaps the most ironic or surprising aspect of his teaching, being a former theology professor and a true jnana yogi, was his exceptional focus on being practical. While many of his writings, including here, showcase his brilliant mind, he always emphasized the most down-to-earth understanding—he was the opposite of lofty.

Once during a lecture at the Institute of the Himalayan Tradition he shared a dream in which his master, Swami Rama, was about to give him the next profound teaching. However, when Swami Rama

3

spoke, he only curtly said, "Do the dishes." This was exactly his style of spiritual teaching, focused on the real-world.

And so, while this book includes his virtuosic verse, his teachings are always relatively straight-forward and sensible. Keep your feet on the ground. Easy in the saddle. Practice wellness to stay healthy. You have a body, but you are more than the body. You have a mind, but you are more than the mind. You are the thinker, not the thoughts. Real life is only now, the rest is shrouded in unknowable mist. Do not be afraid of the world, be discerning of it. Get out into nature often, for it emits a radiance that empowers you. Enjoy a chai or a mocha with friends. And most importantly, love life!

I hope you enjoy reading the wisdom of Swami Jaidev. Knowing and learning from him has been a great blessing.

Andrew Johan Korsberg, May 2022

One | Explorations in Theology and Philosophy

The Voyage Begins

The voyage begins
Hidden alone in the night
My search for the Self.

With senses quiet
No comfort left in desire
My ego abandoned.

Motionless I sit
Awaiting the dawn again
Where's my hidden goal?

A barren calmness
Haunts my yearning awareness
With fallow fruit still.

My soul adrift on
A sea of dark clouds without
The stars to guide me.

An endless journey
This path of meditation
Where has my soul gone?

I endure darkness,
Empty tears, impatient for
The quest of being.

Ah, faint echo heard
In the murmur of my heart
Chanting life anew.

The Dumb Ox

Everyone admires St. Francis of Assisi. The fond memory of this man carries through the 700 years since his death with an inspiration even for those of us living in a decidedly technological culture. Who would imagine in our world that the story of a monk "married" to poverty and deeply in love with nature could inspire modern people? And yet in our ecological sensitivity, St. Francis seems fitting as a reminder and a solace for city dwellers to return occasionally to nature. The remembrance is more than nostalgia; modern man needs this experience, to sense the rhythm of nature, in order to find himself. Amidst the pressures of commerce and industry, he can easily lose his bearings, caught up in the frantic pursuit of livelihood and career only to find later that his career has become one-sided, draining his energies without replenishing. Here precisely Francis calls to us in the depth of our nature to re-experience the natural realm of creation.

Born in 1225, the year before St. Francis died, another man entered the Middle Ages. In the castle of Roccasecca near Aquino, a small town between Rome and Naples, Thomas Aquinas began his life. The youngest of the family, he was sent at the age of five to the most prestigious monastery of the time, the Abbey of Monte Cassino. From the beginning, the parents royally decided to "sacrifice" Thomas to God. To designate a son to the service of Christendom was not unusual among titled families. What was unusual in Thomas' case was his own initiative in later refusing the Benedictine life. No doubt he would have emerged one day as the Abbot and thus brought luster to the family name. Instead, while a teen, he resolutely determined to join a revolutionary group that was barely older than himself. The Order of Preachers, or more commonly, Dominicans, "the hounds of the Lord," were a new, approved band of dedicated monks who embraced, like St. Francis, the solemn vow of evangelical poverty. These monks, for the first time in Christendom, combined a life of practical activity with meditation and contemplation. Education was the forefront of their training. To relieve themselves of encumbrances, they renounced the world by their dedication to evangelical poverty and inaugurated programs for sending out their teachers to the various universities of Europe. Thomas, like so many of the flocking students, went unnoticed. His reticence and physical stature quickly earned for him, from his classmates, the nickname of the "dumb ox." Only his teacher, the renowned Albert the Great, recognized his genius. One day he felt the students had gone too far with their teasing and proudly declared that someday all of Europe would listen to the bellowing of this dumb ox!

These itinerant monks—a radical innovation for Europe since people were accustomed to seeing their monks and priests located for life at one place—were formed for the expressed purpose of manifesting early Christianity and intellectually combating the errors of the day. They roved about depending upon the alms of the villagers.

For all his love of peace, Thomas was to enter vigorously into one of the most turbulent periods, politically and intellectually, of the Middle Ages. As a monk, he entered on the comparable path of a *sannyasin*; as a priest, he engaged in the ritual pursuits of a *pandit*; as a philosopher and theologian, he entered into *jnana* yoga. All his life he practiced asceticism, not for its own sake, but out of love for the discovery of truth. While St. Francis may be called a lover of nature, the epithet that best fits Thomas is a lover of the truth—both uncreated and created. For unlike Francis, Thomas did not turn from the cities but instead embraced the total world of man as the creative image of God. The cosmos and man in history were his fields of study.

Thomas was sent to the "Harvard" of his time, the University of Paris. Later he would assume there the Chair of Theology and command the largest audiences for his lectures. His confreres mentioned how he never wasted time himself and slept but a few hours each night. He could dictate to three secretaries moving from one subject matter to another and back again without losing the train of thought. After his thirty-fifth year, he never remained but two or three years at any one college and traveled between Italy, France, and Germany, continuously lecturing, debating, and preaching until his premature death at the age of forty-nine.

A CENTURY OF INTRIGUE

To appreciate the atmosphere in which Thomas labored, one has to recall the bitter conflicts of the century in which he was ordered by his superiors to take part. First, there was the continual struggle between the bishops and the secular princes to influence the shape of Christian Europe. Thomas wrote a treatise on government in which many ideas foreshadowed John Locke's version of democratic government. Secondly, he was constantly involved in justifying the mendicant orders—the Franciscans and Dominicans—from unscrupulous clerical propaganda that attempted to undermine their Christian base. Thirdly, there was the "new learning" of ancient sources—Plato, Neoplatonic, Arabian, Hebrew, and Greek thought, especially Aristotle. Fourthly, the growth of empirical science, the foreshadowing of Bacon, Galileo, and Newton were inaugurated now and not later as some modern historians maintain.

The thirteenth century was undergoing importations of Eastern and Greek learning. Latin translations of heretofore undiscovered works were provoking excitement at the state universities. The leading professors were writing their commentaries and creating schools of controversial thought. Students were flocking to these teachers by the hundreds; this is why history has denominated this century as the "Golden Age" of scholasticism. This period of "Schoolmen" produced more intellectual challenges than any previous century for Christendom.

THOMAS THE TEACHER

Above everything else, in spite of his many travels and administrations, Thomas excelled as a teacher. He was fearless in combating error. Equally, he was utterly respectful of the personal character of his opponents. He remarked how difficult it was to come by truth in any form and therefore he stated, "we must love them both, those whose opinions we share and those whose opinions we reject. For both have labored in the search for truth and both have helped us in the finding of it." Narrow-minded polemic was beneath him. The object of a public disputation was not to pounce on the weak spot of the opponent's argument, but on the contrary, to seize the kernel of truth and nurture the dialogue into the rich discovery of the topic. Thomas in his writings would always formulate the oppositions' words in the best possible light. Again, this shows his lack of self-importance and his overbearing concern for the dignity of man in his effort to discover reality.

To know reality, to arrive at truth, was more than a severe straining of brain power. To read Thomas on the qualifications for grasping reality sounds strange to modern ears. Only he who wants nothing for himself, who is subjectively "uninterested," can know the truth. The selfish will to pleasure or egotistical gain blinds one to the clarity of life. The sanity of this insight, as well as its refreshing openness, gave Thomas the quiet courage to assert that in the Book of Job, where Job boldly converses in a seemingly irreverent manner with God, the truth does not change according to the standing of the person.

His dedication to teaching was not to score a victory over the opponent nor to dazzle first-year students. The act of teaching displayed the greatest act of service one man can render to another, for by teaching a man is led from error to truth. The love of truth and the love of persons—only the two together constitute a teacher. An intellectual dispute was a common effort for truth and not a competitive showing off by one of the contenders. His personality is further revealed in a prayer he wrote. He requests God to let him be cheerful without frivolity and mature without pompousness.

The intellectual dynamics of the thirteenth century further reveal Thomas' character as a teacher. Frequently, scholars and lecturers select from other writers those phrases and arguments that bolster their predetermined theme. Thomas, on the other hand, chose everything. He was under suspicion by over-zealous censors for his weaving of so-called pagan learning—the Eastern and Greek writings—into his synthesis of Christian theology. He dared to use Aristotle's works and Moslem writings when the former was under interdict and the latter source was viewed as extremely dangerous to minds. He borrowed from the Islamic interpreters of Aristotle, Avicenna, and Averroes; his writings reveal quotations from the Jewish genius Moses Maimonides; Roman writers like Cicero, Seneca, Boethius abound; Plotinus as well as Augustine, the Fathers of the Church and the philosophers and non-Christian theologians of antiquity are found in his major work, the *Summa Theologiae*. This unfinished opus was his crowning masterpiece combining philosophy, positive sciences, psychology, history, biblical exegesis, and theology into a truly comprehensive framework that measured man's dignity by his contemplation of reality, which activity finally led him back to his divine origins. Thomas labored almost eight years on it and it remained unfinished, not by accidental circumstances, but from his deliberate, though quite unexpected, choice.

The *Summa Theologiae* was a summing up of reality at its deepest principles. It was not a "scholarly" research piece. He wrote it for "beginners," those who are embarking upon the journey toward grasping the wholeness of reality. One does not read it in between appointments or at a resort while waiting for the dinner bell. Modern students may find it dry, resistant to their attempts to penetrate its meaning. The reason for this resistance is not due to the inherent content of the *Summa*, as much as the agitation of our current lifestyles, where even the neophyte in hatha yoga and meditation finds it surprisingly difficult to coordinate his body and mind slowly and silently.

In this masterwork, Europe found the most positive philosophy of life that had ever been exposed in university circles. For until the thirteenth century, there had crept into the Christian outlook a tendency from Augustine to view natural reality as somewhat suspect, as slightly tainted and therefore beneath man's dignity. What this attitude does to one's understanding of the body and emotions is still felt today in certain quarters. For Thomas, the entire universe was good, intrinsically so. Life was basically wholesome. There need be no fear of the beingness of things. True, evil was there but it was not anything substantial. Man's ignorance was the root cause and perpetrator of the ills of the world. Reality was sound because it expressed the divine intelligence, the cosmic consciousness. As profound as he could be with the most obtuse topics, it is interesting to see what he recommends in the *Summa* for curing depression: a good cry, the sight of an old friend, the facing of the issue involved, laughter, and lastly, a good warm bath. He never lost his touch with basic common sense.

THE END IS SILENCE

As a teacher, one could expect Thomas to complete his life in communication. A final opus, the reworking of his earlier, less mature writings, the dictating of his memories—these sometimes occupy a great personage when he knows the end is near. But Thomas answers the summation of his life work in a different manner. Let us recall the unusual incident that transformed him more than anything in his busy years. Remember that we are talking about a man who was the consultant of kings and princes, even the Pope himself requested Thomas' judgments on occasion. His balanced and serene replies to questions and contests were sought by every major department in the universities. He was respected and honored by all the faculties wherever he went.

The episode is this. His favored secretary, Brother Reginald, noted one cold, December morning in 1273 that Thomas was strangely altered. Instead of his usual exuberance in dictating the final pages of the *Summa*, he just sat staring into space. This amazing man who had shown that there was no conflict between science and religion, that man's consciousness was the key to the mystery of life, that there was nothing bad about human nature, was sitting, almost in a stupor, refusing to do the very activity that meant life to him—the communication and continuation of his basic insights about reality. His secretary urged him to pick up the pen, reminding him that Europe was waiting for his final analysis of these philosophical and theological matters. His response to these pleadings was the same short words. He simply refused to write any longer, knowing full well that his masterpiece would remain incomplete: "All that I have written seems to me nothing but straw . . . compared to what I have seen and what has been revealed to me!"

His selfless pursuit of truth led him experientially beyond the rational formulas of philosophy and theology into the realm of their origin. In his remaining months he became a citizen of a different world, a world whose inexhaustible horizon could only be communicated to others in silence. How paradoxical that this monk who had begun his search for truth as a quiet, retiring student should now return to those same circumstances, but in the fullness of enlightenment. Once again, Thomas became the dumb ox. The following March he died in his fruitful silence.

Contemplation is the goal of man's whole life.

Dedicated active living disposes one to the life of contemplation.

Human happiness does not consist of knowing God through reason, but in a participation of Divine Life.

In loving, man expresses the Divine Life within himself.

Contemplative happiness is knowledge of the highest truth.

The happy life does not mean loving what we possess, but possessing what we love.

Without love there would be no contemplation.
— St. Thomas Aquinas

Yoga and the Jesus Prayer

In some Christian circles an ancient form of prayer is stirring interest. The "Jesus Prayer" is currently enjoying an unexpected resurgence among Christians who practice serious prayer or contemplation. It is an unfamiliar form of prayer to Roman Catholics and Western Christians in general, but its modern story appears under the title, *The Way of a Pilgrim*.

It is the story of a Russian peasant who spends his life learning and practicing a special way of praying. The setting is Russia in the middle of the nineteenth century. The pilgrim's identity remains unknown. The methodical use of his practice has been described in the Russian version of *The Philokalia*, a compendium of maxims from the Desert Fathers, Greek Fathers of the Church, and theologians of Byzantine spirituality, but for some unknown reason St. Benedict, the Father of Western Monasticism, did not include the prayer in his Rule for monastic life. Only in the twentieth century has it been rediscovered for the modern West.

There are four points to note about this special technique. (1) *The Philokalia* ("The Love of Spiritual Beauty"), composed in the eighteenth century, contains the written material required for the practice. Its theoretical foundation is grounded in the Bible and the Greek Fathers. In 1351, an orthodox council officially approved the doctrinal justification for the prayer, largely due to the defending efforts of a fourteenth century monk, Gregory Palamas of Athos, who later died as the Archbishop of Thessalonica in 1359. (2) The simple, invariable formula, "Lord Jesus Christ, Son of God, have mercy upon me" comprises the entire prayer. (3) Ideally, in learning the prayer, the aspirant approaches a geront or staretz (a spiritual advisor) for the proper instructions. (4) The purpose of the prayer is not merely ritualistic, nor is it merely paying homage to Christ; rather, through it, an interior transformation is sought that leads to what the Greek Fathers called theosis, or the spiritualization of the personality.

Prayer has always been appreciated by the Christian East as a primary means for growth in self-knowledge. In fact, Hesychasm, a spiritual tradition that dates back to the third century, uses the Jesus formula as one of its forms of inner prayer. A Hesychast is someone who lets ". . . the memory of Jesus combine with your breathing." As the monk Nicephorus suggests,

> You know, brother, how we breathe, we breathe the air in and out. Oh this is based on the life of the body and on this depends its warmth. So sitting down in your cell, collect your mind lead it into the path of the breath along which the air enters in, constrain it to enter the heart together with the inhaled air and keep it there. Keep it there, but do not leave it silent and idle; instead, give it the following prayer: "Lord, Jesus Christ, Son of God, have mercy upon me." Let this be its constant occupation, never to be abandoned. These are the words of this blessed Father, uttered for the purpose of teaching the mind, under the influence of this natural method, to abandon its usual circling, captivity and dissipation and to return the attention to itself, and through such attention to reunite with itself and in this way to become one with the prayer and, together with the prayer, to descend into the heart and to remain there forever.

For a Christian who is practicing yoga the above description is not merely similar to, but the same as japa yoga in which the constant intonation of a sacred sound, mantra, is commonly referred to as japa. Unknown to the West, there is an ancient science of sound that permits the aspirant to use sounds for the precise purpose of effecting an internal change in his consciousness. The inherent power of the sacred sound, however, is not released in a mechanical fashion merely by repeating it. Unless one is prepared, unless the sound is intoned properly, and unless the spiritual master is qualified to impart it, the practice remains futile. Thus the function of the geront/staretz served in the same capacity as a master teacher in the yoga tradition, and the qualifications embodied by the master determined the germination of the seed-sound.

There is a certain naivete in the Western attitude that one can choose an appropriate mantra for himself. This thinking finds its logical extension in the attitude that the laws of japa are a matter of taste, or fashion: if one is not satisfied with a mantra, why not select another? To their eventual discouragement, people will find that unless the laws of transmission are respected, their effects remain dormant.

The Hesychast method involved the combination of breathing into the locating mental concentration in a definite area of the body. The combination of these two factors immediately identifies the process with ancient yoga. By this recognition I do not mean that these monks were yogis; rather, the Hesychast practice of converging breath, concentration, and silent intonation at the heart region is a recognized yogic form of meditation. Whether these monks were informed yogis is not the issue. The descriptive facts of their method involve the laws of yoga, whether the monks were cognizant of the tradition or not.

With the Jesus Prayer we have a historic event in spirituality which links the traditions of Christianity and yoga. Just how far back in history the monks started to pray in this manner is difficult to trace, but the psycho-physical emphasis which is placed on the invocation of the name of Jesus corresponds to particular aspects of yoga. Thus the ancient science can shed light upon this Christian method of prayer.

The yoga laws of concentration can contribute to a greater under-standing of this methodical prayer, for according to them, there are definite glandular and nerve centers in the human body which, when interiorly focused upon by the mind, bring subtle alterations of energy into play. The stimulation of the area in question, such as the heart region, through breath and concentration, can provoke a gradual expansion of those positive qualities associated with the spiri-tual development of a person's heart. The increase in love, of course, heads the list.

In Christianity, as well as in other Oriental traditions (and even in the Occidental world of poets and philosophers), the heart has always been identified with the quality of love. In the yoga schema of spiritual development this heart region, or *anahata* chakra, when properly stimulated, awakens a conscious increase in the aspirant's ability to love. He becomes more sensitive, affectively, especially to concerns of other people. A change of heart, a conversion, takes place, and this change now influences his vision of reality. He reverses his selfishness. His personality unfolds in compassion, and he is led into a new level of emotional integration.

In yogic terminology, the stimulation of the anahata chakra puri-fies one of his tendencies to egocentrism. The same thing is meant by the monks when they speak of the purified heart as being the abode of God. The Hesychast technique involves what the Fathers call a "natural" process—a retraction from the excitement of the sense, a silent intonation in rhythm with breathing, and an absorption of con-centration upon the heart. Often accompanied by a feeling of warmth about the heart, the technique gradually leads to the intuition of a previous identity that had been obscured. Starting from the human situation ("fallen nature" as described by the monks), the Hesychast technique can bring about a return or restoration of human nature to its original identity.

THE GOAL OF THE HESYCHAST: THEOSIS

The ultimate goal for the Hesychast method is nothing less than divine consciousness. A process of conversion is undertaken in which the flow of attention is reversed from the external, created reality towards the inner man. In this way a return, or ascent, inwards to a divine status of theosis transpires. The entire method parallels Patanjali's classical yoga. *The Yoga Sutras*, like the Hesychast writings, outline a bodily and mental regime that gradually disposes one to greater self-knowledge, and the coordinated disciplines involved bring a sense of mastery over human nature, spontaneously inducing a calmness of spirit that spreads throughout the body-mind complex. Amid that profound peace the Hesychast and the yogi intuit their real nature.

Hesychasm postulates an organismic connection between body, mind, and spirit. As a result of poor living habits, according to its tenets, man's constitution is weakened, his emotions embarrass him, and his thinking is disoriented. Prone to grandiose illusions and selfishness, man's inflated ego obscures his real nature. By employing a psychosomatic regime (including posture, breathing, attitude, and concentration), man's nature is rehabilitated into full spiritual actuality. But for this conversion to theosis, the aspirant must struggle with two stages of inner development called *praxis* and *theoria*.

PRAXIS

Praxis, for the Hesychast, is similar to the moral code of yoga, the yamas and niyamas. It is a comparable asceticism that aims at rectifying the dissipation of the senses as well as the egotistical tendencies, and daily practice in bringing the senses and imagination under a more rational direction results in fewer and fewer superfluous images and thoughts to distract concentration. In this way *enkrateia*, or mastery of self, emerges. The Hesychasts insisted that the experience of divine existence remains outside of man as long as he is unable to deal effectively with his thoughts and passions. Patanjali, likewise, remarks that unless one controls the fluctuations of the body-mind complex, his essential nature remains obscured.

THEORIA

The second phase of inner development emerges from the virtuous efforts of praxis. The purifying struggle to reorder the bodily and mental faculties throws more light upon the nature of the world. The inner rectifying of the appetites, along with the restraint of egotism, affects a cleansing, as it were, that allows one to be more objective. The tempering of the senses produces a correcting effect upon the mental faculties. Self-deception wanes. One contemplates (theoria) the entire cosmos (physis) without imputing personal designs to it. Balance returns. The created world is seen with its relative merits. The purgative virtues, like yoga sadhana, enhance one's powers of discrimination, and the Hesychast lives with what the yogi calls meditation in action—the ability to live in the world but not be deceived about its nature.

According to St. Maximus, praxis purifies the intellect as well as the body. The reintegration of the intellect and emotions leaves the power of intelligence open. No longer dominated by his descent towards the material world, man's cleared intelligence now discerns the "divine wisdom invisibly contained in creatures." Purgation has increased his sensitivity, enabling him to recover a higher, intuitive approach to reality. Instead of relying upon the limited framework of his rational faculty, he knows the world in a superior way—from within.

Passing beyond the superficial knowledge of created things, the Hesychast now apprehends their eternal essences. With an immense expansion of discernment his "purified heart becomes an interior sky with its own sun, moon, and stars, and circumscribes God, the Uncircumscribable, by the secret ascent of his vision." Simultaneously with this illumination, the heart consciousness enlarges into a cosmic love: "the heart is aflame with love for every creature." St. Clement calls this *apatheia*, the cathartic control of the emotions that enables love to be strong and consistent.

The similarity between the Hesychast method and theory with Patanjali's *Yoga Sutras* is evident. Both methods describe an applied psychology for transforming human nature into its full actuality. The validity of either tradition lies not in authorative declarations but in the personal trial of its methods. In daily testing, through self-practice, the student can verify their intrinsic worth.

Both traditions respect the various levels of the body-mind complex. While the terminology can often be interchanged in either methodology, the Hesychast descriptions retain a religious symbolism and are less detailed in their presentation of the psychological stages than the *Yoga Sutras*. Both traditions agree from the start that the student's emphasis is on "enstasy," a re-entering into oneself, as opposed to "ecstasy," the energetic moving outward from oneself to things. Both postulate that the preliminary ascetic practices lead to the interiorization of the mind, culminating in an expansion of consciousness.

Both traditions respect the fundamental life principle as it functions in the entire body-mind complex. Since breathing and the heart's action are indispensable for life, both methods incorporate these processes into their techniques. The intrinsic relationship between these two vital functions, however, is the basis for more than physiological techniques. While breath gives life to the body, the Hesychast considers the body to be the "temple of the spirit." He accepts it as fact that there is an interdependence between breathing and the infusion of the life spirit, or *pneuma*; air serves as a vehicle for vitality to enter into man. From the spiritual point of view the Hesychast sees pneuma, or the divine life breath entering into man and making him a holy temple. Already manifesting God's image, man thus becomes and continues to be enlivened with God's life force through the action of breathing.

To the Hesychast, then, the physiological connection between breathing and heart action (for physical well-being) corresponds to a higher level of psychological and spiritual integration. The rhythm of breathing indicates the condition of one's health as well as his spiritual vitality. The same life force (*prana* in yoga) promotes physical health as well as spiritual development. The Hesychast, like the yogi, recognizes the reciprocal communion between proper breathing and the lucidity of consciousness. According to St. Nicephorus the Solitary:

> *You know that our breathing is the inhaling and exhaling*
> *of air. The organ which serves for this is the lungs which*
> *lie around the heart, so that the air passing through*
> *them thereby envelops the heart. Having collected your*
> *mind within you, lead it into the channel of breathing*
> *through which air reaches the heart, and together with*
> *this inhaled air, force your mind to descend into the*
> *heart and to remain there . . . the mind when it unites*
> *with the heart is filled with unspeakable joy and delight.*

The union of mind and heart in Hesychasm unexpectedly concurs with the meaning of yoga—the science of the unification of all of man's powers in order to bring about his full realization. Specifically, the heart region is only one of several areas available for expressing various dimensions of man's personality. Although not described in the literature of the Hesychasts, these other centers of concentration are fully elaborated in the yoga scriptures. The unfoldment of personality, or spiritual restoration—however one views it—proceeds in both traditions from bodily disciplines and social virtues to inward concentration.

The Hesychasts, as well as other early Christian communities of hermits and lay people, couched their various practices in religious symbolism which relied upon their close resemblance to biblical terms. Although the Gospels were their constant resource in clarifying their aims, still terms such as, "becoming Christlike," "the spiritual ascent," or "theosis," can be just as lucidly interpreted from the holistic understanding provided by the yoga tradition. Both traditions assert that man's human nature is fundamentally sound. St. Simeon remarked that man's deification is not a supernatural addition to his mundane nature; theosis does not make man into a two-tiered being of nature plus supernature. Rather, the monk continues, beneath man's ego and his emotional cravings (which injure and blind him) lies his pure nature which "subsists fully, just as it was created."

The Hesychasts do not speak of attaining something new through their practices but of recovering an inheritance already intrinsically possessed, the kingdom of heaven which lies within us. In order to discover this hidden kingdom, they felt, man must enter into himself, establish an interiorization of consciousness, which they refer to as an "unknowing" or agnosid. But unknowing does not imply a condition of ignorance (or *avidya* in yoga terms). The unknowing here means an unblemished awareness of reality without vested interests. Egoism retires. The ego's liking for conceptualizing reality, even God, is the last temptation. From this pervasive tendency, the ego must be purified. Man must leave behind his preference for the rational mode of uniting with the objects of his knowledge. He must actively seek an inward retraction from egotistical conceptualizations. As he interiorizes, he must abandon the effort to objectify what the mind most wants to idealize—God. The Divine essence is not an idea. Neither is the experience of divine life. Unlike the cosmos, God's intelligibility can never qualify as an object of rational knowledge. According to the Hesychasts,

> *The prayer of the heart must sweep away all imagination, both proper and improper . . . as wax melts in the fire, so does imagination disperse and disappear under the action of pure prayer through simple, imageless cleaving of the mind to God . . . since every thought enters the heart through imaging something sensory . . . so the light of the deity begins to illumine the mind when it is freed of every-thing and totally empty of form . . . as the Lord dwells not in temples built by human hands, neither does he dwell in any imagings or mental concepts.*

Often Christians consider that prayer and meditation involve mental content, at least for the necessary imaging required for eliciting devolution to the desired object. In the Hesychast tradition the effort is to wholly eliminate any fluctuation of the mind complex. The normal, ordinary mode of discursive knowing contracts the mind, thereby focusing attention upon a limited particle of reality. Instead, the Hesychast desires to eliminate contraction, allowing the light of Divine consciousness to fill his heart.

In the late Middle Ages books on Christian enlightenment reiterated this same approach to spiritual development. One finds in *The Book of Privy Counseling*, for instance, such passages as, "reject all thought . . . see that nothing remains in your conscious mind save a naked intent stretching out toward God, leave your thought quite naked, your affection uninvolved and yourself simply as you are. . . ." The Flemish monk, Jan van Ruysbroeck, in *The Adornment of the Spiritual Marriage*, remarked that ". . . enlightened men are, with a free spirit, lifted above reason into a bare and imageless vision wherein lies the eternal indrawing summons of the Divine Unity; and with an imageless and bare understanding they reach the summit of their spirits." John of the Cross states that, "the soul must be emptied of all these imagined forms, figures and images, and it must remain in darkness in respect to these internal senses if it is to attain Divine union."

The student on the path must be alerted, therefore, to conceptual traps, lest he misidentify the level of ideas about God with the experiential intuitive knowledge of Divine consciousness. In their writings, the monks Callistus and Ignatius note: "Since every thought enters the heart through imagining something sensory, so the light of the Deity begins to illumine the mind when it is freed of everything and totally empty of form."

Hesychast means, "the tranquil one;" its path is strikingly similar to that of yoga. In both, the positive unknowing, or naked intellect, is achieved through the process of stilling the mind. Dissociated from the slightest mental activity, subconscious or conscious, one breathes in undisturbed equanimity. An inner peace that exceeds all description reigns. In the undisturbed being of pure awareness without an object, the Hesychast, or yogi, realizes his absolute nature. Through reversing the externalization of consciousness, the vision of God becomes one with the vision of self, and in perfect stillness, according to Evagrius, one has recovered his original state. Theosis and samadhi unite.

It is important to note that our brief study has examined only the form of Hesychasm that is found in the Jesus prayer. But widely speaking, Hesychasm can apply to all forms of inner prayer. The riddle of why Western Christianity lost this treasure of spirituality may be traced in some measure to St. Benedict who, the Father of Western Monasticism, opened to his followers in Europe a path of spirituality based on the imitation of Christ as witnessed in his moral virtues. Although he did not in any way minimize the role of prayer or meditation, there is not the slightest hint of the prayer of the heart nor any direction towards a phychophysical incorporation of spiritual principles in his famous Rule for the monastic life. As a monk of his time, he was familiar with this ascetic approach found both in the Rule of Basil, which Benedict relied upon for the composition of his own Rule, as well as in the Conferences of Cassian (360-435 A.D.). No doubt the Hesychast method was known to him. Whatever his reasons, he preferred not to introduce it in his writings nor apparently to his order of monks. And thus an invaluable tradition of meditation was lost to the West.

Can a Christian Practice Yoga?

In the first book of the Bible, when God had completed his priceless handiwork, he remarked that it was "very good" (Gen.1.31). God qualifies only the goodness of man and woman with "very." Everything else in the cosmos is "good." Only people are "very good." The peculiar use of that adverb makes the achievement unsurpassable—God couldn't have done better if He tried.

It is disconcerting to see how, in general, people treat themselves as God's image. In the midst of scientific and technological advancement, Christians enjoy a poor state of health. Most people tend to ignore the most elementary physiological laws, and yet demand of their bodily and psychological energies efforts that are only compatible with a healthier body and better mental outlook. How to bring body and mind together to appreciate fully the goodness that they are in their nature?

Yoga responds to this problem by affirming the divine judgment about human nature. As a most positive and comprehensive approach to health based on the proper use of those elements with which Nature affords us so liberally—water, sun, air, light—along with the training of our natural faculties at the physical, emotional, social, moral, intellectual, and intuitional levels, yoga confirms the Christian's acceptance of his human nature as a priceless gift to be preserved and developed. In yoga, he learns to live with the seasons, facing life as a whole, not just with his mind or muscles. For a Christian, the techniques and philosophy of yoga are there as an invitation to foster his own peaceful perfecting of himself as God's image.

The science of yoga belongs to an ancient source of perennial wisdom. As a science, it is hardly recognized in Europe and North America. Often Christians mistake it for an Eastern product or activity without understanding that both yoga and Christianity are founded upon a similar base of wisdom. Like Christianity, yoga is broader than the Orient. To speak of yoga as a wisdom means that it transcends cultural labels, that it shares with other wise traditions a timeless quality that makes it a continual resource for human enrichment.

Yoga, then, is not an Oriental import. That its traditional ground for thousands of years happens to be the Himalayan mountain region has a significance unassociated with Oriental culture. Yoga remains free of ethnic, religious, political, or social influence. Does one speak of the circulation of the blood or the law of gravity as being Eastern or Western? Much less should anyone subscribe to yoga on the mistaken association that it is indigenous to the Eastern world.

As a non-cultural contribution to human development, yoga is applicable to any citizen of any country. It is concerned about the basics of human nature as such. In reading the translated yoga primer—Patanjali's *Sutras*—one cannot decipher what ethnic background influenced these thoughts. It is impossible to state in what country these words were first composed. The 196 terse statements defy being located in a geographical setting. The *Yoga Sutras* make statements about human nature without relying upon the cultural or religious symbols that naturally reflect a definite historical period. Yoga attempts to interpret man, not for a particular period of history, however beneficial, but on a perennial basis. To put people's minds at ease, it is important to remember that yoga is not interested in displacing religions. Yoga can no more threaten genuine religious beliefs than, say, a basic course on dental hygiene opposes one's faith. Yoga's interest lies in the study of human nature and its unfoldment from the primary perspective of consciousness. It investigates questions concerned with the range of the human mind and body, the normal attitudes one should have in order to cope with life calmly and intelligently. These and other similar questions are treated extensively by the philosophy and psychology of the *Sutras.*

For society, yoga poses a critique of culture. Whenever society becomes complacent or discouraged with its current level of civilization, yoga quietly insists upon a special feature of human nature. No matter how bogged down or overwhelmed man may become with his involvement with society, he possesses, according to yoga philosophy, a transcendental nature. In spite of his endless worries and tribulations, yoga reminds man that he is more than his body, his mind, his career, his success or failure with life. For he possesses a center of wisdom and strength within that makes his nature wider than history.

In yoga philosophy, a distinction is made between human nature and human culture and its manifestations. People can't help but identify with their ethnic origins or national territory. As a result, they forget that these qualifications denote, like the chopsticks of China or the saris of India, only a cultural preference. Within a society, cultural protocol only expresses the imaginative art of human communication; it cannot disclose universal insight for human development. Cultural appeasement is only temporary, it can't resolve the quest for human happiness. On the other hand, yoga being outside cultural frameworks, addresses itself to the root problems of life and the means to human fulfillment.

People live in culture and history. They grow accustomed to their habitudes and cannot easily avoid being provincial and sectarian in their desires. Yoga recognizes that beneath the multitude of desires lies a fundamental one that everyone shares but rarely satisfies—a desire to know experientially the ultimate meaning of their human existence and the nature of human happiness.

What human existence means to you may not be what it means to me. True, as long as we are speaking at a relative perspective. But is there a broader perspective, one that satisfies everyone regardless of race, creed, or locale?

If one speaks in ultimates, there cannot be a diversity of goals— means, yes—but goals or ends, no. For if the case were otherwise, if your version of ultimate human existence were as valid as mine, though opposite, then there would be the necessity for positing a diversity of human natures. Your nature would be type A, while mine would be type Z. We could not speak of the human family as being one. To some extent, people already practice this shortcoming by insisting on what (in an accidental sense only) makes them different from others. Human nature, though, is not composed of those aspects or items that make someone different from his neighbor. Race, color, creed, bank account, vacation home—all are not essential to appreciating the basic sameness of those living organisms called human.

Human nature is, without exception, one in its kind of being. The differences in personality are obvious but still this amazing variety does not prevent thoughtful reflection from discerning a common nature shared by all. Appraised of cultural differentiations, people still uphold themselves as one human family, one kind of being. The paradox is that people's actions don't always substantiate this universal truth. The wars continue.

Yoga, in its study of human nature, outlines its remarks from a universal perspective. Yoga does not explain how to be a better carpenter or Icelander. Yoga goes deeper and explains how the carpenter's or Icelander's similar human nature can reach its inner potentials as a human being.

Let's take the unexceptional aspect of human nature called breathing. Yoga does not want someone to appreciate breath from a static point of view. Understanding yoga is not like reading Grey's anatomy classic. In selecting breathing, which is essentially important to yoga, the emphasis is on a dynamic appreciation of human nature. Right at the start, yoga parts company from various fields of study by insisting that it can't be authentically understood except as a dynamic discipline; yoga is yoga and understood as yoga only in the act of applying it. The meaning of yoga dawns in the act of performing it, not from reading about it.

Breathing is an excellent example. Human breath offers little stimulation for reflection by most people. Yet the rate, depth, and rhythm of your breath constantly influences the way you feel, the thoughts you think, and the zest with which you face life. Specific exercises in breathing unify the mind and body into a healthier relationship. Everyone breathes the same air with the same organs. Breathing is not a theoretical reflection, but an activity that engages the entire person. Recognizing that breath affects the whole nature of man, yoga probes the mystery of breathing by practicing different techniques for different effects upon human nature. People practicing a simple form of diaphragmatic breathing come to know—through experience only—that a real change can take place in their overall feeling and thinking. A person's concrete state of being can be altered, sometimes drastically. The act of proper breathing promotes a coordination between the body and mind that is obtainable by no other method. The end result is there because the laws of breathing, when properly stimulated, produce definite effects upon one's being. These effects can be verified under controlled experimentations. Thus the laws of breathing, discovered by yoga practitioners, are not the result of authoritative faith or persuasion; they remain the positive truths of using human nature according to its inherent laws.

From the continued practice of yogic breathing, one's self-understanding increases in and through the breathing practice that directly affects the expansion. A kind of inner learning takes place during the practice. An academic knowledge of the human respiratory system does not affect the overall status of one in the act of this knowledge. Yet knowing the human respiratory system in the act of breathing—a different kind of knowing than concepts—provides a self-knowledge that is unavailable to the book description of breathing.

The regulation of breath is not an isolated act in the full appreciation of yoga. One is not merely exchanging gases. Regulated breathing lays the foundation for self-understanding. The experiential performance of breathing improves the practitioner's sensitivity to his inner nature. One gains an awareness of controlling and studying his nature in a direct and immediate sense, a dynamic knowledge rather than a theoretical knowledge of one's being. Yoga establishes its rightful claim to true knowledge through practice, not through intellectual coherence. Verification is always made by the individual. One can immediately submit a particular practice to personal scrutiny. To embark on the practice of yoga is to enter, not an intellectual adventure, but a transformative process for which one accepts responsibility.

Obviously, yoga can be described with concepts. The reflected ideas of yoga are systematically and coherently outlined in Patanjali's *Sutras* and the *Samkhya Karika*. The concept of yoga, however, is not the revelation of its truth. Yoga's power comes not from the idea, but from the actual evoking of the interior laws of man's nature. Yoga postulates that people carry within themselves the impulse or appetite towards self-perfection. People want to actualize their total nature, to experience life as richly, as enjoyably, as maturely as possible. The personal troubles man encounters, including emotional distress and disease, are symptomatic of his inability to regulate and develop this inherent appetite for life.

Yoga further recognizes that man's nature is multi-leveled, a combination of vegetative, sentient, rational, and intuitional forces that should function organically for his wellbeing. His inability, moreover, to achieve this integrated condition as an abiding state results primarily from his self-ignorance. Yoga treats suffering as the temporary product of man's failure to understand himself, which can be eradicated through the discipline of true knowledge about his nature. All the dimensions of his consciousness and all the levels of his nature must become involved in this holistic enterprise.

Yoga, therefore, is an applied philosophy of human nature. This definition departs from the modern conception of philosophy as a theoretically coherent version of life. Yoga's purpose is not to arrive at correct concepts in order to satisfy the intellect, but rather to stimulate the latent potentials in man that will bring him to final, conscious realization. With that aim in mind, it offers itself as a systematic program for peaceful living in full self-awareness. On that prospect alone should yoga pass or fail.

Death and Dying

A young lady called the IHT office recently and said, "I would like to sign up for death and dying." After the laughter died down, the woman was signed up for the seminar of that name which I was scheduled to teach. Ma Devi then remarked that she wouldn't be caught dead coming to the seminar.

For some people the topic of death fascinates; most, however, would rather avoid the subject matter as too emotional, too personal, and with no room for options. Let's look at the topic from ground level, placing it into an unlikely but understandable gross context. Contrary to ordinary assumptions, your body in its current form—despite your birthdays—is not very old. The reason for this predicament is that the body continually dies and rebirths itself. Bodily tissues last but a few months; some barely a few days. Your stomach lining hardly makes it through a week. Your skeletal system appears but for a season. Every organ undergoes death and replacement. Nothing very dramatic; they just die quietly. As you live, you are daily undergoing death. And, simultaneously, you are growing yourself a brand new body also. To your advantage, you do not feel the tissue cells' demise, because that process would terribly distract. Thousands of cells are dying right now in your body as you read this article, but you don't feel their termination.

With astounding regularity, your body rebuilds itself. This enthralling enterprise has been in operation since birth. The question arises: If my tissues regenerate, why do they look and feel the same as the ones that died? The answer to that question requires that one investigate the "blueprint" that regulates the business of new tissues. The hidden catch is that you can influence the blueprint. You can alter the quality of the new cells by the quality of your life.

Staying at the gross level and working out physically, for example, performing hatha yoga, aerobics, or weight lifting, produces profound results that affect the vital quality of the incoming, new cells. When your soft, muscular tissues die, you don't have to start rebuilding their strength from scratch. The new ones take up where the old ones left off. Your negotiable blueprint renovates the composition of your body while you live constantly within its context of death and rebirth.

PERSONIFICATION OF DEATH

To leave the subject of personal biology and walk back into religious history, we can find an entirely different approach to our topic. In casting about for a vivid description of personal demise, many ancient authors portrayed death in terms of something that we are all too familiar with: sleep. Staying within the Western reliance on Judaic and Christian scriptures, the metaphors utilized by various authors compare death to an endless sleep in which even God forgets you. An examination of the Torah would support this loathsome depiction. The dead person ". . . is no more," leaving the impression upon the living of non-existence, for an after-death is beyond the control of the living. The dead is delivered to dust, without hope or knowledge of God. The Hebrew mentality understandably personified death as an ominous shepherd who enters homes to strike down children. Death is an exterminating angel, a cunning executor of the vengeance of God against his enemies. The Psalms and Book of Job, among others, are full of these dire descriptions of death.

The Torah, having been written over several centuries and constantly undergoing redaction due to the cultural pressures and inspiration of the day, does not lend itself to a precisioned, unequivocal notion of death. Among the writers, it is more in terms of human testimonials than clinical judgments. These descriptions do not, nevertheless, make their assertions less real.

DEATH AS SHEOL

Jewish scriptures associate the termination of life with a summary notion called Sheol. "What man can cling to life and not see death? Who can evade the clutches of Sheol?" (Psalm 89.48). Sheol is the common lot of the human race. Once past its portals, there is no return. To appreciate this depiction, one has to briefly examine the Hebrew notion of anthropology. The Hebrew language uses a flexible term *nephesh* to designate a human as a living, personal entity. The Hebrew God created man by breathing into his body, or "spiriting him." Thus it becomes a nephesh. At death this spirit-principle, *ruah*, leaves man and returns to God. The ruah is on loan only. This resulting loss of ruah now characterizes man as going "the way of all the earth" as being in Sheol (Josh. 23). It is important to view the result never as a separation of body and soul—an incomprehensible distinction for Hebrews— but simply as the sad and irretrievable separation from the realm of the living, for he "who goes to Sheol never ascends again" (Job 7.9).

At the same time, descriptions of Sheol ambiguously indicate some sort of semi-existence. The state of being dead is compared to an eerie place, a sort of underground territory, a nether world "beneath us," where a shadow of the dead person resides. Nonetheless, "there is no man who is master of the breath of life so as to retain it, and none has mastery of the day of death" (Eccles. 8.8).

Antecedent to the inauguration of Christianity, Hebrew writings underwent an astonishing reversal inspired by curious revolutionary stories and ideas from the books of Maccabees, Wisdom, Daniel, Eze-kiel, and others. Under the circumstances of the times, reflections now indicate that Sheol may not be the boundary line that halts the power of the living God. The old antimony of the "just" having to endure the same final retribution as the godless seems surmounted. A new kind of re-creation awaits "the dry bones" of those who have kept God's laws. While Sheol touches all, it does not consume everyone. Sheol now becomes a juncture. For some it still is an irretrievable disaster where one remains among the waste of the dead. For the faithful servant of God, however, a transition occurs: a triumph over the wicked, enabling an entrance into the peaceful vineyard of the new divine "kingdom" with an astonishing bodily resurrection. This highly controversial redaction challenged the inherited conventional view of man's total demise and produced aggressive religious party splits in the Hebrew orthodoxy. Faced with this inherited context, the Christian scriptures regarding death reinterpreted the phenomenon.

CHRISTIAN CONCEPT OF DEATH

Orthodox Christian scriptures take up the Jewish controversy of death and fill out its resolution in unique terms. Christian writings do not, nor could they, deal with death strictly as a natural phenomenon. Their consciousness of the human event was subsumed into a religious jargon that attempted to contend with the conflicting religious issues surrounding the Jewish understanding of Sheol.

More than any other author, Paul writes in his letters that death is both a natural and a religious condemnation for humankind, since it manifested the final dissolution of humankind's relationship to God. Paul especially portrays the central figure of Christianity, Jesus of Nazareth, as the second Adam, who rescued humankind from the dead-end reign of Sheol. Jesus breaches the discontinuity between the human and the divine.

In the Semitic religions, death appears as the termination of each person's life, and associated with that idea there is a strong moralistic context that measures the consequence of the individual. Death, in the Christian version, ushers a judgment, as it were, that qualifies one either for eternal life with its scriptural God or for the horrendous experience of eternal perdition. There is no appeal to this latter sentence, which is rendered in the most equitable way. Metaphors were introduced to foster the elaboration for these two contrary resolutions. Thus, heaven was conceived as up, while Sheol became Hades, conceived as down below, the nether regions. Just as there was a guardian angel to watch over heaven, St. Michael, so his counterpart, Satan or the devil, was the managing director and sentinel of hell.

Interestingly, Satan, as encountered in the Torah, is not classified as an enemy but actually as part of God's entourage. He pressures the challenge of visiting earth and, with God's acquiescence, of proving Job's integrity. Like a prosecuting attorney, he probes Job's allegiance to God, shrewdly out to ascertain the facts in the case, testing the human to see if he keeps his allegiance when things get tough, really tough.

MODERN RESEARCH ON DEATH: THE SLEEP OF DREAMS

Leaving aside religious mythology characterizing death, let us examine recent explorations. For example, consider when you go to sleep at night. What occupies your attention? Being unconscious, you don't remember tangible events around you. Nevertheless, events are taking place outside you and, especially, inside you: dreams. During approximately twenty-five percent of your sleep time, dream episodes occur. Dr. Nathaniel Kleitman of the University of Chicago carried on extensive experiments with his students to verify how often we typically dream, and whether we remember them or not. Some people deny that they ever dream but if they don't, according to Dr. Kleitman, they will go crazy.

He experimented with students by having their nightly repast interrupted every time a dream occurred. The inspectors could tell by noticing the movements of the eyes beneath the closed lids. Hence the expression REM—rapid eye movement. The unexpected result for the participants being awakened whenever they dreamed showed them having erratic behavior throughout the day, becoming discernibly imbalanced. Needless to say, the professor immediately ceased the experiment and concluded that eliminating dreams becomes hazardous to your well-being. Your mind and body, it seems, take advantage of 40 winks in order to cope with the emotional frustrations of the day. Through the symbolic induction of dreams, the daily stresses are diffused. Interestingly, the dreamer rarely undergoes genuine death even when the dream portrays it convincingly. And then there is the strange reoccurrence of dreams foretelling future events. One wonders if Adam knew while he was asleep how Eve was to emerge on the scene?

NEAR-DEATH EXPERIENCES

A few decades ago, a remarkable little book came out called *Life After Life*, by Raymond Moody. The author, both a doctor of philosophy and a medical doctor, wrote about people who had experienced apparent clinical death and then reversed the verdict. A kind of spontaneous resuscitation. From the subjects' reports of the experience, hallucinations were suspected in spite of the sincerity of the persons. Later, a careful analysis of some patients' reports, verified independently, recall vivid descriptions of the surrounding environment that would not have been discernible under anesthesia. The author also noted common features outlining the structure of the interlude near death that were cross-culturally similar. Curiously, many people undergoing their experience altered their life afterwards, admitting a loss of the fear of death and a stronger sense of immortality.

For most people, however, in spite of religious assurance, death looms as a hauntingly, fearsome reality. Some perturbance regarding death would be understandable because one of the most basic drives is the sense of bodily self-preservation. The confusion and perplexity of death may be due more to lack of sufficient facts and knowledge with the result that too many people approach their longevity with suspicion.

A NEW PROPOSAL ON DEATH

With the use of philosophy and yoga, let us attempt a different tack with this enormous task of understanding death. "Death is a habit of the body," was a refrain that Dr. Swami Rama repeatedly spoke to his audiences. Along these lines when the eighth-century master, Shankara, was asked, "Why do people age?" he answered, "Because they see others do it."

Reflecting on my years of teaching optimal wellness and experiments on aging, these two assertions make more sense with the facts than with capitulating to the number of your birthdays. Chronology is not as important as most make it out to be. Lifestyle takes precedence. To ask, then, in spite of sudden and unpredictable catastrophes, "Why do people die?" let us propose the refrain, "Because they see other people do it."

For the moment, place death and aging among human habits. A singular thought of death, dying, or aging does not immediately take its toll. The question goes further: What occurs to one's vitality when those thoughts of death, dying, and aging become directives of a lifestyle consistent with their meaning? Do suppressed fears and anxieties regarding my demise and the possible crippling effects of aging play a role in my renewable metabolism? Am I frightened by dreams of death?

However nerve-wracking the thoughts about these forbidden topics, there resides within humankind the fundamental urge to stay alive. Self-preservation dominates everything. No one wants to go out of existence, whether biologically, emotionally, or in business. Life comes back to that one principle. How can I best preserve myself? Fundamentally, it is an ego-centered principle, but it's very sound. It's based upon the subtler reality within a person which ancients revered as the spirit, the real self, the Atman, that spark of the omnipotent divine. The Atman, according to perennial philosophy, reigns eternally in you. In other words your spirit is the perfect self-preserver. And as its sublime omnipresence shines itself through your body and mind, you experience its power as an embodied being, with all the earthly and cultural limitations accompanying its presence. Your ego-centered urge to sustain your daily self is a fundamental reflection of the Atman in its eternity. The question of how much one can extend the power of the Atman into human preservation remains to be seen.

EXPLORERS OF DEATH

In the last century, a yogi explorer named Aurobindo from Pondi-cherry, India took this challenge as a major mission of his life—or death. He wanted to change the DNA of death and he spent the last decades of his existence at the molecular level to see if he could alter the blueprint of human demise. He passed his adventure on to his co-pioneer, a French woman who carried on the task. There is no final answer yet.

We all have a natural fear of death since we desire to continue to enjoy life. Yet that basic fear can be so strong that at times it interferes with life's very purpose. Fear as a caution can be a good thing because it alerts us to avoid recklessness. The inevitableness of death, when it finally comes, is such a horrific anticipation for many individuals because they fail to understand its reality.

We have two kinds of fear, two great categories: internal and external. Walking through the Boundary Waters area of Minnesota and noticing a moose or bear in the distance may alarm some. Some people are afraid of fast traffic. The object of alarm is outside of them. Those are easy fears to label.

The internal fears are subtler. You have fears of not making it in life, of losing your job, of not being loved—all sorts of ways in which you can see yourself being diminished. That is another way of saying death. With our internal fears especially, we often attempt to substitute some-thing to relieve the discomfort. So our response to that fear impels us, or we might respond to it by getting very dependent upon people, or things, or food, or certain kinds of pleasures. In that process we don't realize that we're starting to identify in a very subtle way, first with the fear and then the mind will start to identify its own preservation with this particular dependence. "I've got to have it. I've got to be around this person," or this thing, whatever it is.

Once the mind identifies with a reality, we take on its characteris-tics, and now we're caught. If something is temporal, sooner or later we'll catch up with the border of that temporality. In other words, sooner or later, it goes out of existence. You lose a friend, a spouse, a child, or your job. What are you going to do when it's not there any-more? Death comes in many guises.

In yoga we learn something called *karma*. Karma simply means action. Be careful not to put more into karma than what is really there. You cannot live without action or desire, which means that you cannot live without karma. And when you initiate an action there are always consequences, or effects. That's the nature of the dynamics of life.

These associations are not arbitrary; they can be negotiable. It is like our law of inertia or our law of gravity. If I let go of a heavy object, it drops. It does not matter for my subjective desires; it is going to drop. Your life and your behavior in the world exert this kind of dynamism because you have an effect produced by your actions. This gives you an edge, meaning you can rely upon it. You do not want arbitrariness, because you would not know the effects. When you repeat the practice of a particular posture in hatha yoga, that posture gets more and more efficient. You have monitored it with attention and self-correction so it becomes easier, more pleasurable. You had a desire, you thought about it and you do it, and it produces an effect, which you like so much that you come back to it again.

Your whole life is composed this way. When you come to the point of death in your life, you have composed yourself over decades and formed a lifestyle thesis about death. You are the summary of your desires, your thoughts, and your actions. That makes you the persona you are.

When you meet death, you have a momentum already because you are living from a certain lifestyle. And while it may not be as wild and fast as the earlier years, it still perdures because you still have certain thoughts that guide you. You have a way of thinking, a way of looking at life. When we go to death, we pass through its portals with the phi-losophy of life that we have forged ourselves, replete with the under-standing of our fears and our joys. All we leave behind is this sluggish body that is locked into time and space in our three-dimensional world. We are no longer in a three-dimensional world but we're able to move in and through it from our dimension, because we are in a fourth dimension now.

Because we are on a long journey, we still have things we want to do; we may have died with incredible desires, which were never fulfilled. And that's what gives us the momentum, according to perennial philosophy, to come back and continue on again. That is why we sometimes have children who are handicapped as well as children who are prodigies.

Back in the early seventies a family experienced an episode that occurred with their four-year-old little boy. On one of their holidays they went to Pearl Harbor. At Pearl Harbor today many ships that were sunk are still in the water. It's a very revered memorial. This couple took their son and read the description of the terrible bombing. As the parents finished, the boy continued the description of how he and his shipmates went down with the ship. And he told his mother: "I'm down there, Mom." He also gave his name as a sailor. They went back to check the records and sure enough, there was a sailor by that name and had gone down on the USS Arizona.

Along these lines, one could read a fascinating study by Ian Stevenson, M.D., entitled *Twenty Cases Suggestive of Reincarnation*. Notice the modest title. He approaches the topic like a forensic detective, critically deciphering the evidence and weighing the social facts, letting the reader draw his or her own conclusions.

While the yoga tradition informs us that death in itself is painless, the self-generated fear of death is something else. Individuals are not entirely responsible for this plight. Cultural sentimentality and theological accretions over the centuries have cast death variously into an emotionally strained scenario, weighted down with questionable morbidity and juridical morality that belies its simplicity.

To speak of death as the natural release of the body so that one's spirit can get on with the business of self-realization sounds almost atheistic if not grossly irreligious. To refocus our understanding of death more in a natural light without these historical accretions does not demean the normal sorrow and temporary grief that accompanies the shock of human loss. Our concern, for the moment, is to separate or leave aside frameworks that could be construed as exploitations of human sentiment to support an institutional ideology about death.

The fascinating questions about death, disembodied realms of after life, and returning to embodied life cannot be pursued only in an intellectual manner nor by a dogmatic dismissal that outlaws the latter notion. For cultural preference or religious persuasion to banish the question of the possibility of an individual's re-entrance into corporeal life compares to the A.M.A.'s denying and opposing the role of consciousness, emotions, and volition in the individual course of pathology or health simply because it's not found in the tradition of medical textbooks. The pursuit of these inquires has been and seems obviously a part of the journey that we are collectively embarked upon.

Since the modern era issued in its grand flourishment of materialistic science in the seventeenth century—an approach that can certainly achieve success up to a point—the realm of the conscious human spirit and its territory has been marginalized to the precincts of religion and theology. Demarcation between empirical science and the investigation of the human spirit has not been entirely amenable to either side. Like in-laws that kept their Victorian distance, suspicions of foul play persisted into the second millennia.

An unexpected new vista opens upon the discussion of conventional death and its limitations once we examine the implications of the Menninger Foundation experiments conducted by and upon Dr. Swami Rama under the direction of Dr. Elmer Green over thirty years ago. There, for the first time, in full view of the audience, spirit and matter danced a tango with each other in unique fashion. The volitional rejuvenation of tissues—as in the experiment with Dr. Rama producing cancer cells and then reconstituting his body at will, along with the evidence that sensory awareness was not necessarily localized in his organic structures of sensation, as when he demonstrated his empirical knowledge of his tangible environment while his brain and senses were verifiably asleep—strain the conventional paradigm of the limits of human consciousness to the breaking point. From the versatility of biological and mental control demonstrated by the subject, taking into account the total range of his demonstrations, one could propose that physical matter may not be the implacable deterrent that measures the time clock on longevity—that the human spirit possesses a dexterity that yields enormously more freedom over the death of matter than heretofore suspected. Could not physical death be just that—the temporary termination of an embodiment of spirit? From pondering with the vast array of clues from sleep and dream investigations, the creative display by human savants and prodigies, the inventive spontaneous recoveries from terminal illnesses, the accumulations of stories from déjà vu events and human predictability, and the cultural and religious traditions on the meaning of life and death, could not one suspect that the human spirit may have the power to return to pick up where it left off?

When we add the study of the perennial Himalayan Tradition along with the solitary practice of exploring the landscape of our spirit, we may yet provide a challenge to the apparent inevitable.

Whose Soul Am I?

The Golden Age of Scholasticism excited European students during the twelfth and thirteenth centuries with rediscovered methodologies and reflections from the Greco-Roman era for scientifically investigating the entire range of the world at large. These medieval pioneers were known collectively as the Schoolmen.

FROM HOLISTIC UNITY TO DUALISM

The rediscovery of holistic procedures met severe opposition in the seventeenth century when the French mathematician, Rene Descartes, introduced an irreconcilable dichotomy between mind and matter. His compulsion for unblemished certainty drove him to endless skepticism about trusting the natural proclivity for knowing Nature through the fallible senses. His anxiety for any knowledge that displayed less than the clarity and assurance of mathematical statements made him separate, irrevocably, the existence and study of mind from matter. As for mind and body, never the twain shall meet. Unfortunately, his furtive separation took hold in academia till this day when, once again, a more balanced, holistic comprehension of Nature is being reluctantly recognized.

The ancient era and the medieval period proposed the study of the mind walking hand in hand with the study of biology. Since we experience life as a natural, embodied whole, there is hardly an excuse for an irretrievable separation of intelligence from its corporeal matter. Sensation and reason collaborate in daily life, ideas evoke emotions, and our senses stimulate reflection. To separate the rational soul as the animating principle from its corporeal embodiment would reduce humanity to an Angelic status.

Descartes insisted on this severance of the natural unity and then found himself unable to reunite them in an intelligible composition. Like Humpty Dumpty, he tried to put the broken parts back together. In a kind of desperation to reassure his colleagues that the mind and the senses could still collaborate and arrive at true knowledge about the material world, he presumed the issue resolved by declaring a *deus ex machina*. With this gambit, he introduced the belief that God, being the benevolent creator of this natural world, would protect us from sheer skepticism, and guarantee, as it were, sufficient validity of our ideas and sense impressions. Perhaps, he kept an inspired eye on the Vatican's approval.

Earlier in Western history we had a similar diversion provided by Plato. He decided that the body housed the separate soul. While Descartes, in his way, acknowledged the legitimacy of sense knowledge, Plato would have no patience with this flimsy stuff. Yet, for him, the empirical realm, incidentally, as it were, tipped off the mind to remember the transcendental realm beyond this planet where it contemplates the eternal ideas that are the prototypes of reality. Matter is insignificant, at best.

Descartes' version posed that man was not a substantial, unified nature, but two substances—mind, whose essence is thought—and matter, whose essence is extension. Even with divine protection against skepticism about knowing this world with any assurance, he decided that the only way these two independent substances could function together in a human being was by way of an adjacent, mechanical coincidence.

From these peculiar roots and the growth of Newtonian mathematical science, along with the equally important commercial success of industrial inventions and technology, the reluctance of viewing the human as a unified whole led to the modern cleavage between body and soul called psychophysical parallelism. A contemporary offshoot is found in the field of allopathic medicine, where treatment of patients relies upon chemical drugs and surgery.

THE SOULLESS ENTITY

In the expanding modern scientific culture, everyone praises the mind but doesn't know quite how to connect its accompanying body. An early explanation in twentieth century psychology occurred with Wilhelm Wundt, Gustave Fechner, and E.B. Titchener. No longer household names, these investigators viewed man as a composite of psychic or mental operations and concomitant neural and physical processes. They posed two parallel spheres of activity in the individual unrelated to each other in any causal dependency. Unanswered theoretically is the question of why these independent spheres should synchronize at all?

As this theory became more prevalent in the scientific culture, reactionary, alternative, monistic views commanded attention. J.B. Watson, the pioneer of behaviorism, eventually became dissatisfied with this division of spheres and substituted human behavior for mental consciousness, external observation for introspection, and reflexes for sensations. He proposed that humans, instead of two spheres in association, are simply conditioned machines. This apparent advancement meant that people are without souls, without minds or rational consciousness, entities, in other words, reduced entirely to physiological functions in mechanical fashion.

To return to the Schoolmen. They started their investigations from a broad base by combining astute, empirical observation with introspection, noting the impact of the environment upon their psycho-somatic subject matter. They would concur with many of the empirical specifics of the body-mind findings of the twentieth century attempts to explain human nature but regard their proposals as too narrowly materialistic, thus incomplete, and subject to questionable generalizations based on their limited data. It is more than a stretch to say that we exist only as a succession of life episodes—akin to a walking photoshop—that from time to time obscurely bonds to form a collage called personal identity. For the Schoolmen, the life principle individuates itself by informing its own particular, organic body. Growth and tissue healing would be an instance. The enlivened organic matter or ensouled body together form the complete human nature. The organic senses translate the soul's powers to contact the world at large. Our self-conscious experience attests that this conjunction of mind and its body performs as a unified substance. Several centuries earlier, this intimate arrangement evoked the concept of personhood.

THE NOTION OF PERSON

The etymology of "person" derives, not from the Greek, but from the Latin, *personare*, meaning to "sound through." The Latin expression refers to the stage actor's mask, constructed with a concave open-ing at the mouth, amplifying the actor's voice hidden behind. The notion of person clearly appears in the sixth century, authored by the Roman philosopher, Boethius, who describes it as an individual substance of a rational nature. "Person" implies that one is the sole bearer of his or her acts. The distinguishing characteristic that makes self-responsibility possible as well as unique in Nature is the power of rationality or intelligence. A person possesses insight and volition, ponders and chooses, and loves in a body. The way these powers are exercised crystallizes the person's individuality or personality. Person is born, personality is achieved, and rationality leads the way.

For the Schoolmen, the notion of person affirms a stable status in being, an essence subsisting in Nature throughout the seasons of life. Growth and decay may alter or impair my physical composition, the raw events of life and the randomness of ideas may continually sup-plant themselves, yet there remains a continuity of identity: I am the same individual feelingly and deliberately undergoing this flux of living, the same person with his or her various internal powers, inclinations, habits, and acts, all of which makes up my dynamic presence or personality. The vast differences of people from nations around the world are accountable by the flexible uniqueness of their personalities, of how they have developed their inherent powers within their environment. That individual uniqueness is sometimes referred to as my sense of identity, my I-ness, my ego. The emergence of ratiocination upon life, more than any other single factor, constitutes humanness.

Using his own terminology, Sigmund Freud admitted that *ego* should replace *id's* influence—those stormy instincts within that resist reason's management—in the development of the adult personality: ". . . the ego represents what we call reason and sanity."

CLASSICAL YOGA MEETS VIRTUOUS LIVING

In the heritage of classical yoga, interesting psychological insights converge with both the Schoolmen and the moderns. In keeping with the former, yoga acknowledges that man thinks and undergoes successive mental experiences involving distinguishable aspects of sensing, imagining, desiring, conceptualizing, and remembering, among others. It even admits that for many people the entourage of plans and events happening to them can be interpreted as the whole meaning of their existence. Here yoga cautions that profitable as one's career may be, there lurks the ego's enclosure of oneself with these reputable, but limited values, placing personal security and well-being only with them. Over the years, some can remember later that they had undergone periods of coveting things or defending ideas that, at the time, seemed almost absolutely important to their survival instincts. Yet with reflective experience, they learned to change their minds. They disassociated with their understanding of reality that appeared so indispensable to them then.

Yoga makes a striking contribution at this juncture. Building upon those moments when one realizes that life exceeds anything already achievable, one begins to sense that there is more about oneself than measured by education, credentials, trophies, or bank accounts. Enter the meditational experience, therein derives the unavoidable insight that one can reach an inner peace of mind like no other. The fruit of that experience carries over into daily occupations where the individual knows that he is not held hostage by his stressful accomplishments and can now enjoy brief moments of serenity amidst the hassle of tasks. Even a lightening of the emotional constraints ensues. In our own purview we have assumed celebrity status. We become confused when others do not acknowledge our importance. In the act of meditation, you find a natural, evolving release from the contrivance that you are essentially your grandiose images and ideas.

Now you have an edge to further your creativity. The discerning use of our inherent powers, known as the intellectual and moral virtues, engender a stability in daily living that reinforces the consistency of the meditative experience. With all in hand you can soon emancipate yourself from assuming your resume is the final word. Inexorably, a transformation occurs. One gradually learns to apprehend reality without appropriating it as an extension of personal preservation. An appreciative walk in the forest occurs without swiping the flowers for appeasing one's mood. In this way, your borders of insight expand beyond the irrepressible competitive and possessive reaction to life's opportunities. An uncanny sense of liberty emerges in which you intuit the possibility that all of the grandeur of the world can be within the province of your awareness, but not all of your awareness is limited to any exclusive acquisition of society's allurements. More and more, one becomes fascinated in taking joy with an unconditional spying upon things as they are. A certain independence of spirit arises. Almost eerily, one discovers how self-reliance beckons with simplicity. Less now do I estimate my sole worth by the co-dependent standards of society. The value's there but in no way a compelling necessity. Imminently, meditation and virtuous living prepares your consciousness for a contemplative awareness of life. The *who* that I am is dawning richer than I ever figured.

From our itinerary on this planet, with all its incoherencies, we have learned that life, while unpredictable at times, is not arbitrary.

Unsettling as the principal of natural causality may be for some physicists, the element of chance is not the ruler of existence. Inevitably one must, from whatever tradition, ask the pressing question: how do I bring my autobiography to its summit?

Our previous probing shows that many modern schools of psychology would declare human entities entirely the product of material evolution. To the contrary, yoga, like the Schoolmen, understands human nature's goal as a self-disciplined rediscovery of the dynamic fullness of personal, conscious life. While these traditions speak differently of self, soul, person, or ego, for the fundamental ascription of who one is as a living reality, there rings yet a common element that unities them at their core. Taking human beings in their whole nine yards, warts and mistakes and all, it is the undeniable emphasis upon the yearning, affirming, implacable desire that brings along all the powers of my being into its harmonious quest for happiness. Even that word has various Eastern and Western faces—from samadhi, enlightenment, or moksha—to self-realization, blissful contentment, and unalloyed fulfillment. Unequivocally, though, each speaks to the human *summum bonum*. But this "highest good" would be meaningless without the unrestricted experience of knowing its possession. Thus we relish our happiness, the plenum of our existence, in the unlimited act of intelligent living, within the abiding ambience of contemplation.

Once upon a time, there was a Greek named Anaxagoras, whom society recognized as his own man, and was asked one day: to what end are you in the world? He calmly replied, *eis theorian*—in order to behold sun, moon, and sky. He meant, of course, the ultimate purpose and perfection of his life was to partake knowingly of the whole of being.

The Yoga of the Golden Flower

There are ways but Way is uncharted
there are names but not nature in words
nameless indeed is the source of creation
but things have a mother and she has a name.

Thus begins a Chinese poem. Authorless as it has come down to modern times, the eighty-one stanzas comprising the Tao Te Ching or the Way of Life introduce the reader into the teachings of Taoism. The poem presupposes an attitude toward existence that the average person, caught up in his daily preoccupations, seldom appreciates. For hidden behind the lines is a cosmology that situates man and cosmos intimately together. Human consciousness and the vast complex universe are viewed as the inner sphere and the outer sphere of the same existence. Both spheres are inseparable from mutual influence. Both, in the last analysis, obey the same laws. The moving shapes of the phenomenal world respond to the actuated laws, and yet these laws derive from a common, immovable and silent origin: the undivided One.

Only the way of nature is the derivative of the One. Someone living through the four seasons is hardly aware of their transitions. Nature is still while it works and keeps control over all. Nature's way of acting without action became the foundation for Taoism.

The way is always still, at rest
and yet does everything that is done.

Taoism intuits the One as the cosmic, mysterious, ultimate, absolute principle underlying form, substance, being, and change. Omniscient, though beyond reason to comprehend, it remains immanent and transcendent, omnipotent and eternal. As inexhaustible, it stays nameless. In poetry and experience only can one hope to brush against its presence.

From sticks and stones to men and meteors, everything in the fluctuating world achieves its goal by following its natural path. With his feet on the ground, man can still see that the star-filled sky exposes constellations moving in their distinct ways. The tireless order and beauty of the evening heavens persistently awakens within man the wonder that he too has his inexorable path to travel. All things, then, in heaven and earth are governed by path, the Way of Tao.

> *Man conforms to the earth*
> *the earth conforms to the sky*
> *the sky conforms to the Way*
> *the Way conforms to its own nature.*

Since heaven and earth are the terrain of man, he participates in their phenomenal activities, subject to the multi-colored drama of nature. Success along his path depends upon discerning the laws of life and returning himself to them just as the stars, knowing their course, proceed along it.

> *The movement of the Way is a return*
> *in weakness lies its major usefulness*
> *from what is all the world of things was born*
> *but what is sprang in turn from what-is-not?*

The Way is not concerned with the Chinese moralism of the School of Confucius (551–479 B.C.). In the *Analects*, Confucian thought, together with the Way, places emphasis upon order and returning to the roots of life. But these similarities are only temporary; the more one compares the works, the earlier their directions part. Confucius was preoccupied with civil living. His writings are the formation of codes of conduct and deportment. He stipulates more than 3,000 rules for attending to life's complications, informing the community on how to perform daily protocol with a codified humanism. While brilliantly pragmatic, he never ventures beyond the moral sphere.

The Way, on the other hand, serves not a philosophy nor a moral code. These human creations easily become self-contained in academia and political systems, each momentarily enjoying favor from the reigning court before falling into historical oblivion. These ways are limited, artificially contrived, halting the pursuit of life. Nature's secret, the constant, normative Way from which no event and no pretext is exempt, is disclosed only to those who can be rid of personal ambitions or prejudices about life. Otherwise, busy about his accomplishments, one further obscures the Way. While expressive of the Way, the phenomenal world is not the One. Man can easily abstract a particular cycle in nature and rearrange its energies for his external goals. By imposing the laws of his ambition upon nature's plasticity, he merely forestalls the inevitable. Grasping a fraction of nature's laws, man identifies his portion as the whole of life and settles into its brief pattern. A rich man to his wealth as a beggar preserves his poverty, both in their wayward patterns staying within the Way, dissipating their life's energies, competing without finding the One. Competing against the Way eventually breaks rebellious man. In his bankruptcy, nature compassionately gives him a chance to breathe. The sense of loss may lead him closer to the Way, for loss gives pause and rest. Not the rest of the inert, the repose of the dead, but the rest of the unborn. Being unborn from the brittle pursuit of competing in the phenomenal world, one gradually returns to his primal spirit. The return to the unborn state enters one into the silent ground that seeds the Golden Flower. Normally, man scatters his energies through his senses into the flux of life, producing ever more epicycles of action. Pursuing these cycles attracts in turn the birth of convoluted desires vying for external completion. With action and desire compelling one another, the inertia of life wears endlessly on.

The secret waits for the insight
of eyes unclouded by longing
those who are bound by desire
see only the outward container.

Nature, however, can hardly avoid action; it fulfills itself through action. And yet, wayward action is the problem for man in nature. But pausing, resting enters man into the very experience of the root of action. Stillness is the clue. The secret of the magic of life, of discovering the Golden Flower, consists in using action in order to attain non-action. Instead of externalizing action, man allows it to subside. What action is our concern here? The action that underlies and sustains every human action—the action of breathing. Thought, muscular activity, local motion, any mental or bodily activity of a living human is inconceivable without breathing. Man's problem of restless action resides in his excessive outflow of breath.

As nature circulates through the four seasons fulfilling its path, so the circulation of his breath allows man to live through the year. By studying the seasons of his breath, man discovers the laws of breathing. The first law is that he can patiently bring it under his control; controlling the breath controls external action. Returning into one's breath is the process of being unborn from the restless world. At the time of his physical birth, the primal conscious spirit inhales the vital energy and thus dwells breathingly in the phenomenal world. The primal consciousness is breathing. The bodily spirit thus loves movement, and in action remains bound to its feeling. Night and day it wastes the primal energy by excessively discharging it in desired movements.

What is to be shrunken
is first stretched out
what is to be weakened
is first made strong
what will be thrown over
is first raised up

what will be withdrawn
is first bestowed.

The primal energy must be retrieved; what the Way refers to is the backward flow of breath. The return to the Oneness of primal consciousness is through subjugating the diffusion of breathing. The gentle subjugation of the circulation of the breath reduces the discharge of the vital energy. Sensation and thinking subside. The circulation of controlled breathing continues, but quickens an inner circulation of awareness. When the Chinese characters for Golden and Flower are vertically touching, the combined figure means "light." With the practice of the backward flow, the gradual diminishment of the movement of breath increases the circulating light of awareness, bringing the primal energy more and more under self control. The expanding stillness brings one into silent intuition with the formative processes found throughout nature. In knowing the silent essence of heaven and earth, nature yields up her laws. Man is born again inward.

The light, the awareness that flows within him is not in the body alone. He sees those mountains and rivers; the great heavens and earth are lit by the sun of his awareness. This light-flower fills and covers all spaces. As the light circulates, heaven and earth circulate. But the practitioner must be strong on the path. He has many seasons and climates to pass through before the flower emerges. All seasons will end in silence. The rhythmical breath and the circulation of light nourish the roots of life, revivifying the primal spirit. Actions return to non-action. Movement flows back to its rest. Heaven and earth recede into the One. For man has recovered his divine nature, the Golden Flower blooms.

Then peace is the goal of the Way
by which no one ever goes astray.

The Master-Disciple Tradition

An amazing emigration has taken place to the Western part of the world in the last 50 years. Masters of the yoga traditions of the East came to reside in Europe and America. These acknowledged teachers invited thousands of new students to pursue their quest for spirituality; the invitation was fully accepted. The yoga masters adapted to Western culture ancient training protocols that echo back to revered formalities between a master and a student, a gurudeva and a chela. Americans can now train in a yoga lineage on their own home ground.

That yoga tradition may come as a surprise to contemporary Christians since the roots of their own spiritual heritage has more in common with the far older yoga teacher-student tradition than ever before suspected. Christianity encompasses a 2,000-year-old history; it should not be surprising that there are many concepts in the early years that are not remembered today. Among the forgotten truths of Christianity is the fundamental relationship that Jesus developed with his chosen followers. It is the same Eastern relationship of apprenticeship involving master and disciple.

With this concept generally unknown in Western culture, a modern seeker reads the gospels, sees the clearly marked clues, and usually misses the nature of this relationship in the recorded biblical scenes. A reader will scan the gospel narratives that use terms like *master, teacher*, and *disciple* without always realizing their unique significance. By carefully inspecting the textual meaning of the gospel words in their cultural use at the time of Jesus, however, a modern seeker—both yogi and Christian—can hopefully gain an important understanding for our times.

THE MEANING OF DISCIPLE: PURSUING APPRENTICESHIP

In the New Testament there are many scenes that involve Jesus' role as a speaker to crowds. Those followers that Jesus chose to instruct at close range, however, are given a consistent designation which sets them apart from the ordinary. The texts utilize the Greek word, *mathetes*, or 'disciple,' more than 200 times. We are familiar with the words 'disciple' and 'master' as these words appear in the standard English translations, yet we have little regard for the word 'master' in Western culture today. 'Master of the house' or 'master teacher' are anachronisms, but in the East the term is still alive and well. There, one can legitimately refer to qualified individuals as master artists, masters in martial arts, or spiritual masters. This notion of master is quite common in the Mediterranean region as well; Jewish rabbis, for example, are still known as masters.

The concrete meaning of the word 'master' (Greek, *didaskalos*) conveys more than professional competence in a field of art or science. When it is utilized with the word *didaskein*, which means 'to apprentice' (found 50 times in the gospels), it implies a very special relationship with students. Throughout the biblical texts when reference is made to Jesus teaching his student disciples, the word *didaskein* is exclusively employed; it is never utilized in texts with public audiences. Unfortunately, our twenty-first-century's appreciation of the word 'teaches' does not capture the impact of its cultural use in the gospel context. In the scriptures, disciples are disciples not because they listen to the teacher, but only because they apprentice to the master who has accepted him or her.

More than remnants of this model survive today when yoga aspirants seek out competent masters. When a master chooses to accept someone as a student, that person commits his or her lifestyle to the requirements of the relationship. This profound alliance between master and disciple has little to do with registering for courses and attending formal classes. As much as possible, the relationship becomes a daily, lived association. The British notion of tutorship approaches, but does not convey, the wider intensity of the ancient notion.

Biblically, to be called a disciple, *mathetes*, means that one apprentices, *didaskein*, to a master, *didaskelos*. This arrangement is more akin to the rapport between a parent and child, where the child strives to model itself upon the parent in a day-to-day association. Discipleship further implies that one undergoes serious self-care practices, known as *sadhana* in yoga, with the guidance of the master who is well accomplished in them. Then a continuous tutorship ensues wherein the disciple undergoes a training regimen leading to self-transformation.

Let us take Matthew's gospel for illustration. The gospel writer of this text identifies Jesus' mission with the fulfillment of the Jewish Torah. As a master of the Torah, Jesus' business was to demonstrate how his students could attain the Torah's purpose, namely, to become as perfect as one's heavenly Father (Matthew 5:48). This teaching mission may explain the prominence (no less than 45 times) of the designation of Jesus as master, *didaskelos*. It is the most frequent title given to him in the synoptic gospels. Curiously, in his public career, Jesus was addressed as prophet, *prophetes*, only 13 times.

In the Jewish culture a prophet publicly announced religious news that affected the community's spiritual survival. He searched out crowds, seeking to deliver a shocking message, a wake-up call, in a provoking oratorical style that moved the people to action. The prophet's urgent appeal was not in the interest of attracting followers, but rather in the interest of jarring minds to change the direction of their lives. Less interested in acquiring disciples, the prophet sought to arouse the audience to take his message to heart.

The master's approach was entirely different. He or she gradually gathered a select group of disciples, spoke to them intimately, and worked with them on a daily basis. A master's instructions were not meant to deliver a timely message but to instill ways for the trainees to alter their perspectives of reality, and from that self-knowledge pursue their life work. The master was concerned with the state of mind and the lifestyle of the disciples with an intensity and intimacy that was reserved exclusively for them. Crowds need not apply. Jesus enacted both roles, speaking occasionally to the public as a prophet, but primarily to his disciples as a master. "Daily in the temple courtyard, he sat apprenticing" (Matthew 26:55).

THE SIGNIFICANCE OF SITTING

"Seeing the crowds, he went up the mountain. There he sat down and was joined by his disciples. Opening his mouth, he apprenticed them." (Matthew 5:1-2). These words open the famous Sermon on the Mount. Technically, it is not a sermon, nor is it for the crowds, for they listened only to parables. It was a training manifesto for Jesus' initiates.

In the ancient spiritual tradition of the Himalayas, sitting near a master in this manner was the norm. The recorded oral transmission of those ancient sittings was collected as *Upanishads*. These writings are the *Vedanta*, the cream of the *Vedas*, and summarize the realized wisdom of the Vedic seers. Yoga masters initiated their chosen students, *chelas,* into the ways to personally arrive at the same universal insight taught in those scriptures. The apprenticeship of the disciples involved a strict training program for body, mind, and spirit. The goal of this master-disciple apprenticeship was to bring the chela's level of consciousness to the same awareness that pervaded the upanishadic master.

In the collection of Upanishad scriptures available to readers, one can peruse the stories and statements that distill the original state of consciousness of the writers. The actual training methods, however, those psychosomatic exercises that eventually produce the conversion to a new state of consciousness, are excluded. Revered practices—the implemented *sadhana* or *prayoga shastras*—are the essence of an apprenticeship. They are deftly inculcated to disciples when the master decides that the aspirants are ready. Without continual practice, there is no assimilation. It is the disciple's job to become established in them; the master's power cannot be a surrogate for the incompetence of the disciple. In that way, the disciples experience the power of the shastras' meaning in themselves.

Advanced practices are withheld by the master if the integrated readiness of a disciple is absent. Hence the gospel admonishment: "Many are called but few are chosen" (Matthew 22:14). Superior athletes and artists recognize the indispensable necessity of undergoing an *ascesis*, an unrelenting, self-training that alters one's biological and psychological make-up so that one can withstand the energy demands required for exceptional performance. Spiritual training is even more demanding.

CONTEMPORARY MISREADING OF THE GOSPELS: FAITH AND APPRENTICESHIP

Our analysis of the master-disciple relationship shows that a direct English translation of the gospel texts does not convey the proper meaning of these terms. The usual Christian interpretation carries the impression that Jesus was a holy instructor giving lessons in religious information. Among the many church denominations emphasizing biblical indoctrination, Jesus is seen to have preached in the hope of making his audience believers. To ensure that the disciples got the message, it is taught, Jesus' God mysteriously worked in the minds of the listeners the disposition necessary to accept instructions. The disciples then received the 'mental change'—modern Christians call that faith—which transformed their lives. This explanation, however, resembles a very passive process in which the disciple's personal initiative counted for little.

An entirely different perspective is constant in the cultural and textual elaboration of the classical master-disciple relationship. It is clearly shown in the gospels that Jesus initiated his chosen students into a lifestyle which revolutionized their consciousness. They trained themselves under his guidance in performance skills that were to match his own. They were not spectators like the vast crowds who listened to their teacher; they were practitioners.

If there is a single word that characterizes the disposition that Jesus' followers held towards him during his public life, it was the word 'faith' but with a very different meaning. The English language uses two words—'faith' and 'belief'—for the original Greek verb, *pisteuein* meaning 'to rely on, to trust, to believe.' Thus, one speaks of 'having faith' or 'the act of believing.' Scholars admit that the New Testament writers preserve the Greek meaning of the word exactly.

Placing faith within the context of apprenticeship, as the gospels do, underscores a meaning that is not obvious in churches today. When listening to a good speaker or coming into the presence of a dynamic teacher, one feels an attraction toward that person. The speaker's presence and message can draw to the speaker an angry or an admiring crowd. Individual listeners may want to pursue further their spontaneous acceptance of this personage. All the reasons for the attraction, however, may not be rationally evident until later reflection, but somehow the listener is touched by the experience. This positive disposition to trust in the speaker was called 'faith' in biblical times.

Faith, then, is quite an ordinary response in daily life. One trusts another person for herself; one believes a speaker because of what he stands for. The more exposure to a person, the more one's trust or mistrust grows. In this way credibility becomes established or abolished. It can apply similarly to trusting or having faith in oneself. In English, we apply the word 'confidence' to ourselves: *con* meaning 'with,' and *fides,* meaning 'faith.' Having personal confidence means that we rely upon ourselves.

The initial phase of an apprenticeship could very well be either infatuation or a certain ambivalence. One could be emotionally thrilled by a teacher's message and thus believe uncritically, or one could be intrigued and yet have reservations. Either response would be understandable. Unfortunately, many religious instructors today urge the 'good news' to people in the form of a less than cheerful dilemma:

either believe or go to perdition! When Jesus announced his vision of life, the scriptures recorded a whole spectrum of responses. Some listeners felt hostility, others were awed. A few decided to entrust themselves for a while and become apprenticed to him: "Immediately they left their nets and followed him" (Matthew 4:20).

An act of faith is the ordinary human initiative to trust another person. Faith is one's choice. Then, as the relationship develops, there will, no doubt, be opportunity for correcting earlier presuppositions. In the Eastern tradition of master-student relationship, *gurudev-chela,* the master is very much aware of the student's struggle with trust. The master carefully guides students through life experiences that challenge their current understandings. These life experiences become the vehicle for learning how the students impose restrictions upon themselves, thus expanding their self-awareness. Clarification is not always sweet and easy, but disciples must struggle with their understanding of reality in order to fathom the master's teachings. Without inner struggle, trust remains naive and even delusional.

Faith or trust in the master, however, amounts to more than an abstract credal statement. The circumstances of the master-disciple interplay involve a series of trying experiences for aspirants. The cunning master assesses with clarity the specific ingredients necessary for the student's spiritual improvement. The disciple fails, at times, to comprehend the master's unconventional deeds and words. Insight comes hard. The master often appears unorthodox. His or her ways sometimes baffle since the disciple is so limited in conceptions of spiritual growth. The master's purpose is not to check disciples' enthusiasm, but to encourage them to follow out the implications of the practices. Often a disciple's improved understanding of the lessons of life follows less upon the master's inspiring words than upon personal practices. These prolonged exercises, *sadhana,* produce in the practitioner the dynamic inner alteration of mind and heart that enables a new vision of life. Without this change in vision, the admonitions of the Sermon on the Mount would not make sense.

Consequently, these exercises amplify the practitioner's capacity for self-knowledge, bringing about drastic personal changes. Practice effects vision: vision enriches behavior. The disciples of Jesus, for example, were taught how to use their inner energy for the plight of the ill and the crippled. Through the experience of this dynamic ability, the disciples would not only realize anew their own worth, but also appreciate the value of their master. It was through this marvelous performance of their innate powers that the disciples were enabled to estimate how far they had come in their apprenticeship.

FAITH: A LEAP IN THE DARK OR AN ACT OF SELF-CONFIDENCE?

On occasions when Jesus, the master, would demonstrate his wondrous healing powers to his disciples, they would naturally be more in awe than comprehension. Later, after being trained in the augmenting and application of this inner power, they could realize that they, too, shared in the same life force. Contemporary theology unfairly restricts the miraculous events narrated in the gospels as beyond the pale of ordinary believers. In a sense, though, this is true.

Most believers, then as now, would not have undergone the necessary training to prepare themselves for expressing their inner power. Being unfamiliar with the possibility and nature of this innate legacy, believers view it as exceeding their nature. In other words, they have no faith in themselves. This kind of deficiency reflects in the puzzled reactions narrated in the gospels about Jesus' identity. The problem is not with the master's proficient and discreet exposure of his power; the problem is with the believers' lack of faith in themselves.

The same would hold for a disciple with self-doubts. These weaknesses confound one's understanding of a master's identity. Without self-trust, without relying upon the human power within oneself, a disciple remains constrained by suspicions and irresolute in action. Thus, the master remains an enigma: "Who do men say I am?" (Matthew 16:13).

Faith by itself remains incomplete. Faith is really less a kind of special power to overcome rational hesitation and make a leap than an attitude of mind with emotional readiness that will not limit the possibilities of human consciousness. The disciple says in effect, "I will venture my trust in this individual, rely upon my training, and see what happens." Faith assumes a working hypothesis. Although proof is not available at the moment, one goes about life giving it a chance. Through words and deeds and especially through silence, the master coaxes, pressures, stimulates, inspires, even commands a disciple to continue practicing until the disciple's blind faith hypothesis is proven through experience. The master's job is to challenge any cultural and personal restrictions within the disciple's mind that restrains potential growth. In time the feedback from the training will establish the hypothesis either way. In a positive way, blind faith, with self-training, collapses into the light of self-evident conviction.

THE DISCIPLES' FAILURE IN SELF-CONFIDENCE

A disciple's association with his or her master will have human sentiments about it that need correction and maturing. Students often fantasize about their progress and the power of their master. Typical infatuation leads to exaggeration. Having made those same mistakes as a student, the master knows how difficult it is to always stay grounded in reality. Consequently, he or she will not be averse to selecting harsh measures to bring students back to the facts of life. Apprenticeship can be trying, upsetting, and prolonged. There are moments of disillusionment for the master does not necessarily fulfill the student's expectations.

Revering the master is not enough. Having faith in the master is an elementary beginning, but faith is not a substitute for experience. Fervent admiration may provoke interest, but it will not affect transformation. The master does not need praise. Masters desire disciples' actualization of their inherent capacities. Masters assist the process; they are not a substitute for it. The work of apprenticeship requires, indispensably, the disciple's efforts to lead to new self-awareness.

An illustration of this principle of self-training occurs dramatically in the gospel of Matthew. Having performed successfully in the art of healing, Jesus' disciples took on a new challenge and utterly failed. They were obviously chagrined at this embarrassing situation as they reported it to their master. Matthew's account of their failed attempt to cast out a demonic influence from a boy (Matthew 17:14-20) becomes, for Jesus the master, the occasion for teaching a subtle lesson.

The boy's father, still seeking a cure, implored Jesus to rectify the lad's disturbance. He related how the healers-disciples failed to do the job. In response, Jesus stunned everyone involved: "Faithless and perverse generation! How much longer must I put up with you?" (Matthew 17:17). Then, in spite of the strong rebuke, he immediately cured the boy. No explanation was given for his exclamation. Instead, the gospel narrator depicts a later scene where the disciples are apparently alone with Jesus. They press him to answer, "Why were we unable to expel it?" (Matthew 17:20).

Let us interject here. If these disciples understood healing the way modern Christians do, then they should have revised their question along these lines: "Why didn't God work through us to heal the boy?" or "Why didn't you, our master, extend your divine power through us as your instruments and thus effect a cure?" There is no hint at this interpretation. On the contrary, the disciples expected to cure the boy. It was not their first attempt, and they were already experienced in healing. Did God ordain to hold his grace of healing from the disciples' efforts? Did Jesus hold back some technique required in that instance? Did the disciples, as it were, run out of healing power? Speculation could wander in many directions.

Jesus' actual reply to his disciples' consternation is almost too simple. They failed, he said, because they had too 'little faith.' The master then made his point with his faulty students: "If your faith were the size of a mustard seed, you could say to this mountain, 'move from here to here,' and it would move; for nothing would be impossible to you." (Matthew 17:21) The striking use of the metaphor, mountain, would remind the disciples of their prodigious potential. Physically moving a mountain seems absurd, yet if the disciples could overcome their lack of faith, less than seed size, even a mountain could not resist them.

A modern reader might easily leap to the inference that the disciples lacked faith in God's omnipotence to heal, but upon closer inspection the question of weak faith pertains to them. Jesus did not remind his disciples to pray next time and then God would work the healing miracle through their humble submission. In fact, earlier he advised them not to multiply prayers (Matthew 6:7) and not to pray in public (Matthew 6:5). Jesus did not hint at their lack of faith in God. The issue is much closer to them: their lack of trust in themselves. Their question was not, "Why did God fail to act in and through us?" but "Why did *we* fail?" Jesus' efforts had not been to instruct them in the conviction that they are nothing and God does it all, nor is there any textual evidence that the disciples viewed themselves as inadequate to the task while God's power is everything. The disciple's failure to procure the anticipated healing was neither Jesus' nor God's fault; it was nothing less than their own failure of nerve. Jesus bluntly told them that they did not have enough trust in themselves. They, not God, were to move mountains.

Jesus' sarcasm is consistent with the master-disciple model. The ages-old, master-disciple pattern of spiritual development is a personalized process whereby disciples mature into masters themselves and they, in turn, pass on the spiritual heritage, *traditio*, to their initiates. The master's responsibility is not to pick up the pieces of student's failures, but to induce in them the authority of self-confidence. If they do not build their self-trust, then their inherent powers remain sporadic and weak. The master's impatience reminded them just who was responsible.

Insisting in this way on the disciples' need for more self-determination does not detract from their acknowledgment of the Divine. Showing pious deference to God, however, is not the issue.

Jesus' students were being trained to discover and use their powers properly. Substituting God's agency in the face of a challenge to personal powers dodged the purpose of their training.

Once a reader recognizes the consistent use of this master model in the gospels for designating Jesus' most frequent activity, then many other biblical passages will become clear. To the crowds, Jesus preached; to his disciples, he taught through the mode of apprenticeship. Modern Christians do not view themselves as trainees but as believers, followers of his words, with the Christian Bible as the guide. They are followers of Jesus like the crowds mentioned in the scriptures. Jesus spoke to these people on occasion, but he did not consider them his disciples. The crowds may have believed and hoped in the words of Jesus, but they could not realize the achievement of the disciples without the necessary apprenticeship.

PRESENT TIMES

Lingering questions remain: What happened to that spiritual self-trust since the apostolic era? Where is the tradition of apprenticeship in today's churches? With whom does one find the performance skills demonstrated by the disciples in, say, the book of Acts?

As Christianity developed westward after the first generation of disciples, the double trend of ordinary believers and apprenticeship grew. New converts in the believer's tradition were initiated—baptized—into the town communities and given their instructions and offices of responsibility. The Christian religion slowly became institutionalized with all the advantages and disadvantages that accompany consolidation. The apprenticeship tradition of the master-disciple relationship proceeded in a different way. Individuals preferred a more contemplative and meditative lifestyle to preaching and working in public and retired to forest dwellings and caves. Christian historians refer to this period as the era of the Desert Fathers.

It was not long afterwards that the ancient master-disciple pattern receded into memory in the West. By the post-Reformational years, it was no longer even endorsed. The former monastic and hermetic atmosphere of the early centuries yielded by the end of the Middle Ages into a type of religious preparation to meet the needs of the institutional Church in its confrontation with secular society. From the sixteenth century onwards, all the various denominations of Christendom stressed variously a fidelity to the scriptural word as written, a fealty to religious authorities, a need for devotional prayer, and attendance at community services. Roman Catholicism, for example, emphasized mandatory attendance at certain rites as the principal means for spiritual growth under the regulation of the clergy. Even in monasteries and convents where there was still some echo of the older master-disciple association, it was still secondary to the formal sacramental activity of the monks and nuns, regulated now by canon law. The Protestant churches, in their various ways, shifted the emphasis to individual allegiance to the words of the Bible and private acceptance of Jesus Christ as one's personal Savior.

In the East, however, the master-disciple tradition held some sway. An extraordinary series of translated texts known as the *Philokalia*, "The Love of Spiritual Beauty," reveals the journeys and diaries of men and women who trod the master-disciple path from the third century. Although Eastern Christianity is, like the West, generally influenced by modern institutionalization, evidence for a lineage of the master-disciple tradition can still be found on Mount Athos in a number of monasteries dedicated to the contemplative life. There one could be fortunate to meet a *startzi* of Russian orthodoxy or perhaps a *geront* of Greek orthodoxy. These technical names describe spiritual masters who embody the realization of their *ascesis*, or in yogic terms, their *sadhana*.

While entrance into the ascetic lifestyle is no longer restricted to celibate monks and nuns in Western Christianity, there is today a definite, but uneven, return to the strong yoga pattern of master and disciple. Due to the influence of writers like Thomas Merton, Irina Tweedie, William Johnston, Tessa Bielecki, and Bede Griffiths, Christians are becoming reacquainted with the enlivening power of the yoga meditative traditions. Masters such as Anandamayi Ma, Swami Rama of the Himalayas, Shree Maa of Kamakhya, Swami Amar Jyoti, and Ammachi have brought the master-disciple relationship to thousands and influenced nuns and ministers to join the laity in learning yoga techniques of meditation from acknowledged masters. Some older monastic foundations, as the Benedictines, are now deliberately restructuring their mode of spiritual living along the lines of Eastern *ashrams* and *zendos.*

These voluntary experiments in self-knowledge are answering an increasing desire in Westerners to broaden their personal responsibility for their spiritual quest. American yogis trained in the ancient apprenticeship have the wonderful burden of continuing their lineage for succeeding generations. If this healthy trend continues, then the twenty-first century may well see even Christian seekers transformed into enlightened beings through the master-disciple relationship that Jesus used.

Justice, Prudence, Virtue, and Reason

Q: Reading on *ahimsa* in the *Bhagavad Gita*, I came to realize that I do not have a clear distinction between prudence and justice. How does one really make a distinction between the two?

A: Quick response, each has a different job while they work in collaboration. Let's start out by keeping a commonsense approach and gradually focus closer. As an example to start things off, briefly recall Arjuna's plight. His primary goal is to reclaim the rightful inheritance that belongs to him and his clan. If someone has cheated and stolen what is rightfully yours and, in the context of the times, the only recourse you have is to strategize how to take back your rightful goods, then the situation becomes a matter of justice and prudence.

Justice in classical Western schools, from the Greco-Roman days through the Medieval times, into our beginning modern era, means to render what is due to someone. It also implies that if you are due something, then it is your right to that reality. If your opponent admits that they have stolen but refuse to return the goods, then you must decide a prudent plan of action or not to regain your property. Common sense would uphold this basic definition of justice with accompanying rights. Justice is about detecting the balance of the scales in an objective, fair manner. It implies seeing the truth of the situation and acknowledging the facts for what they are; in this case we have, indisputably, stolen goods of all types that won't be returned to their rightful owners. In the face of these facts, the thieving family has a moral obligation to fulfill a just return, yet they refuse to restore the goods. In justice, Arjuna has a reasonable right to demand these goods. Given this situation, Arjuna now has to decide a stratagem to regain what is rightfully his. This is a shrewd matter for prudence, doing the right action at the right time in the right way, in order to regain his rightful goods that are justly his and the clan's.

Here is how justice and prudence connect. The objective estimation of justice clarifies the scene then prudence inaugurates and supervises the right choices to see that the task of justice is carried out. Justice establishes what is owed, the issue itself; prudence discerns and executes the how, when, and where, the best way to resolve the issue. Prudence mandates that the task of justice is to be actualized, usually eliciting the help of fortitude. They mutually cohere in doing what is good while each has its own distinct, operational responsibility in relation to the truth of the situation. They are distinct but inter-connected rational powers rooted in one's intelligence.

Knowledge, will, and action reach their zenith in an act of prudence. The apex of prudence is liberty and happiness. Bravery is rooted in justice, and without truth leading the latter, only injustice. Bravery is the defiant calmness of a fearless heart. Then the unbiased silence and alert poise before the unexpected stands ready for definitive resolution.

Q: In the *Bhagavad Gita*, Krishna tells Arjuna that he must fight and slaughter a lot of soldiers. While Krishna tells him that the *atman* cannot be harmed since its eternal, immutable, etc., Arjuna still must harm a whole lot of people in battle. How do I reconcile non-harming and harming?

A: The context of the verses is important. Students forget that the story is a religious myth. They tend to take it as literal history and that's their first mistake. Myths, like fables and legends, can bear or give insight into certain truths presented in a dramatic manner, often reflecting the mores and social history of a country. The verse is hard to make sense of by itself. It seems to me that if this is your attitude then you will just stand there. This kind of neutralization won't bring about any action. Without motivation or intent in reference to the situation at hand, no action occurs. Those "holding things the same" is unrealistic.

Q: Also in the *Bhagavad Gita*, "Surrendering all your acts unto Me, with a mind dwelling in atman the Self, free of expectations, free of a concept of mine, having freed yourself of all feverishness, then fight." How do we accomplish this?

A: This is a dream admonishment. This verse is hardly self-explanatory; it stays an abstract idea, at best. Keeping in mind the religious context, the entire verse is a preachment. Each of us is the agent of our acts, thus the one responsible; you can't forfeit that to anyone. In battle, you can't get away from the expectation, at least implicitly, of self preservation; you wouldn't be normal otherwise. Surrendering is hardly the concept one wants in the face of battle. The whole verse seems surreal. It presumes to prepare our hero with the best attitude, but its preachments defy common sense.

Since we are dealing with religious proclamations, they are simply asserted. They miss the point, however, and are unnecessary for an intelligent response to the task. His Holiness Dalai Lama, the great contemporary proponent of non-anger, has stated that sometimes force becomes necessary to combat evil. Here I give a story I have repeated numerous times in my lectures on the subject. It comes from the Sufi tradition.

A Sufi soldier was in the middle of a battle. It came to hand-to-hand combat. He was fighting the enemy skillfully with his dagger. Soon he had the enemy down on the ground and sat astride his chest, raising his hand to drive the dagger down. The enemy, in his helpless anger, spat on the Sufi soldier's face. The Sufi soldier's hand hung in midstride and did not strike. "What are you waiting for?" asked the fallen enemy. "I am totally under your power. Go ahead, kill me!" The Sufi soldier replied, "I cannot. I was doing my duty and you were doing your duty. I do not know you and you do not know me. Now you have introduced a personal note by spitting on me in anger and I have become angry. Now killing you will not be an act of duty, but it will be murder."

In simple terms, Arjuna is being told to kill but not to commit murder. What Arjuna is taught is the essence of all oriental martial arts where one is trained to hit the opponent but inside oneself remain in the center of stillness. That is ahimsa in the battlefield. This is the resolution of the koan of *Gita's* non-violence.

This is a rather naïve account. In war, both sides are there to maim, plunder, and kill. Whether you dispatch the enemy keeping a cool attitude or surging with emotion, it's all the same: you slaughter the opponent. Personal or impersonal, the outcome is the same. You are the agent of his death. Given the outcome, to speak of ahimsa is an oxymoron.

Arjuna's duty is to defend his clan against the injustice of his relatives, who are prepared to slaughter him and his immediate family, should he dare remind them of what is rightfully his. The circumstances are unavoidable. Once he gets past his chagrin, which is understandable in the social context of having to battle with fond relatives, who cheated, mocked, and humiliated his clan, then he can recall his just duty. He is fighting for the truth of what is legally and morally his clan's reputation, property, and honors. There is no disgrace or "sin" whether he does it full of heart and emotion or not. Just because one does violent actions with a cool head, does not obviate the fact that mayhem is being committed and you are responsible. Otherwise the just actions would not be to your credit.

His primary goal is to reclaim the rightful inheritance, not to commit murder. In the unavoidable circumstances, since the relatives are violently opposed to submitting to the just demands that they had originally accepted, the objective circumstances force the only intelligent decision by Arjuna—I want only what is properly mine and if you knowingly get in the way, that's your problem. Given the intransigent stance of the relatives, Arjuna has to go to extremes, which is a moral action on his part. To pose the fact of the relatives' immortal soul is true but not pertinent to exculpate Arjuna's actions. It's a clear case of acting justly.

Q: What is virtue?

A: Virtue is the realization of the human capacity for goodness. One's primordial will for the good exerts its momentum into life's territory. The strain of self-mastery is for beginners. Whereas the maturity of virtue means freedom from constraint and self-conscious tension. The "yes" or "no" of my will no longer follows my mood at the time, rather it seconds the truth of the matter. The motive to enforce goodness as the standard of real living complies with objectivity as its calling card. Sentiment is fine but without overriding the issues at stake.

The authenticity of virtues lies in the fact that they are in subjective accord with objective reality. Therein is a keen docility toward the facts and an alacrity to respond that stays in step with the shifting forms of changing circumstances so that one's action connects with the weaving target of life. Living virtuously, one gains a greater understanding of inner and outer life, a discovery of human nature, self-knowledge, an inkling, even if partial, of knowing "who I am."

Q: What is reason?

A: Reason, or the rational faculty, is the unlimited power to understand reality. Reason and the senses apprehend and scrutinize the evidence before them. The purpose of this discursive activity is to weigh in on the data and seek to determine a true judgment about the facts. Or at least the most probable conclusion, given the evidence at hand. Curiously, the conclusion of reasoning becomes an instantaneous act of contemplation. Could one propose that the ultimate extension of reason is contemplation? Does a possibility further exist for the intellect to amplify its contemplative power into a superconscious state?

From another angle, can the dynamics of contemplative perception augment the power of reason into a heightened state of critical awareness? One still retains the discursive ability in cahoots with the senses but the avenue to contemplative intuition of the truth broadens. Understand liberation with a festive contemplation of reality. Contrary to Eastern writers, we don't arrive at or gain liberation from afar, we already exist in its ambience. The proof is that the faculty of reason, by its very use, powers liberation. It becomes self-evident that knowing the truth and acting upon it evinces freedom. Nor is ignorance, as they write, our only problem; bad choices destroy us. Hence, the reason that the odyssey to fuller liberation begins with the virtues is because their cultivation, with the help of meditation, can overcome profound ignorance of both our nature and our dealings with the vicissitudes of life.

Could one not say that reasoning is comprehending (an understanding) whereas contemplating is apprehending (a knowing). Both can reveal truth and a sense of unity, but through different modes. But pure contemplation resides outside of reasoning, thus potentially revealing aspects of reality unobtainable through reason alone.

Q: Consciousness, as you say, has various modes of cognition. I am wondering if there are preexisting forms: reasoning form, memory form, sensual form, rational form, intuitive form?

A: I am much more comfortable using the notion of power rather than form; the reason is that once the power is activated it takes on the forms of the objects. The eye sees a pine tree and thus takes on the form of the tree as a sense impression. Also, consciousness itself is a cognitive power capable of knowing or apprehending all the forms or natures of reality. I view human consciousness as an unrestricted power capable of knowing all of reality. And within itself it has subsidiary functions (or specific powers) such as imagination, memory, and the use of the senses through the body. And the ego chooses what part of consciousness to use. For example, I will listen to music, I will read a book, I will reflect on the winter, I will meditate, and in each instance, the ego chooses how it wants to use its consciousness in relationship with its body. I think all these potential powers or functions of con-sciousness pre-exist, as you say, in our natures. It seems to me that our job is to discover them and use them optimally.

Q: Is the one who is having the thought the same aspect of the self as the one who is aware of the thought?

A: In the act of knowing an object, I am united to that object. Then, my mind can turn around and ponder, contemplate that which it knows. In that sense, the one, same self has two functions. I can't justify assigning lower or higher to the mind. For me the mind has different functions and powers that are all needed and my ego, I, can coordinate them at will. The division of higher/lower mind, e.g. that Vedanta holds, is clumsy and does not match human experience. Awareness is the natural, pervading quality of consciousness in the act of knowing. Again, I view the mind and its powers and functions operating on the same spirit plane, each in their respective manner.

Consciousness

Q: What is the difference between consciousness and the life force?

A: No difference. Consciousness manifests itself as the life force. There is a life force in a tree, in an animal. Life means consciousness. Anything that lives has a type of consciousness, since it shows vitality. Nature is full of grades of consciousness, as evidenced by the different species. We have all the grades but need to discover them in ourselves.

Q: Using Swami Rama's words from *Sadhana the Path to Enlightenment: Yoga the Sacred Science, Volume Two*, "When they probed into the depths of their own consciousness, they discovered that all consciousness is one and permeates the universe." The *Upanishads* state: "There are no diversities in the universe; all is a single infinite expanse known as Brahman."

A: Common sense says otherwise. Everything that exists shares in beingness but with differences. I have a growing impatience with this one.

Q: "There is only one gold, but there are many ornaments made of gold. Gold does not become many by changing its name, shape or form."

A: If gold is being compared to the vastness of the universe, then gold becomes many in "name, shape, or form." What is curious for me is why the Eastern writers want to flatten the diverse world instead of appreciating the amazing diversity and marvelous complexity of things. For me, everything shares in being but in its own unique manner, which dazzles at times. What is intriguing, and absent in Eastern writers, is that things can be and yet be different and their difference is real being. It's hard to find the exact words but being covers it all and admits diversity. Being is the unity that encompasses its own diversity-beingness. Finally, let's be practical. Daily human survival demands an appreciation for the various "name, shape, and form" of things. Walk about life and deny the differences in society and watch what happens to your personal "goldness."

Q: Beyond the diversity, in all its forms and levels, yoga teaches unity?

A: The unity is not separate from the diversity; it is found amidst the diversity and keeps the diversity existing. By analogy, the complexity of your body may be compared to the functioning unity of the diverse powers of the universe that hold it together in that the intelligent force of vitality keeps the unity of all your bodily components functioning as an integrated whole. You can ponder them separately as concepts, but you have to juggle the unity and the diversity together to grasp their relationship.

Q: Is part of that uniting the mind/body/spirit of the individual; the self with the higher Self?

A: What higher Self? You are an embodied self, nothing else. You are born united and grow that way with greater awareness of it. It takes time and experiences to come to that insight. There is only oneself, capitalized or not. Period.

Two | Meeting Adversity

The Meditation Journey

Entering the void
Vast silent darkness awaits
Where is my refuge?

It seemed so easy
Restless I sit endlessly
No satisfaction.

Where's tranquility
Thoughts and images badger
Is there no reprieve?

Peace of mind nowhere
Wasting time without result
I feel so alone.

Head full of nonsense
Must be more efficient way
Welcome grasshopper!

Alone on the path
Beyond judgments of others
Stalking the silence.

Hear whispers somewhere
Hidden trail among the stars
Darkness veils her.

Adrift and alone
Nowhere to turn without pain
Is it all worthwhile?

Quiet without light
Weary in a barren land
Endless nights too long.

The winds of time sweep
My soul yearning through history
Emerald isle waits.

Can I go on
Where does it end
Peek-a-boo says Self.

Be Agile

Let's assume you're a stroller through the Universe. You're getting on with life and suddenly you meet Mr. Adversity. You didn't expect it. You can't get rid of it. But is it the whole story? You can't remove it if you try. It has all seasons captured. It comes in different shapes, tonalities, postures, and we might raise the question "Why is it there?" Nothing seems to work for long. How come she's got the biggest piece? You always think you're right. Is adversity like a bush or a flower that causes allergies? Is there a vaccine like for the swine flu? Is it all bad or all good, this adversity? And why does it seem to collide so much with my life? It's almost as if someone is out to get me. Everybody is playing tricks when I'm not looking. You're going along and you just keep turning your head back and forth because adversity might follow you. Then you meet Mr. Agenda. And like adversity, it exists.

So, agenda exists and that has all types too. I'm going to bake a cake. I'm going to babysit the grandchildren. I'm going to visit New Zealand. I hate paying the taxes today. But again, why can't I live without an agenda? Everyone has one—or more. We've got projects, lifestyles, wishes, dreams, even worries are a type of agenda as you well know. When agenda meets adversity, someone else comes along. One is really grumpy. Don't look at me that way. And one is rather interesting. One is called adversarial and the other is called agile. Now, both have consequences. Adversarial puts up his mitts right away. Let's go at it. As I said, it has consequences and some of the time those consequences can hurt because of the way you involve yourself with Mr. Adversarial. Is that the only recourse? Not necessarily. Mr. Agile comes in and says "Whoa! Wait a moment." And he has written across his chest "Learn the ropes," what an interesting phrase! Swami Rama once said and I never heard him say it again, "If the world is getting to you, you don't understand the world."

The moment you have an agenda, you are going to have adversity. Because there's all kinds of agendas that are bumping into each other. They're colliding. Not necessarily on purpose. They just do. This is a complicated world. We live in a world that has to have adversity because it's the natural consequence of agendas. But that doesn't mean we can't work it out. We can be adversarial and belligerent and try to plow through and demand our way above everything else and overpower situations. Or we can become a little agile. We can learn to understand how things operate. That is called resolution. In order to appreciate resolution, being agile means to take a certain perspective on life. I'd like to explain that by a note that was given to me today by a young man. This young man came to America three weeks ago and unbelievably in his second week he decided to visit me. He was twenty-four years old, had a master's degree in computer science, spoke very good English, and his home was Taiwan. He stayed here for two weeks approximately. He wants to visit all of America he told me. He likes words. I found this note this morning at my door. Keep in mind adversity and agenda.

> *Thanks for giving me a wonderful experience at IHT. I learned a lot, especially a simple and contented lifestyle. Every day was beautiful and everything was great. I also got to know the importance of breath, sound and meditation, which is a totally new and different perspective on life for me. I was also was amazed by Swami Rama's wisdom and insights. [I had him read the book* Walking with a Himalayan Master.*] I read it and it was as if he was talking to me. I learned that most people who are*

not enlightened only care about reaching enlightenment while Swami Rama, enlightened, cared about people and their feelings and their needs and he loved them. And most important of all he didn't have a high ego. He was really into matters. He was exceptional and no one could replace him.

Now during these two weeks I learned more than 600 new words thanks to reading your book. But I drafted a blueprint and I set milestones for the upcoming year for myself. I read a book and another book and I took an adventure to the Mall. After the Mall I slowed down my life and observed people. In Taiwan most of my time was spent on work, schedules, countless meetings and making money which made me empty and greedy. I thought they were the safety nets which turned out to be an abyss of demanding more and more. Everything was not good enough and it made it so hard to try to please people and it made me unhappy. Anyway, I've learned a new attitude on life. I got a lot of things in such a short time. Wow and it's incredible! Thank you again. Live long and prosper. Sincerely yours, Eddy.

How about that for meeting adversity and resolving it? A young man who had never seen the shores of this land until three weeks ago. It was amazing. He loved every cuisine we offered to him.

So A, A, A, and A: Adversity, Agenda, Adversarial, and Agility. We decide our perspective. It's that simple. You have to step back and say, "Where is it all going? How much do I want to contribute? How much do I want to get involved?" You have to. That's just life. You are caught by the current. It's not so overwhelming but you've got to move with it. You've got to do it.

I was talking to a mother the other day and she was telling me, "I can't understand why my son just won't straighten up his room."

I said to her, "Well, does he eat all his spinach?" and she looked at me.

I said, "Mom, how old is he?"

"Well, he's fourteen."

"Well you know as well as I do, you are not part of that room. That's his world and he's going to run it the way he wants to. I know it opposes your schema but that's the way it is, isn't it? You have your perspective which you grew into and he has his, which he is growing into, and they're not going to be the same. Your agenda is not his agenda and so he sees you as simply adversarial. You've got to work that out. And you know as well as I do you can't tell him how to live his life. You can give him directions, you can give him guidance, you can set down certain house rules, but ultimately he's got to run his own life. You know that. I know you want him to be immune from pain and sorrow and suffering. That doesn't work because that's part of adversity. It just *is*, but it doesn't have to be the total story."

Look how far we have come. Some of you have been with us, Devi and me, for a decade or more. A lot of things have changed. A lot of things will continue to change. As you grow on the path you are on, do not think that adversity subsides. No, you have changed your perspective. You can take things on today that you couldn't have five years ago. They would have irritated you. Now you can ride with it. You are learning the ropes. You are not having grandiose expectations nor are you becoming cynical when people don't measure up to your high standards. That's just the way they are. I can continue to be who I want to be. There's no real standard that can be used as an objective measure. We know the insights. We know when we recognize, when we see beauty. No one has to spell it out for us or prove it to us. We recognize it because we can trust our own powers of discernment. And these grow precisely because you have learned to handle adversity. Adversity is not evil; it is simply a challenge. You've had different agendas over the years. You've altered them, you've modified them, and you've dropped some and added more. You always have to have one because you are on the path. You are not sitting still. You haven't retired from life. You're not making yourself obsolete. No, it's not possible. The human spirit wants to express itself. It wants to engage, through the body, the reality that is there. Because in that engagement, in that give and take of life, that's how you enrich yourself. There's no other way. Nobody is going to whisper something or pour something into your head. You have to go through adversity to get it and as you're going through you develop new kinds of agility. You become a nimble spirit. You are now going to resolve questions, arguments, that you couldn't before. You're also picking up the sensitivities of others faster. You're perhaps seeing things before they do, because you are more and more seeing things as they really are. There is a profound expansion of awareness that goes on in your soul because you want it.

When you see someone and you're attracted to that person, there is something that resonates in you, otherwise you wouldn't have that affinity. It's like vibrations meeting vibrations. If they're not on the same wavelength there's perhaps a little static. But your job is now learning how to read the rhythms of life and you're doing it. You know yourself better today than you did before. You don't have to keep repeating the past just because it's there. It's an old chapter, that's all. It has as much meaning as you want to give it. That's one of the hardest things that you have to finally get to—that often things have a meaning that you've either exaggerated or underestimated instead of seeing it for what it is. Once you do, there's a new kind of security that enters your blood stream. It's hard to explain. It's more profound than a science. But as you get to know yourself, as you get to know life, you feel more at ease with living. The old worries, anxieties, they don't exist anymore. And it's so easy to recognize them in your friends sometimes, because they haven't gotten to where you are as a stroller through life.

You rest for awhile at different encampments and then you move on. You acquire friends and then you lose friends, not because there is something wrong with you. No, it was meant just to come in for awhile and say farewell. I have none of my early friends from life.

They're all gone. We all went different directions. It's not a sad thing, perhaps a little nostalgic but that's just the way it is. Look at all the new ones I have acquired. You're open to life. You say, "Come on. Give me it. I'll take it on." You're careful and yet you're not a non-risk-taker. You're willing to take a few risks occasionally. You occasionally get scraped. Oh, we'll mend that. It'll heal. You will console people when you see they need it yet you won't make them dependent on you. You are a sovereign being. You don't need anything beyond what you already have. Swami Rama said, "You are complete but you are just unfinished."

That's what life is for, to finish, to go this whole gamut of this magnificent cosmos, to travel through the stars and the gardens of life, smelling the flowers and realizing you need very little. Your love grows much deeper. You are more subtle in your love. It's not demanding. It's there in the most subtle ways of offering it to others. You are not overwhelmed by feelings that it is rejected. Sometimes people can't help it. They really don't see what you're offering. So you have to just be patient again.

You've learned to calm down your breath and look at the results—profound results that occur in your metabolism, in your awareness, in your thoughts themselves. As you cultivate that particular skill, you enjoy the magnificent healthful fruits it brings to you all the time. You've got skills that you can return to again and again. They do not fail you. They get stronger. They resist and contradict entropy. The more you use it the stronger you get. You pick up on things and people. You walk into a home and you can size it up immediately. This is a good feeling. You are agile. You are not imposing yourself on people nor are you allowing other people to run your life. You're becoming a human being. "You're already divine," as Swamiji's master said, "Go out and find out what it's like to be human."

And that is one of the biggest challenges to all kinds of schools of spirituality. Too many of them want to make you an angel. We want you to become a full human being here. So enjoy the chocolate. Drink the chai. Celebrate the birthdays. Bring forth life and learn to forgive.

Mindtraps

A friend emerged in my life recently. Born in Hastings, he went West from the farming country. Arriving without references or leads in the Twin Cities, he surveyed the scene and wasn't quite sure what direction to seek. He landed his first job as a valet parking cars at an educational training Institute. It wasn't very glamorous, but he made nice tips. He said he tried to do it very well. Well, the boss noticed him and assigned him inside the school. The month being November, he was quite grateful. Inside he became a general handy man, folding towels, stacking shelves, and other mundane chores. He did his labor with a certain panache. The boss continued to take note and finally made him his assistant. That man today owns six stores with four hundred employees under him. He mentioned to me what he thought got him where he is today. Whatever the task he always gave it, unhesitatingly, his full attention.

Another friend is a talented par golfer. He restrains himself to that status because he doubts he could be a full pro. What's interesting is that everybody else is doubtless that he could. His colleagues envy his stunning swing. They wax poetic when he splits the fairway. They scramble to canonize him for his unerring putting. He privately revels in their remarks and knows they are rendered without hyperbole. His consistent skills would easily attract sponsors. Though he yearns, he won't, in spite of the evidence, envision himself at pro status. His restraint is his secret.

Two talented individuals and yet minds apart. One fulfilled his choices into his future, shaping it along the way; the other evades the evidence and meanders, unfulfilled, in what could be.

Pertinent to our subject matter here is that before anything meaningful can happen in the real world, it has to happen inside my inner world. Obvious. The possibilities we entertain and the emotional flair with which we infuse them affects what eventually comes about outside. Manifestation is less the product of hearsay than purposeful intent. Willfully ponder an idea long enough and it begins to have repercussions, first in my metabolism, and then in the outer world. Who doesn't attempt to shape the forces of life the way he'd like them to be? Yet, as any golfer knows, sand traps lurk along the way.

Following that lead, it's no exaggeration that most traps are generated by the same power that guides us into life and through the game. Let us explore some of these entrapments that lie in wait. Up front is the ever-present verdict that thinks something will inevitably go wrong. Nature and society somehow, without doubt, plot against us in subtle ways. Gleaned from that assumption, two more offspring occur: one called doubt and the other, conflict.

Being prone to doubt is often cast as a bad thing. Let us pause here with a caveat. On the contrary, in important activities a certain caution seems appropriate, lest we jump headlong with the familiar retort: what have I gotten myself into this time?

As I sort through my sense impressions from the outside world, I weigh them and begin to see where they might lead. Imagination, a very powerful tool, spreads out the options. Possibilities loom. In this way, my capacity to doubt is hardly a cumbrance, for it keeps me sharply solicitous for fine-tuning the options at hand. Who says doubt's the main adversary to bringing ideas into action? Instead, doubt stays handy as a consultant but submits to the higher manager: rational analysis. Now doubt gets a fair assessment instead of just badgering your emotions. No obligation for doubt to run rampant and disturb your health. Call for arbitration and let the calm light of reason assess their worth and pass judgment. It hardly needs mentioning, but the only compulsion doubt achieves is what we allow it.

As for that other encumbrance, conflict, consider, "Beauty does not ensnare men, they ensnare themselves." Here especially, we need to get at the crux of things. Conflicts do not grow on trees nor enter from outer space. We whine that it's always the situation or the other person that's at fault. Curiously, conflicts seldom stay lean. They expand exponentially. One could say it's their ambitious nature. Conflict is also cousin to hate. Like hate, it easily generalizes, spreading out into other issues, looking for an excuse.

Passing people as we walk in a commercial area of town, we have no idea what's going on in their heads. Some appear pleasant, others grim. But the contents of their minds as they stroll along are privy only to them. Some may be carrying a lot of heavy baggage with our favorite twin labels. Somehow, they insist it's almost morally necessary and God help anyone who reminds them or attempts to talk them out of it.

With sufficient exposure, we can admit that doubt and conflict, while quite different, can amass quite a toll on our personal endurance. No one's immune to their presence but they aren't contagious. The advantage of admitting their source, however, is that the remedy becomes surprisingly evident. Unpolitically correct as it is to admit, I am the evacuator. Without my abiding consent, it's all a charade.

Now the typical response to this declaration is indignant denial. Some proffer an immediate protest, an accusation of unfairness, even a spark of rancor. Please catch your breath, if you would, and ponder a moment. Do you have to submit to every doubt? Could you not stare them in the face and note what substance they show, if any? Instead of giving in, as that rascal Frenchman Descartes did, why not turn around, as it were, and doubt your doubts? So there!

For conflict, does it not take two to tangle? Whether it's marital wars, driving on the expressway, or cage wrestling, where's the contest if only one shows interest? Again, return to yesteryear. Not what but where does it originate? On the playing field or the player's mind? Any guesses on the table? Carrying conflicts around is wearisome business. But who's commandeering you? Someone insults you. . . . Well, a friend once handled it along these lines. He politely asked the loud perpetrator to repeat himself. Then he requested the same three successive times with different words. Then he demurred that he did not quite get it. Throughout, my friend kept an even keel with voice tone and cadence. No trace of arrogance, but a certain hint of puzzled inquiry. The insulter finally retaliated by swearing and departed the room.

My friend courteously failed to comply with the opponent's terms. Sure, that's his style and it may not be functional in every instance. But without cooperation, words fly by. Another point: conflict resembles a co-dependent conspiracy. Do you really want to be a colliding partner? Is asperity your best shot? Didn't we admit that reality offered more opportunities than we suspect? Or is that only on the eve of a full moon? Where has imagination gone in today's world?

Opportunities for recurrent conflicts abound. If I keep bumping my head as I descend the basement stairs, it must be the ceiling's fault. If people don't appreciate my outstanding qualities, what's wrong with them? The beauty of rehearsing an accepted affront in your mind is that you are the master of ceremonies and the sole audience. You can even enhance the script. No one's there to oppose your offended righteousness. You're running the entire show.

Human beings, in bearing their doubts and conflicts, demonstrate an amazing capacity to generate the accompanying pain in all its variety.

The other day a friend came by and mentioned, "Boy, I wish life didn't have any problems." "Really," I replied, "Without your problems, would you have gotten this far?" He had to think about that.

No one, to my knowledge, is yet born with a warranty declaring that life will be without problems. Like the neighbor who insists, "Well, I have to worry. How else do I know that I love my kids?" She resolved her self-doubts about her motherhood in an interesting manner. She proposed a unique equation: love is in direct proportion to worry. At last, a way to overcome her conflict of not loving sufficiently. When she becomes a nervous invalid this will certainly prove how valiantly she loves. Careful, the assumed problem may not always be the real problem. Can we be talking here about it's more in the eye of the beholder?

During a Middle Eastern conflict, a series of dog fights occurred above a capital city. Watching from the roof of the radio station, the local newscaster gave his personal blow-by-blow radio description of the fierce battle in the sky. Suddenly he excitedly declared that one of the home field's planes was shot down and, without any official confirmation, gave the plane number. Listening on the ground was an elder gentleman who recognized that the number belonged to his air force son. Almost instantly, the grieving elder collapsed with a coronary arrest. Some seconds later, the announcer apologized, wrong number. What we assent to in our minds makes it so regardless of the objective reality.

Two entrepreneurs, fast friends for twenty-years, entered into innumerable business investments together. Quite successful, they even shared vacations. Occasional differences were always ironed out, till one day a severe difference of opinion provoked such malicious anger and denunciation that they could hardly restrain from blows. The lover's quarrel brooded for nine months, each waiting for the other to apologize, till one day, within the same month, their enduring conflict stopped their heart beats. Their survival, however, left them no smarter: they choose to keep their offended reputations. They could not leave home without them.

Then there was Viktor Frankl, who, when asked how he could endure years of savaging degradations and inhuman privations in the Nazi concentration camps, quietly replied: ". . . there were always choices to make. Every day, every hour, offered the opportunity to make a decision, a decision which determined whether you would or would not submit to those powers which threatened to rob you of your very self, your inner freedom, which determined whether or not you would become the plaything of circumstance, renouncing freedom and dignity to become molded into the form of the typical inmate." Yes, he mentioned how the guards relentlessly deprived the prisoners of every liberty possible, except: "... the last of human freedoms—to choose one's attitude in any given set of circumstances, to choose one's own way." He firmly concluded that this was possible due to "the defiant power of the human spirit."

To succumb to doubt, to nurture conflict, to confuse love with pain, to give credence to self-generated traps, all are in your hands, Grasshopper. Or are you in a defiant mood? Your choice.

Evil and the Quest of Life

The interaction between consciousness and life promotes an enduring quest to know more about reality. Thus, in a way, man becomes a question unto himself. Probing and pondering, he tackles, with varying degrees of enthusiasm, the challenge of discovering and understanding the world at large.

In examining the heritage of knowledge that is available to him in his inquiries about life, man is helped in his quest by an enormous history of attempts similar to his own. His effort to make sense of life is not the first, nor will it be the last. In every new generation, it seems, there are those who demand the right to fathom the mysteries of existence irrespective of the vast heritage of knowledge offered them. They insist upon finding their own new way amidst the opportunities of today.

In his pursuit of the meaning of life, however, man is frequently obstructed, prevented from accomplishing his task. This opposition or that hindrance—however one may describe it—lessens or even halts the goodness of his desires, and concretely, man feels blocked or hemmed in by these unexpected circumstances which leave him in a not altogether pleasant situation. He feels hurt. He has met what he conveniently calls *evil*.

The problem of evil arises so often in life that most people come to identify human existence as essentially involved with it. One can't get away from its enclosures. It seems at times like a sinister power, waiting to pounce upon one's best and most innocent efforts.

Evil takes many forms, and it is often poignantly seen in the melodramas of every day. Soap operas such as Peyton Place and As the World Turns serialize the events that overtake many people in their struggle to live a "good life." In their endless plots, the problem of evil is rarely resolved. One finds only a slight reprieve until the next episode when circumstances and human desires once again forge a new scene for the emotionally charged battle between good and evil.

Most religions tell us to "offer it up," saying that "God will provide" or that "your reward will be greater when it's all over." But many people use this as an excuse to avoid confronting the real issue: why does evil occur at all? It is not a sign of maturity to remain naively fatalistic when the stakes are high: you could lose more than your submission. When something threatens your life, a passive attitude that tells you to back away from it may be playing right into its hands. How could life not go sour on these terms?

Let us examine, then, what it is that we call evil. Let us assume a certain working hypothesis. The major thrust of it is: life is fundamentally sound. In spite of the hazards of living, existence is felt and thought of mostly in favorable terms. So the first practical suggestion that results from this insight is that we should see everything that happens against this positive background. Another offshoot of the hypothesis is that life, or reality, enriches. Our appreciation of life increases, thanks to mother nature and human culture. Given these preliminaries, let us now examine more concretely the problem of evil and its reconciliation with life.

When we were children, our instinctive, or spontaneous, understanding of good and evil was very egotistical. I, like most children, usually considered everything from the point of view of my individual well-being. Certain realities held more interest for me than others, and it wasn't long before I set up my priorities. A toy, for example, was very important to me in my daily existence. If my older brothers or sisters took it from me, my whole world seemed threatened, and I would cry my eyes out over the pain of the loss. In my small world this breach of justice was not a minor incident; it was a catastrophe that shook my whole being. My day was ruined and my future happiness blighted, for it would probably take a miracle for me to recover the toy. While it was no consolation, at least now I knew my enemy. Evil had been met in both the personal form of my older brother and in the sense of objective loss—the irreplaceable possession, my teddy bear.

The very fact that I had favored this toy among others, that I had enjoyed it, thought about it, and played with it endlessly, made the entire experience with it "good" (goodness here being that which pleased me). The additional, but unfortunate, fact that the toy got broken, stolen, or borrowed without my permission made the entire experience "evil." I wanted my toy, and it wasn't there. I wanted it in the condition in which I left it, and now it was broken. My reaction to this situation was experienced as pain, and I questioned, as a result, the overall soundness of life. Our basic hypothesis is now in jeopardy.

The tendency to respond to life on the basis of what is good or bad, nice or evil, likeable or displeasing, is not left behind in childhood. It is a basic attitude that pervades one's whole existence through time, and adults are not exempt from its compelling force. All the emotions, in fact, derive from what we apparently experience as good or evil. Very early in life we learn to gravitate towards those people and events that somehow give us a certain satisfaction; conversely, we try to avoid, or at most grudgingly tolerate, those things that dissatisfy us.

A curious change, however, takes place during human growth. During the years of growing up there is often a voluntary reversal in our thoughts and values. Those toys and particular activities that so fascinated us at a certain age or period of life, gradually lose, in the least imposing way, their attraction. Before, one was ready to spill life's blood in the defense of a possession. Now the recent months of growth, biologically and emotionally, have prompted new interests that have eclipsed some of the older ones. A special object that we lavished with undying attention receives hardly a cursory glance as it gathers the dust of the passing seasons. Not only can my older brother now borrow the things, but in the most casual manner it is dismissed forever to his domain.

These former possessions or activities haven't suddenly become evil or repulsive; we have simply lost our interest in them. Now that we are older, occupied with our teenage interests, the objects and activities that formerly engaged our attention at, say, the age of ten, have only a distant relationship to our current interests.

Our center of attention has expanded. We don't look upon these former playthings as sinister or infused with evil; we have simply lost interest in them. The energy that we invested in them is no longer there. This analogy continually repeats itself, under different forms, throughout life's journey. We begin to recognize that what we considered good at one time in our lives has proved to be only temporarily "super" in our estimation. While we may very well recognize its intrinsic value, still its attraction wanes with no hard feelings. Life moves on, and we try to keep up with it.

Likewise, some of the "bad" in life, when we look back, may not have been so appalling after all. Those events that seemed to be so ominous, provoking fear and trepidation, may later be experienced without negative feelings. Thus, there is a certain dimension of relativity to whatever we considered to be good or evil. This flexible feature of reality is based upon the reflection that every concrete object in this world has its limitation, and in that respect it can only offer so much satisfaction. Experience reminds us that no single, concrete item can utterly satisfy our quest for what we may hypothesize as the "perfect good." And to the extent that something is less than comprehensively good, we can, due to our dissatisfaction, view it as something evil.

Conversely, there is nothing that may be called completely evil. People may be efficient in their actions and thoughts, things may be imperfect in their makeup, but no existing reality can embody evil. In realizing that both good and evil are relative, and even convertible depending on the way one looks at a situation, one can learn to become less intimidated and overwhelmed by their impact. In understanding their function in life, through experience, one begins to balance the presence of good and evil in the overall context of personal growth.

Our daily experience tells us that we grasp reality in partial installments, a little bit at a time. As we gradually accumulate exposures to life's crosscurrents, we connect these partial and limited exposures into a coherent whole. At least this is what we attempt to do in our quest for the meaning of existence. We make mistakes, and that's bad; but we learn from our mistakes, and that's good.

Nothing we experience through our senses is perfectly good or perfectly bad. Most of the time life can be improved upon. When evil asserts itself, for example, in conflicts and among people, in natural catastrophes involving injury and even death, our personal investment in the situation may prevent us for a while from coming to a reasonable judgment on the facts. On the other hand, a strong personal interest, painfully endured, may be a surer guide to the truth than merely being an aloof bystander.

When the problems and reverses of life can be balanced against the good of continual growth, then there is room to confront the pain of the day within a broader context. Life seems to be a continual preparation, painful at times, for the next stage of experiencing—this time with greater richness through the insights gained from the pain. This can be compared to the cycles of the seasons, in nature, where winter is followed by spring, death by regrowth. In many religious scriptures, too, death is seen as the threshold of a new life. Thus, the evil of nonexistence gives way to the greater goodness of the next stage of development. The evil, or fear, of pain is only temporary; it is endured for the sake of something more abundant to come.

Evil, surprisingly, thus helps us to discover the meaning of life. From experience I have learned that when something hurts me, when I feel the evil in myself in the form of pain, this is a signal for me to grow beyond this restriction. If I fail to understand the various kinds of limitations, or restrictions, that are placed on me, then my lack of discernment may cause the effect of pain. For example, if I eat something that doesn't agree with me, my stomach aches. The felt evil of this pain is the direct result of my not understanding, here and now, the correct relationship between this kind of food and the current condition of my stomach. In this way, the distress is good, for it reminds me to make an adjustment in this area. It signals that something is in disorder and, thus, needs reordering.

So evil is not a primary principle in life; it is merely a limitation that occurs in a situation of overall good. If our stomachs were not substantially sound, we could not become upset. While the stomach ache isn't good, the fact that we can detect it is good; we can use that knowledge for our benefit. This disclosure is possibly only because of the overall health in that region of the body. Consequently, evil always presupposes something good.

On a larger scale, the question is often asked: "If God is good, then how can there be evil at all?" In current Christian theologies—both Protestant and Roman Catholic—there is the conventional reply that evil is permitted so that greater good may come out of the situation. Human suffering and destruction is tolerated in order that, with the help of God's grace, virtue and spiritual growth may result. A mother loses her child at birth; a good and wholesome person is found to have cancer; innocent visitors lose their lives because of big-city gangsterism; abductions take place; wars break out; a plague devastates a village—a multitude of evils continually perpetrate themselves.

If God loves all, and if man's relationship with the divine is enclosed within a single lifetime, then the disparity between the various levels of human existence is all the more pronounced. In terms of world population, the few born into an abundance of enriching opportunities for personal and cultural fulfillment stand in shocking contrast with the majority of people who will never even hear of these opportunities. Viewed in this cosmic context, the easy answers limp.

Can the imbalances at birth and throughout life in so many cultures be somehow "tolerated" by the belief in divine bounty? From a survey of the living conditions confronting most of the world, one could draw the inference that God loves, but not uniformly. Yes, this contention would eventually undermine the belief in the essential justness and infinite goodness of the divine. So in attempting to resolve the ambiguity of global evils in its most personal and horrendous forms, it becomes increasingly difficult to restrict our field of vision to a single lifetime.

If we look, on the other hand, at the dynamics of human thought and action as they shape one's personal history (rather than theorize about the structure of divine providence), then fresh questions open up a wider vista from which we may explore the solution. Given the imperishable core of man's nature, must his journey through life be kept within the parameters of sixty or seventy years? Is it unreasonable to suppose that the experiences necessary for human fulfillment, in a total sense, may require more than one life span? Without being fatalistic, we can admit a certain causal principle underlying nature's workings in general: certain effects normally, at least for the most part, follow from determinate causes. If this principle isn't true, then there is no good explanation for existence. Life would be sheer chaos; there would be no coherence whatsoever. Anything could happen at any time. In other words, every form of existence would be self-destructive. There would be no rhyme or reason for it as far as the human intelligence could detect.

Presupposing, then, a sufficient degree of rational consistency behind life's complexities, each individual may have more responsibility for the fate of his personal and collective environment than suspected. The circumstances surrounding my birth, for instance, in conjunction with the subsequent opportunities for growth unfolding within the family and community, may be more of my determination than Providence's. Perhaps birth in this century is not my first initiation to life, but a continuation which I chose, one that allows for new phases of my development. The personal and social texture of birth may be the product of past decisions that now opens a new future for me that will provide the experiences for further development. In other words, is my current situation not a result of past decisions and their consequences?

There is still enough room between my decisions and their effects to permit me to reevaluate the resulting situation and decide to make new adjustments. Hopefully, we learn from our mistakes, and this shows that there is room for us to make a choice in the face of unexpected, or dire, consequences. Life thus beckons me to work through the pending obstacles I will meet.

The question remains: could human progress take palace in a responsible way without my choosing a total life plan? If it becomes a working hypothesis, in combination with the statements at the beginning of this essay, then the good and evil that befall me can become opportunities for spurring my progress. Instead of blaming God for the woes of this world, then, I can exercise my human freedom and go beyond the limits of "evil" restrictions. Even if the circumstances of my present life are the consequences of what I have accomplished through my choices in the past, the exertion of a life plan for self-emancipation can ultimately free me from the bondage of the past. I am not doomed by my past unless I choose to be.

In overcoming petty evils, one can gradually realize, through painful experience, that the exercise of choice and discrimination increases one's personal freedom over these restrictions. I thus shape my future by sustaining a personal, enduring responsibility for it is progress. Anything less will impose the constraint of suffering—and suffering consists of self-imposed restrictions that prevent me from overcoming evil.

Meeting the challenge of life's obstacles, then, increases my power to overcome them. Instead of being evil, they are invaluable signs that urge me to transcend their restrictions through the immortal freedom of my spirit. The achievement of this goal dissolves evil into a mirage.

Be an Artist

I got an email where the person said, "I've been trying to get away from tracking all that stuff going on today in this country. I've seen enough. The group who is doing it will never be held accountable. It's not worth my time to meditate on it for even a minute. It's just the nature of this place these days. It will always be, as long as people think that they are their body, their party, their race, their family, and their country. All I can do is do my own *dharma* as best I can and follow out my vocation. Beyond that I will only upset myself over things that I can't change and it's not going to serve anyone."

The most wonderful gift that we have is between these two ears. It's the source of our appreciation of life as well as the source of our discouragement at times. People see only what they want to see. People believe only what they want to believe—even if the facts say otherwise. People sometimes put their life in the hands of a symbol. They somehow confuse the fact that in striving they have to suffer. So how do you decode their belief systems? How do you get them to give up the sense that somehow they have to be impaired, wounded, or suffering in order to get someplace in life? Like the letter that I got, the individual finally came to the realization that there are some things that you just can't change. You can't blame the weather if it rains on the picnic. It won't help. It won't change a thing, but we get ourselves all upset, don't we?

I think there are certain remedies here that are available. At first they don't seem to be very effective and they don't seem particularly attractive, but if you give them a chance you might be surprised. Again, it goes back to the mind. Your mind is not alone in this life. It's in a body. In fact, you are an embodied spirit. You've chosen to be in this three-dimensional format which grows and declines, grows and declines. Our cells don't last very long. Your body is dying and you're being reborn, so to speak, all the time. There are things that are going to go on in your body that you don't have very much control over. But there are many things that you do in your behavior and your exercises in your life that you do have control over to some extent, sometimes more.

You're all on a path. You have your own preference for the way you want to review it. Some will say, I'm a *bhakti* yogi or I'm a *jnani* yogi or a *raja* yogi. I would like to look for a common element there. You're really on the path of being an artist. You are to create your future. Think for a moment. You have no idea what tomorrow's going to be like. You have no idea what next week is going to be like. It could even snow, much to our displeasure. But the point is the parameters in how we live have a great deal of liberty. You have to choose how you want to use that liberty, how you want to respond to the situation that can't be improved immediately or in the near future. We don't always like what's going on today in our country, in our city, in our workplace. And yet I keep saying that you are meant to be an artist. You are meant to create something that's an expression of you. You are to recognize how to put the energies together, however modest it may be, to bring about something that you feel is worthwhile, because you can't live with yourself unless you do.

You are meant to live a noble life. I know that sounds almost strangely corny, but that's true. You can't live without having a sense of nobility otherwise your health will suffer terribly. But you have to realize how to use the tools you have and that's often forgotten or not sufficiently paid attention to. You have to discern, what is the best way for me to act as a human being in the circumstances of today, in any situation I find myself—at home, at work, at play. That's what I create. That's where I express my humanity, my humaneness. Often times it takes a crisis to find out what you're really made of. Just what do you do when a crisis comes? What do you ponder? It means you have to follow your nature, because that's all you've got. If you oppose your nature and try to coerce it, sabotage it, you're going to end up with a lot of suffering sooner or later. And the strangest thing is we all talk about how we've got to be disciplined. We've got to get things done the right way. Discipline simply means following your nature. There's nothing particularly harsh about that. Discipline simply means understanding who I am, what I've got, and following it up. You're a body, a mind, and a spirit. What is the order there? What is the reality of those three, and how can I work with them in such a way that I can be proud of my artistic creations? So, the remedies for the ills are to follow your nature.

Nikola Tesla is probably the greatest scientist of electricity who ever lived. He's the one who gave us these lights, not Edison. He was asked to look at the reports of the Manhattan Project when they created the atomic bomb in 1942 in the basement of the University of Chicago gymnasium. Professor Oppenheimer and the gang were very satisfied. They were convinced they could smash the atom. He looked at the papers and he concluded, "Gentlemen, you're right. You will smash the atom but you'll pay a terrible price. You're going to put a curse on this earth." "What do you mean?" "It's the residue, the poison that will be released from all those explosions." And then he said something interesting to them. He said, "If you let me, I'll show you how to work with nature and you'll get even more power." They sent him home unfortunately. And we still feel the consequences.

The point is, you and I can't change what happened in '42. We have to somehow protect ourselves as best we can. But you will always have the opportunity to work with human nature, to find out what's the harmony here. How can I resonate with my spirit so that I can be the artist, the noble person, in spite of the circumstances? In that way we discover our potentials. We often don't realize that if we force things, if we coerce things, we won't really gain that much headway in the mystery of who we are, the hidden regions where the treasures reside. So in recognizing the importance of working with your nature, in understanding it, exploring it, testing it, what you're really doing is you're leading yourself to freedom, a freedom that you don't have right now. You only have a little bit. And so you are dissolving the ignorance that is confining you to your suffering, to the limitations that you feel in life and wonder, why can't I do better?

Want to do better? Study yourself. Study how this works. Two things occur up here all the time. First, you are constantly getting impressions from the outside world and you are turning them into ideas, concepts, thoughts. Second, as you do, there is another part of you that gets a little excited about that. We call this emotion—passion if you will. Those two walk together as partners: thought and emotion. Your job is to work with them. It can be done because you have a power within you that can step outside and examine them. Why did I get upset there? Why did I get so emotional? We have that ability to discern, to penetrate what occurred. Without it you would be just bouncing around.

You don't have to constantly repeat or rehearse the past. You can say, whoa, what's going on here? And because of that innate ability, it can never be taken from you. It can give new meaning to your actions in the future, now. You can determine how you want to respond. Just ponder. You don't deny the emotion. You don't deny the harvest of thoughts that you have but you simply want to say, let's inspect them. Let's do a little introspection for a moment and find out, which ones do I really want? Which ones do I like? Which ones are helpful? Which ones are useful? Which ones are beneficial and which ones just trip me? If I do that, this is likely to happen. Is it? Well, do you want that to happen? Well, no. Then why do it? Why think certain thoughts if you know what's likely to happen emotionally? I'm not trying to indict anyone, I'm just saying this is the way our minds are. At times you've got to say, could I be enjoying myself more in life? You don't want to pass any serious judgment. Now, wait a minute. Am I tense? Why do I wake up tired in the morning if I'm getting enough sleep? Am I taking things to bed with me that are unsolved, that I'm not paying attention to? If I'm waking up every morning all stuffed and I feel a little grumpy, maybe I should use the neti pot. It helps so many people clear up in the morning. You understand to get the breath flowing, to clean up the channels in the face, and then you'll feel better. You understand your nature.

So again, in attempting to be the artist that we're meant to be, there are certain things we want to do to improve the instrument. So we go for a walk. We make the time to take a break and leave work. It's not going to run away from me. It's going to be right there when I get back. Go for a walk and just be aware of your environment. Did you ever examine the architecture of buildings where you live? Did you ever wonder why they were made that way? Get your mind off what you were doing five minutes ago so that you give the mind a break. You come back a little calmer, more restored, ready to hit the wheel again.

Aristotle defined happiness in a very interesting way. He said it's a life that flourishes. How can you flourish more? He wasn't talking about riches. He was talking about your energy, your attitude, the way you respond. Do you flourish? And can people sense that in you? You say you want to help others. Are you willing to sometimes put yourself behind to give a break to this person? Some spiritual paths call it service, *seva*. But again, there's a little challenge here. Because to really perform service well, you have to discern what's the best way. You don't want to be a busy-body to somebody. You don't want to just simply impose yourself because you feel you've got to do service. Now you're just satisfying yourself, not the person. Being nice is not a substitute for discernment.

The Dog Whisperer, Cesar Millan, runs into problems when he comes to help rehabilitate the dog. The owner thinks that lavishing a lot of attention on the dog, giving it treats, is how to get the dog to do what they want. The dog just runs wild and keeps saying, more, more, more. Why? Because the owner is satisfying themselves and not trying to recognize the nature of the dog. So again, it goes back to discerning the realities that you're dealing with—people, situations. When you have a little tension with people at work, try to understand them maybe. Understand the situation. Are you leaving out something? Just step back. The power of discernment is broader than the occasion in which you use it. It can see almost around corners at times. Swamiji used to say, "You are a nucleus and the universe is your expansion." That's consciousness. That's meant to be an awareness. It's a cognitive situation. It's knowledge. It's learning to be in contact with reality and staying in harmony with it. Then things will flourish. Then happiness ensues.

The first time he made the following statement, he stunned me. He said, "Most people can't be happy because they don't train themselves for happiness." I had never associated those words together: "train for happiness." We somehow think it's just going to happen. He said, no, it doesn't happen that way. You have to train for happiness. Now I started to pay attention in that lecture and he brought it all back to understanding yourself. How can you take the powers you have, your cognitive powers, your emotional powers, your physical powers, how do you express them? How do you bring them into action? How do you engage them with life? Do you know what you're doing? Can you have a reasonable expectation: if you do this, that is likely to happen? That's how you train for happiness. You must recognize you are at the center of all that. Happiness is not the responsibility of your spouse or your mother-in-law. It's yours. That means it's self-training.

People sometimes used to ask Swamiji, "Oh, enlighten me, please. Touch me with *shakti*." He'd just look at them, "If I ever touched you, you'd just explode." No preparation, no self-training. What do you really think is going to happen? May I ask you for a moment, what do you think is going to happen if you suddenly could become enlightened? What do you think is going to happen in you? Biologically, emotionally, intellectually. Think for a moment. What does that mean? In the body. I remember him saying there is a holistic preparation that must be there so that it takes and stays, so that you can hold it. Because you are going to see with such clarity, such discernment. You are going to see with such vitality and it goes on and on. And then he pulled back and said that's enough.

So we are preparing by realizing we are the artist of our life. We make things happen by our actions or our omissions. The more you use matter, the more it breaks down, loses its strength. Not so with the human spirit. The more you engage yourself intelligently, calmly, the stronger you get. The less likely you are to fly off the handle when the crisis comes. There is a kind of enrichment of your being as you begin to work with yourself and sense what's going on inside you, how your thinking changes as you calm down. How your walk, your whole demeanor, begins to alter itself in conjunction with working on yourself. You'll see life differently, but not because life has changed. Something else has changed. It's like the teenagers who grow up finally and have their first child, they realize, "Gee, my parents have really grown wisdom over these past few years." Keep it simple. Don't rush. Don't try to make the enlightenment Olympic team the first month. Grow into it. We do that in our tradition. We could hit you early like Paul of Tarsus. You know what happened to him when he fell off the donkey. He couldn't handle it. We want you to open it up, walk into it like a bright sunrise and just be astonished. Peaceful, no friction, just awe. That's the way Swami Rama wants to bring the students along.

You are in a tradition; remember, this is not a beginners' tradition. This is a finishers' tradition. You are on the last leg otherwise you wouldn't be here. You are meant to be finishers in this life. They will do half for you. They'll do the bigger half because they know what we're up against. Swamiji said one day, "You have a harder life than I did when I grew up." He will factor that in and give you more help as a result. He said you have chosen the greatest vocation. "Be in the world and yet remain above." You haven't taken refuge in a cave. He didn't have much respect for yogis that did that. He didn't think they were helping humanity enough. But you are by being the person you are at work, at play, and with family. So you have embraced the highest vocation and the enjoyment is to find out what that's all about. You are a work in progress. You're flying as you're building the airplane. That's part of the fun.

If you would have told me years ago that I would end up being what I am today, I would have said you're nuts! Things just happen, don't they? You make choices. Something else happens. It's like opening up a present somebody gives you. You don't know what's in there. Ah, and there it is. It touches you. That's the way you are meant to be. You are meant to be surprised sometimes by the way you act, what you say, a gesture, and it's so delightful to catch people off guard that way. Then you can feel the affection coming towards you too. Swamiji used to say, "All life is nothing but relationships." So you have to build them, you've got to foster them, you've got to mend them. They go on and on. You're built for being around for a long time, not necessarily in this body but a long time. That's what immortality is all about.

So, like the email I read at the beginning, we don't always like the stuff that's going on today in our environment, our government, our schools, but we're not going to let that hold us back from being the kind of person we want to be. Don't ever condemn yourself, regardless of what has taken place in the past, all the mistakes, the flounderings, the betrayals. Let it go. You're still intact. Your powers are here. No one can steal them. Just use them. Use them the way you see what the truth is saying to you at this moment. You've got something in you so beautiful. It's called conscience. That's a hidden power that speaks to you. Listen to it. It shouldn't speak harshly. If it's harsh, you've got to take a look at it. At times you'll be called to extend yourself. At times you'll say, oh, I've got to stay out of this. It's not for me. Fine. Your freedom will continue to blossom as you follow your nature and recognize that, in this book of life, you are the author. You might cite other people but you are the author and you have to keep writing those chapters. And as we see you, we see where you are in the book of life.

So, we all have the same vocation ultimately, to build a community in which we can share, respect, and help each other when we can. I don't always have to like what you do but I can always be kind. I can always walk away if it's not for me, but I can always be kind even if you're not. Kindness goes a long way. Speak kindly. There is a wise person in you. All you have to do is speak to that person. Sit down quietly. Ask this remarkable mind. If you're stuck and things aren't working out just ask and listen. It'll come forth.

The other night someone told me a story. She wanted something. She wanted to take a certain training course and she didn't know where or how. She was getting a little discouraged. She went to bed and Swami Rama appeared to her. He just smiled at her as if to say, "Don't worry. Just wait." The next day when she woke up, in the mail out of nowhere, came the application for the very thing she wanted to take. This happens all the time, doesn't it? We're in it together. We help each other. Be kind.

The Journey of Self-Discovery

Creatively, the twentieth century dazzled in its abundance of inventions, societal innovations, artistic presentations, even wars. One may say that engagement with nature and matter is only hampered by a dreary imagination. And who is responsible? Why, the mind, of course.

Ah! The mind, such a phenomenon! We use it to contact life and to fulfill all our ambitions. But it is also a sort of tricky reality. As much as the mind can produce wonders, it can show other sides as well. There are moments when the mind foists upon us the idea that it is a dire necessity to be admired by significant others for almost everything we do. When the admiration does not arrive, how upset we feel. Who made me upset? Could it be the mind? Of course not, my mind would not make me feel that way. When things don't go the way we like them to, distress is felt. Instead of just saying, "Well, it's just too bad," the mind thinks that its distress is obviously caused by a nemesis. From weather conditions to the political situations, from my neighbor next door to my kids or colleagues, the idea that what's making me feel this way might be my view of these unfortunate circumstances is not entertainable. My sense of entitlement would be compromised.

Throughout the day, the mind loves to play with its ideas, especially about itself. To really solve our problems once and for all, we absolutely need something other or stronger or greater than what we currently possess. Reflecting and acting less dependently on externals seems too risky. My work environment, my home life, people at large, just need to recognize my importance.

Then there's the striving ideal that one should be thoroughly intelligent, competent, achieving, beautiful at all times, and beyond apologies. Then there's also the idea that if something is really good, as one sees it, the more quantity, the more the good accrues. Try that with coffee and find out how your body responds. The mind also slips into the attitude where what we really want is uncontestable control all the time over the situation. Play the market and watch what happens on that one. Headaches are just waiting when the mind insists that life and every task has "got to be perfect." There's the idea that in the midst of troubles if I just act professional and get emotionally detached from any involvement, then I've done the spiritual thing. Well, if you want to become a zombie, it may get you some mileage. It's a choice, but that's not what life is all about. When we're afraid to devote ourselves to people and projects, aging prospers. Then finally there's that marvelous idea that we have virtually no control over our emotions. I'm victimized all the time, and we cannot help feeling disturbed about life in general.

These are just some of the comical traps, but I'm amazed at how often I bump into them. I have a lady who comes to see me about every two or three months. I can predict before she walks in the door what her complaint will be. Because this is the fourth time she's informing me and she can't understand why life isn't any different. She's ready to end it all. I'm saying well, please remember me in the will. She gives that look because I don't take it as seriously as she expects.

It's amazing how we can keep playing around this way. Sometimes it's hard to figure out exactly what to do. I think it's very dangerous when we start to play with the reality of the mind and we forget what's out there, the empirically based things that meet you every day. You get up in the morning. It's cold. You don't want to leave that warm bed, but you go and wash your face, time for ablutions, walk on that cold floor in the kitchen. It's a reality out there. You're hungry, you need a cup of coffee and you're involved in it. So you're always engaged then with something that is more than you, at least more than the body at the moment. That's what keeps you sane. Because there are a lot of people in institutions who just stay up in their mind. They weave tales, stories, scenarios that have nothing to do with baking bread or cooking or tying a shoelace.

So also in yoga, which is not an attempt somehow to withdraw from life. No, it's an attempt to understand it first. Can one find the richness in it even though it's limited, it's temporary, even faulty? Things break down. So what? That's just part of life. And because of who you are, this fundamental, magnificent mind or other that's so mysterious in you, always abiding there, that's what walks you through life. You see, we are really not human beings searching for spiritual experiences. We're spiritual beings journeying through human experiences. When you view life from the latter perspective, it's a different context when the days don't always work out as planned. Those utterly unpredictable events, those moments of frustration that exceed our competency at times, or backfire on us. Yet look who is still surviving.

Yoga, that most natural of all philosophies, certainly endorses the amazing intelligence that we have. It espouses techniques and opportunities to develop that even further, but never at the cost of mundane reality. Remember that. There's an old saying that goes, "God is found in the details." Well, I would like to say, "Your spirituality is not found by withdrawing from the world." So if you really want to find out who you are, you've really got to get engaged in life, you've got to be a neighbor, you've got to be a citizen, a traveler at times, if you can. Not merely to be on a list, that you live here, but to be engaged with the issues, the programs. What are you doing for your community? How can you take your skills, your competencies, and touch the lives of others in some way? You don't have to be a crusader. It's a more comprehensive approach. It keeps you balanced, less veering towards some of these self-pitying traps that the mind gets itself into. We are so sincere in our thinking: if only things were different, why isn't it a better world? Maybe I should move away. Move away and you'll soon discover that you are carrying it right with you.

By staying in touch with things, noting their contours, testing their limitations, sensing what works, what doesn't, risking a little at times, you begin to discover you are freer than you supposed. However, you can't discover this by just keeping to yourself. You first have to engage life out there and then that shuffling back and forth, that ability to deal with the tensions, that is what opens up the reservoir in you so that you don't have to fear life as you get older, as the body starts to weaken.

But there's something in you that can be getting stronger almost in inverse proportion. Your spirit can be getting stronger as you get older, more perceptive of what's true. When you can feel that way, you learn what love is all about. When I lived with Swami Rama, I used to watch him intently when he was with people. I watched how discerning he was, how he adjusted himself to that person regardless of the age or background. I always noticed too that there was such a fostering attitude in him towards that human being. What could he do to enhance their career, their ambition, their special plan that they were all excited about, or where they wanted to go at this time in their life? That was always uppermost in him. So he would make the phone call, coax his friends whom he could trust, and say, "Come on, help me out with this person."

Perhaps even more astonishing was the unobtrusive way he would regard another's assistance. If you gave him a hundred dollars, he would see to it that you got at least one thousand dollars for your trouble—and all anonymously.

Those episodes made me ponder anew what love is all about. Is not love that which enlivens? How do you feel with your friend? How does that person feel with you? Is there an excitement, a joy, a spontaneity? Can you tease? And most of all can you trust? You know you're not going to be condemned because you made a mistake. In the yogic path, there's something very important called *viveka,* discernment, the ability to see the contours, the edges, the different flavors, to recognize "Okay, this didn't work out. Let's move on." Learning to measure the pace, depth, width, and height of events, learning how to relate to them, and learning at times that you're going to be fooled. People may take advantage of you no matter how cautious you are.

But again there is something that you return to in the night or in the morning when you do your practices. There's something there that is blemishless, that has no limits, that always restores you, that can always be called upon as your abiding friend. It can't age. Because of its existence you have an advantage regardless of how cloudy and dark the days can be at times; how lonely and desperate times can become. By taking refuge in that, you touch something that enables you to go on because nobody here can predict what is going to happen in the next five years. We've all heard rumors, some good, some bad, but again, so what? You're going to be around, and *how* you're going to be around is determined now. What's your attitude? What's your disposition toward the future? What are you doing now to prepare to take advantage of that future?

People have the amazing capacity to know their future and yet resist it. Many employees continue working at a job that they secretly find distasteful. Instead of diligently searching for other opportunities, they put up with things, not realizing the cost to their health and spirit over time. They comfort themselves with an attitude of resignation and when challenged by a friend will come up with all sorts of rationalizations. In fact, they resent being reminded of their situation.

There is a battle going on within us. On one side is sloth, that self-deprecative attitude that turns away from the challenges of life. Utterly opposed to this rationalized weakness of spirit is an attitude of boldness, a certain effrontery that arouses one to confront the ordeal of life's unpredictable tests. The medieval masters called it magnanimity. Without this attitude upon life, they insisted their struggles for self-development would overwhelm the aspirants. Even Saint Teresa of Avila insisted that the most important virtue for traveling the spiritual path was not love, but fortitude. Swamiji used to say, "The worst sin a yogi commits is not mistakes; it's laziness, sloth."

In his experience, Swamiji noted three versions of sloth. They're all connected. There's sloth of the intellect. When a good idea comes, what do we do? He used to get so mad at people because he knew what splendid ideas came along. He challenged, "What are you doing about it? Why do you think you have that idea? It's a gift to you, and you're not acting on it. It's not just there to say, *Oh, gee.*" He used to get so frustrated because he knew that if they acted on it all kinds of benefits would then happen. We sit back and say "Well, maybe not, it's a little scary." He used to crumble as people heedlessly dismissed their fine ideas.

Connected to that dismissal is sloth of action. Swamiji used to really hammer at me for procrastinating. You see, we Irish have a slight sloth, very slight. We sometimes put off things saying, "Well, I'll do it next week." No. Now, now, now! Swamiji used to come down on me all the time. He'd say, "Look, it may not come back. Be careful. I can help only to some extent. I need your cooperation."

He told me one day there was one person in the group who slowed him up a whole year. It was one person who claimed to be a great leader in the organization. Swamiji was on a timetable with only so many years in his body. He had to get on with it, so he was terribly frustrated. He lost a whole year on that person's selfishness.

Finally, there's the sloth of the heart, the worst kind. It's when you see something that you could contribute to and you decide you're not going to do it. You're not going to help that person, and all it would take is a little energy. He said those sloths are what will destroy you. He had no patience with people like that.

Ah, the mind, what a clever fellow it is! What an instigator of change, what a perpetrator of self-delusions, what a discerner of truth! What are you and your mind up to today?

Then there is the journeyman mind, the revealer of secrets, the possessor of hidden knowledge. Revelation, however, is not copied down in a revered book. May I suggest that the mind is the source and grandest revelation? Visit the revealed treasures of countries if you will, but how about the journey within? Talk about a change in topography. Metaphorically, the mind's inner journey means you have to grow in awareness. How strange to posit that you become more knowledgeable without pursuing ideas. You will have to abandon some old knowledge, not because it's bad, but because it hasn't the strength to measure up to what you want to know. This new knowledge is translated not into a fascinating idea but a new power of discernment. The inner journey takes you past the reservoir of ideas into what at first seems the new territory of silence and darkness. The mind wants to hold on to its ideas and its dependence on sense contacts. After all, they have gotten you this far, for better or worse. Thus, as you depart from the comfortable light and warmth of familiar ideas into the darkness, the mental distractions abound. As the months roll along, it seems that the same distractions keep cropping up in different guises. You plead: "Have I made no advancement at all?" That rational mind now steps in and protests hauntingly that maybe it's a waste of time, all these hours and so little to show for it. Guess who is behind all this consternation? The mind, no less.

Frankly, you have advanced, but you don't know it. If you only open your eyes (excuse the paradox), you will see that you have arrived at a crossroads. In the darkness you have met Mr. Doubt. Your mind has turned into one of its many unwanted guises. As long as you engage him on his terms, then you are trapped into his lair of suspicion. Now, doubt, like fear, has no substance. It's all bluff. Just turn your mind and face this mirage and tell it that it doesn't fool you for one minute. The reason you doubt is that you want your comfortable ideas back, especially the rational idea that you should have much more to show for your efforts. Laugh at your mind; it's only teasing you, and you are buying it. Give your mind a run for its money, as Swami Rama used to say, dialog with it. Force it to prove itself, and watch what happens. You are on an inward journey without rational precedence.

A singer once uttered the line: "Hello, darkness, my ol' friend." As a medieval compatriot put it: entering into the silent darkness, without the companionship of ideas and images, is like entering a cloud of unknowing. Your role is no less than to get familiar with the new territory. Your solitary mission: pierce the void of the darkness. Once you get a taste for the journey, then you begin to know yourself without masks. Are you up to it?

In the darkness of your inward journey, you acquire the sight to discern the reality before you in your daily life, not as the commercial world would have you view it, but for what it truly amounts to in its limitations. There, amid encountering the tasks and fashions of daily existence, is where you look for your growth. Are you still enthralled or are you beginning to size things up accurately and enjoy them without grandiose expectations?

The mind remains a trickster until we hold it accountable. Learn to be a little reflective. Ask yourself, "Now, why did I think that? Why am I afraid here? What am I trying to protect? Do I think I'm going to lose something or not gain something?" Sometimes one can be clearly right and yet know that insisting on that conclusion isn't always necessary. Probe yourself with an ease and just see what comes forth. What the mind cannot tell you about yourself doesn't exist. You need to just listen. Already pulsing through you is a thrust towards fulfillment in life.

Life's journey takes one uniquely through the dangerous curves, the hills, the dark valleys, and those perturbable cul-de-sacs. Did reality deliberately keep things hidden from you, not out of disrespect but, on the contrary, to stretch you beyond your self-important ideas? Yet when you look back, even now, look at the things you've managed to do in life already. You are still intact.

When our lifestyle puts us in hope's way, there's a gradual loss of anxiety about daily living, a gradual diminishment of fears of the future. These are all symptoms of your growth. One day you have to resign from all the external assurances you've been clinging to for security. No rush, staying on the journey gets you ready. And if you have religious pretensions, one day you will outgrow every concept of your favorite deity. And you will be able to do that not by banishing them and saying what a waste of time. No, your beliefs were almost inevitable, given your circumstances and concerns.

In the grand scheme of your continual journey, you come to the realization that the mind participates in stages of expanding awareness wherein important ideas, images, beliefs, and actions about life at a previous stage inevitably require revision. Why? Because the experience of reality is indisputably richer than any accurate idea of it. The proof of that insight is easy to come by. Just compare your cherished ideas on life held as a teenager with your vision of life in your adult years. One's understanding, although true, based upon one's apprehendable evidence, may yet be seen to be surprisingly incomplete based upon a greater range of discernable reality. How many intelligible ways can one truthfully describe a flower and then pronounce to the world that no more true descriptions are possible? Some may be shocked by the revelation of richer reality and voluntarily withdraw from the journey; others may simply plateau, as it were. The current life's stage is far enough for them. So be it.

Still, a few others appreciate the entire journey from birth. Their quest: "Come what may, I want the fullness of the reality. I don't want to settle for a metaphor or a revered text or icon, however inspiring and consoling it may be."

What we have here is a toughened traveler ready for the journey's final stages, because one is no longer dependent upon anything but one's own mind and heart. You alone prepared your eyes in the dark silence, and so, like the pickpocket who renounces his beggarhood, you see now beyond the beckoning pockets of the one standing before you and instead discern the saint.

Attachment

Q: Is an attachment necessarily harmful?

A: For years I pondered attachment. I knew there was more to it than just plain connection. It came to me that attachment per se is not enough, since our daily life is endlessly filled with attachments, including our body and its operations. Something more was needed to justify the bad press attachment got.

I asked myself, why do only some attachments get you into trouble? Ah, it's the importance you place on some. Attachment per se is not bad or negative, but as one places importance on the attached idea or object, one creates a dependency. The greater the importance, the greater the dependency. One's dependency may lead to an infatuation, an obsession, an addiction, or an absolute need. Unfortunately, this process often goes on unconsciously, creating a more pervasive dependency.

You either select or are forced to accept a host of attachments, upon which you build up a kind of hierarchy of importance, and this arrangement grows into dependence so strong that it becomes your self-identity. The greater the importance placed on the attachment the greater the dependency, which becomes one's self-identity.

Q: Is attached dependency necessary to obtain the absolute pinnacle of one's endeavor?

A: Many who rise to the top of their business, athletic, or artistic field always seem to have a tunnel-like vision, an obsession with the task at hand. Their goal becomes their attachment and identity.

Somewhere along the way, it really starts to kick in when one chooses a particular endeavor seriously. Then the sustaining desire, as you go along, becomes the unconscious pressure, creating a pervasive dependency and the centerpiece of their identity. In a sense they can't live without this self-acceptance. It gives them the primary meaning to their existence. It's who they are. They are at an excruciating loss when it is not recognized or acknowledged or useable by society.

When you get to that high level of achievement or competence, all of life is put on a hierarchical scale and you support the top rungs because that's where you think you are the worthiest. In other words, on that plane, you are the greatest good in your eyes. You are a rock star, you know it, so why quit the venture? It derives meaning in your life. Often this tunnel-like vision brings collateral damage to relationships and family along the way.

People can become exceedingly successful, even a genius, in any field from art to business, and while they enjoy their rightful fruits and benefits, they miss the overall purpose of life. Still, their achievements give them a genuine glimpse of the totality. Some will do it with collateral damage; others will keep their integrity.

People can achieve superior states of awareness, power, and knowledge in any field if they are totally dedicated and do the work. They can also so strongly identify with their acquired proficiency that their endeavor may leave them deficient in some areas of human living, even unknowingly confused about their identity.

Words don't always get a fair shake. Two dire warnings are reiterated to budding students: one, avoid the bondage of karma (human acts) and be unattached to the things of this world. Make sure you surrender the fruits of your actions (karma). These three notions, bondage, be unattached, and surrender fruits, are often associated with each other and mostly designated in a pejorative way. Without making any excuses for spiritual teachers, let us as far as these words are concerned, apply the judicial rule of construction: let words mean what they do in common usage. Taking these mandates at face value, let us place them into the context of everyday life and see how they stand up where cause and effect abounds.

Quite simply, your days are utterly filled with episodes of cause and effect. Not just your private life but the whole world runs on that fascinating combination of action spelled out as karma. Nature and civil society could not survive without it ruling the land. From cloistered nuns to the unemployed, from royalty to the merchant marines, no one remains exempt. In irrevocable words: to gain or receive an effect, there has to be a cause. Moreover, the combination is not arbitrary. Only the appropriate cause has a decent chance to produce the anticipated effect. In leaving aside the reactive emotions and melancholy presuppositions with the word, karma may be viewed as an indispensable and welcome part of the rhyme and rhythm of reality.

Everything just described implies attachment and bondage throughout, unless cause and effect are attached no results. It does not matter whether the cause is mechanical or human. To state this fact in another way: your actions imply and necessitate bondage, or no action comes forth. If hydrogen does not bond with oxygen, there is no water. If food does not bind with digestive juices, no nourishment. If your signature is not attached to the contract, is it binding? Unless cause binds to effect can there be a result? In the real world, bondage is not negligible. Do we not bond with our friends? Is not the human body a bundle of connections? Is not the act of paying attention an act of attachment? Can one ponder ideas without staying bonded to the topic? Curiously, does not the meditator stay attached to his awareness? Does not the meditator also desire bondage with his silence? Does not the act of love seek to unite, to bond, to attach? Is not knowledge, for that matter, the union, the attachment, of the knower with the known? Is not daily life, including the range of Nature itself indispensably filled with attachments and bondages in one way or another, temporarily or longer, that enable it to survive and surpass itself? Is not yoga the ultimate art of attachment in which you bond to the fullest of its fruits, self-realization?

Q: Yes but is not yoga also a concept? Why attach oneself to a concept and a process? Why not attach oneself to its fruits directly; whatever it may be called.

A: Nice comeback. First, conceive your goal. No attachment to the concept, nothing happens. Then, guided by that concept you begin the body-mind practices or process. Gradually, the attachment to the practice of the process matures one. Again, no attachment to the practices, no advancement. These factual advances are the concrete fruits, and these fruits continue to ripen as you continue to practice. Finally, your attachment to the process matures into the fruition of your goal: self-perfection. Jargon like Divine Self, Beingness, Inner Guru are nice, pious preachment. We can leave these gratuitous notions.

Q: Gratuitous notions are just another way the mind labels to dismiss what it cannot fathom.

A: I submit that nothing real is unfathomable. But people love to assert esoteric jargon when they can't grasp something; it makes them feel nice. The ol' principle: what is gratuitously asserted, can be gratuitously denied.

Who's Afraid of Being Alone?

Q: People do not appreciate what it is like to be alone, solitary. To the contrary, they say, "tried it, got restless, became skeptical."

A: My retort: of course you did since you weren't really alone. Instead, your straining impatience evoked a formidable shadow of distrust. You evaded being alone by consenting to that distressing emotion and so became inseparable from it. By adhering to that feeling, your purview of self and life distorts. After all, how could you want to be alone, truly, when you easily arranged to be suspicious of yourself?

To be alone means to be in a plain attitude of sheer awareness. One experiences an inclusive stance so pervasive through sense and mind that it leaves no cracks for doubt, worry, fear, or anything else to seep in. With eyes wide open, desires and ideas flutter by, you couldn't care less. The world surrounds you, yet you merely gaze without any anxious search. You are becoming abundantly poised in alert, silent sentience.

Parenthetically, in the past, you sought the range of deliberate action induced when excitedly involved with friends about a likeable, timely conversation or task. But here, instead, in these imperceptible moments, you are by yourself. Here, no constraints, no timetable, no haste, just the simple presence of solitariness. What eludes people is that their stern efforts, their discursive endeavors, their pressing emotion to obtain the solitary experience, suppresses it. Like an indignant muse, aloneness won't tolerate coercion.

Enter upon aloneness such as sauntering through the cool, autumn woods. Just be willfully easy in the saddle. Before long, a serene feeling issues forth. The radiance of the forest irresistibly beckons your contemplation. Soon a surreptitious mood of wonder widens with gratitude. Now, fearlessly, you are free at last, at home alone.

Q: What are your thoughts on loneliness? Being alone seems beneficial if it is a state you desire, but when you don't want aloneness, it turns negatively into loneliness.

A: When you say that "you don't want aloneness," it's like wanting to be rational without being self-conscious. The dynamic of aloneness is integral to your nature, not a passing state even though we mistakenly assume otherwise. It is essential to our being but unfortunately, we don't recognize it as such. That's the irony. We can gloss over it, refuse to dwell upon it, try all sorts of substitutes for occupying our mind, but we can't eliminate its inherent presence. When we dodge it, then there's a price to pay. We attempt to use our mind to escape from itself. Interestingly, the medieval masters called this escape the melancholy of the spirit (*acedia*). At the street level it means the conscious, ersatz ways you refuse to be who you truly are.

Again, when you say "you don't want aloneness," then the denial effects an inner obfuscation which results in an eventual self-confusion about the meaning of life. Down the road a bit is the inevitable pain of loneliness. Of course one denies being the originator and searches for rationalizations. The hardest thing to get people to see is the conscious, embodied self that they are.

Denying aloneness brings on layers and layers of misconstrued substitutions that may satisfy us academically, socially, professionally, and politically, but can't eliminate that repressed feeling of loneliness which, as long as we covet the substitutions, makes us ineligible to experience the alone self with all its bounty. We don't know how to abide in our aloneness. Like a gift staring you in the face and yet you won't reach out for it.

Discovering being alone opens the universe in new, playful ways. But one has to prepare for the epiphany. Most won't have the patience, and when their previous histrionic and conflictive moments regarding life's meaning resurface from memory, they choose to renew them.

Three | The Promise of Practice

Walking Temple

If one would be aware of each tissue the body possesses,
Like a nest of birds knows the tree branches it lives upon.

If one would be aware of each caress the blood gives to its veins,
Like the shore of sand feels when the sea ebbs and flows.

If one would be aware of each breath,
Like flowers in the field feel the bees and butterflies that come and
visit them.

If one would be aware of the breeze upon the skin,
Like a forest feels a wind.

Definitely for such a person, if it came to exist,
there would be no more separation between the mind, body,
and nature.

They would become intimate companions forever.
In this way, would not one be a Walking Temple?

Meditation: An Inner Science

Modern science is predicated upon its ability to verify its hypotheses. Verification is very important because it allows the investigator to objectify his thoughts. Frequently, for example in astronomy, scientists may not be sensibly aware that there is another planet in space, yet they hypothesize on the data of the movements of the other heavenly bodies. Through their ingenuity, scientific investigators can occasionally predict the discovery of a new body. Some of our planets have been located in this way.

An elementary textbook in chemistry may assert that plain water, H_2O, boils at 212°F. But how does anyone really know that statement is true? How do I know it makes sense? Is the author correct? Does water really boil at this heating point? The author may be a close friend, or he may even possess a Nobel Prize. But are these assurances sufficient to make me feel secure in the knowledge that water boils at 212°? Hardly. I want to know by experiencing the fact. Otherwise doubts arise.

I want to experience the reality of boiling water at that degree. My mind isn't satisfied with anything less. In other words, a scientific demonstration requires first-hand knowledge. Second-hand knowledge, textbook statements, words from an authority can't guarantee the security of knowledge.

Whether we are professionals who are striving to examine or to comprehend a section of reality, or just someone who is interested in life in general, we prefer real facts to wishful hoping. To stay close to the facts of life helps us to deal with the task of life. With facts, we have more possibilities for success in living than just hoping or praying that things will work out.

Today, meditation is being recognized in research circles as a scientific fact with humanistic value. Meditation is a unique experiment because the investigator is his own laboratory. The investigator, in the practice of meditation, experiments with experience—his own inner experience. Broadly speaking, there are two kinds of science: those that deal with outer phenomena, the sensible, tangible world, the world that engages so much of our attention, and those that deal with the interior world of consciousness. This is where the science of meditation lays down its claim.

In its search for secure knowledge, science attempts to establish its hypothesis by eliminating the variables and finding the constant factors in the experiment. Likewise, meditation follows the same procedure. As a science, meditation hypothesizes that the investigator can discover, in an orderly and repeatable fashion, universal knowledge regarding the conscious nature of human beings. Moreover, the methodological procedure carried on in the experiment is capable of verification by disinterested investigators. By submitting to a principle of verification, meditation removes itself from the onus of a private experience and allows for objective scrutiny.

Before outlining the experiment in broad strokes, let us begin with some preliminary fact finding at the commonsense level of ordinary introspection and reflection on human experiences. Introspection will be used as a procedure tool throughout the experiment, but the investigator will refine it as he probes deeper into the experiment.

In a normal day, one notices that the mind and body entertain all kinds of changes. From the endless thoughts and images of the mind to the equally unending sensations and moods of the body, the meditator as investigator undergoes almost relentless alteration. The meditator resembles a constant variable. At this preliminary stage, neither the mind nor the body would qualify as constants in the experiment, for both are clearly variables.

Where does that leave the experiment without the mind or the body? What else is left to human nature but these two components? The question is whether the body-mind complex in its variable status exhausts the evidence that composes the nature of the meditator.

Granted that the body and especially the mind fluctuate throughout the day, everyone still feels that he is always, in some way, the same one who undergoes these changes. I am thinking about the weather; I am feeling the cool rain; I am resenting your intrusion; I am missing my friends—these and many more episodes happen to the same person all in one day, as yesterday so tomorrow. The same "I" persists as the experiencer.

Whether one experiences life as a series of fluid configurations or a stack of contiguous snapshots, something abides that, in spite of the unpredictable and illogical occurrences that blur into each other, renders continuity to these episodes. Life is not a quilt of experiences seamed together by the incidental threads of time, space, and location. While waking, dreaming, and sleeping may comprise my apparent range of experiences, in between these traveled states I do not suffer annihilation. Something about me sustains its existence without changing amidst the changes experienced. Without some perdurable, underlying reality upon which these mental and bodily changes take place, change puts itself out of business. Change can't exist by itself; change occurs or takes place in an existing reality.

Given this brief review of human experience simply to introduce the experiment, one now tests the hypothesis by carefully setting up the conditions recommended in the traditional manner. First, a stationary posture is assumed without stress, eyes are closed, and rhythmic breathing commences—all for the purpose of subduing the fluctuating variables. A systematic process is undergone by the experimenter who attentively directs, controls, and observes the self-induced experiment. The relaxed stationary posture settles the body, and the rhythmic breathing settles the nervous system and calms the imagination. The experimenter gradually focuses his inner attention in a designated manner that permits him to witness the entire quieting process. As the interiorization of his concentration lingers, the latent richness of his consciousness expands into his inner awareness. As the experiment is repeated daily, duplicating the sequence of steps, further enrichment occurs as the experimenter refines the process. Repeated experiments yield more knowledge and the eventual power of control over the full range of consciousness.

Through first-hand exposure the experimenter-meditator now knows that he is not his variables, that he is surpassingly more than his thoughts and feelings, more than the customary states of consciousness that occupy his normal hours. By investigating meditation, he investigates himself; by investigating himself, he discovers the perdurable factor which not only gives continuity to life's experiences but also remains intact through all personality changes. In the experiment of meditating, the investigator-meditator discovers the basic constant: the awareness-presence of his self-consciousness. The experiment is not an isolated event. Samplings of various subject-meditators will concur on similar findings. The experiment of meditation yields not private insight but universal knowledge about human nature. With continual experimentations, the investigator-meditator makes further refinements and discovers that this dynamic constant expresses itself in combined variations that account for the personality and attitudinal complexions of people, as well as their growth or lagging on the road to maturity.

Among his investigations into the experiment of meditation, the meditator will note that his mind assumes certain modifications time and time again. A dependency builds up. The mind becomes fond of its mental habits—its ways of judging, evaluating, reacting—without realizing that there is more inner enrichment to experience, that these mental determinations may be preventing the meditator from understanding and enjoying life more. By persisting in meditation he eventually recognizes his fondness as a recurring variable that needs inner control. This control takes place through proper discernment. He sees that in using his mental outlook as the only way to appreciate life he was paving his own road of suffering.

Meditation is the experimental science of human consciousness. Everything one does, feels, wishes, or imagines is possible because consciousness is the underlying reality. Meditation is not a science of thinking; the reasoning realm is only one of its functions or levels. As a process of interiorization, meditative awareness expands beyond the margins of thought into the regions of creative intuition, exploring the full range of consciousness.

Experimental clues emerge during daily experimentation which vindicate the experiment—increased tranquility, smoother coordination of body and mind, less tension, more relaxed sleep—the data goes on. These signs indicate that the experimenter is proceeding properly. Moreover, the systematic practice gives one a sense of reassurance that the science is not hit or miss. Finally, at the practical, everyday level of jostling with life, one learns through meditation that the seeds of happiness are sown within, and by nourishing them a bridge is built to intelligent living in the outside world.

Meditation and the Future

An appreciative awareness of the future is a strong force in today's society. It is, however, accepted in our culture that we should avoid, almost at all costs, the embarrassment of reexperiencing the past, the old ways, when we cope with the compelling issues of the future. Today, vital possibilities for human development seem unlimited. In the last half of this century man's widened consciousness has given him a fresh impulse to seek beyond the immediate or remote past, and thereby escape those weary problems that bogged down previous generations. Modern man is on the brink of embarking for new destinations, and he must be ready for living in the twenty-first century.

Prompted by his current fascination with the ever-outdated wonders of our technological age, man hurriedly anticipated what the future holds in store for him; he must be careful not to insulate himself from those events that could very well prepare him. Therefore, he feels that what is new must be experienced, but it must not become routine, for remaining with the old only slows down the process of transformation. Since we know that we create our own personal future, staying in vogue assures us that we are secure. In other words, we seem to have to run constantly in order to just stay in the same place.

Since every culture estimates the value of human nature differently, history can disclose some of the limits by which modern man can measure his options. In spite of our frenzy over the future, a very ancient possibility recurs in the midst of our rush towards the next millennium. But the practice of such a venerable tradition as meditation has surprised those who rely on ideas and concepts to bring in the answers to our pressing problems.

Meditation, as a process of self-discovery, does not work primarily through ideas. It works more in what may be called an existential manner, actually transforming the capacity of the mind itself. The meditative way of understanding human nature does not come from discussing ideas about the mind. It is the result of actually observing the complexities of the mind at work, and yet being uninvolved with them. One must be a witness, in other words, to the stream of consciousness, without either coaxing or interfering with its activity.

In charting the dimensions of the mind today, researchers are recovering many ancient truths. Since the latter part of the nineteenth century, we have been aware of the subterranean dimensions of human consciousness—the subconscious, or the unconscious. But this way of looking at the mind has been often limited to the context of pathology.

Meditation, on the other hand, reveals the mind in its healthiest, most wholesome aspects. Here, one starts with a saint, a realized person, who then deciphers how the mind works for the totality of its operations, as embodied in himself.

The ancients can thus broaden modern research so that it reveals a balanced picture. They can show us that there is more to the subtle dimensions of consciousness than has been discovered so far in clinical practices or in speculative theories offered since the turn of the century.

The ancients understood consciousness as something that never retires. It is always alive; it doesn't have to rest. The body, with its nervous system, has to rest, but not consciousness. Nor does it suffer entropy. It cannot wear out with use, although we frequently think otherwise. In fact, the more it is used, the more skillful it becomes. It is just the opposite of matter with its limitations, for the more you use your car the faster it disintegrates. This is not so with the inner spirit of the human being, for the more the inner faculties are employed, the more they are used in a daily way, the more dexterous they become.

For instance, when meditation is introduced for the first time, one can discover firsthand that there are areas within the mind that could never have been found without that experience. Then, in the act of making that discovery, there is always a change in self-knowledge. One can never be the same, for through meditation there is always a subtle advance in insight. Continued practice results in a transformation of the personality.

According to the ancients, one slowly recovers his essential nature through meditation. In other words, one is completing a circle, as it were, embarking on a journey to discover who one is in the world, and through the act of meditation one comes back home to an ancient insight that illuminates the present.

The consequence of meditating is not to insert something new into the mind, however; it is to recover the treasure that is already there. This is a strange treasure, because one expects something material, or tangible when he uses that word. We expect something that has a "sensible" quality to it because we are so used to thinking in "sensible" terms. The student is very apt to say, "Well! All I get out of meditation is tranquility, peace of mind, better health, and a sense of integration, but beyond that there isn't really much to meditation, you know." Without realizing it, the meditator has begun to uncover the treasure.

The mind is never really blank. We are always coming into contact with the world, full of anticipations, regrets, needs, and wants, and these color the way we look at things. Sometimes these predispositions can be so intense that we really cannot see the total reality. For instance, if the pickpocket meets the saint, so the story goes, all he will see are his holy pockets. By the same token, our own personal interests are so dominant in our minds that we cannot appreciate the many facets of life that are right there for our sake, facets that could possibly relieve some of our anxiety about the future.

This is where meditation comes in. The act of meditation is an act of release; it is an uncomplicated act of unburdening, an experience by which you are no longer competing with life. In meditation you let go for awhile, but it is not an arbitrary release. It is not just sailing here and there with the wind; it is a directed letting go, so that as you calmly step back from the agitated contents of your mind, your entire being shares in the unburdening. But meditation does not merely release the tension associated with our desires and plans, for the act of unburdening is also an act of knowledge. One learns something in the release that cannot be disclosed in any other way. Discernment dawns in a natural, but unexpected, way—because you don't work at it.

Our approach to education accustoms us to think that knowledge is the fruit of hard work only. But in the act of meditation insight emerges to the extent that one releases one's anxious intensity in terms of desires and expectations. This does not mean that you abolish them; it means that you release the inner tension associated with them.

Then, when the emotions quiet down, the mind achieves a clarity that it could not possess when it was agitated. In other words, what presents itself as a problem frequently diminishes once the emotional distortion around it subsides. Meditation allows you to see your desires in their proper perspective.

This inner process of clarification is needed today as society rushes toward the future, for because of this rush, pressures, competitive frenzy, oppositions, polarities, can be felt in the atmosphere and observed in tense faces. When one is in a quiet atmosphere, however, something very different takes place. When one is being quiet, simplifying one's daily schedule, living in natural surroundings where one does not have to keep up the defenses that retain our desires, something wonderful, but sometimes disturbing, occurs. Since one is participating in an atmosphere which is extraordinarily peaceful, the unresolved thought patterns that are within the memory, surface; a visit in a natural setting releases some of one's pent-up tension and achieves a gentle restoration. Meditation can also effect these changes.

The process of meditation, then, as it continues, is not primarily for the purpose of creating unusual occurrences in the mind itself. It is, rather, a deepening of this sense of tranquility. Silently, imperceptively, an inner sense of peace becomes the basis of a new process of growth. Tranquility becomes substantial. This does not mean that one becomes dull or withdrawn from life. Meditation is an act of awareness. The mind gets sharper. One becomes more sensitive without losing a peace of mind that is growing stronger. Then, while you increase your sensitivity to life, you are not thrown off center so easily. Meditation contributes to the future by clearing away past attachments in the mind, and thus, in a gradual way, the loss of tension and the reduction of anxiety about the future allows an inherent peace of mind to expand its influence upon the body-mind complex. One's outlook changes accordingly, and the experience of stillness and silence becomes an enduring value that now informs one's attitude toward the future. The practice of meditation directs the inner silence of peace to the tasks of daily life. Seeing in perspective broadens one's responses. Thus, returning to an ancient tradition accelerates tomorrow's progress, for if one meditates, one chooses the future not from the intimidations endemic to high-pressured living, but from the security of an inner vision and freedom which is ever broadening.

Meditation and the Subconscious

Sri Swami Rama tells this story when he talks about the power of the mind to fool us: "One evening, after my brother disciple and I had walked thirty miles in the mountains, we stopped to rest two miles past Badrinath. I was very tired and soon fell asleep, but my sleep was restless because of my extreme fatigue. It was cold and I didn't have a blanket to wrap around me, so I put my hands around my neck to keep warm. I rarely dream. I've dreamt only three or four times in my life, and all of my dreams came true. That night I dreamed that the devil was choking my throat with strong hands, and I felt as though I were suffocating. When my brother disciple saw my breath rhythm change and realized that I was experiencing considerable discomfort, he came to me and woke me up. I said, 'Somebody was choking my throat.' Then he told me that my own hands were choking my throat. That which you call the devil is part of you, and the myth of the devil and of evil is imposed on us by our own ignorance. The human mind is a great wonder and magician; it can assume the form of both the devil and a divine being any time it wishes. It can be a great enemy or a great friend, creating either hell or heaven for us. There are many tendencies hidden in the unconscious mind which must be uncovered, faced, and transcended before one intends to tread the path of enlightenment."

The unconscious is the hermitage of "devils," "angels," and all sorts of paraphernalia. The contents of our unconscious are so subtle at times that we cannot anticipate their emergence. We often mistake certain feelings and thoughts for reality, while it's only our conditioning, a flaring-up of an old emotion or result of something disagreeable. Then there are occasions in daily life—people we meet, unexpected events, episodes in our personal careers—that awaken latent memories that are already tucked away in our minds.

Your mind works through the process of association and that bears upon your faculty of judgment. It is constantly being stimulated by the atmosphere and the environment, and consequently many memories bubble up to the surface from your past history. Your past experiences sometimes tumble into the front part of your conscious mind and create a situation calling for attention. "Why did I feel this way when I met that person? Why did I react so strongly; it seemed out of proportion to the event that was happening." You question yourself in this way because you don't really understand the dynamics of why these thoughts and images occur.

The goal of meditation, in regard to the unconscious, is to expand our awareness slowly so that we can bring all the hidden regions of the mind under the direct light of our awareness. Just think what that would mean if we could do it, just ponder the implications—the very wellsprings of our creativity, our energy, our healing power, our ability to communicate—all of these resources would gradually enter into our self-awareness and be there at our beck and call rather than, as is so often the case, only asserting themselves sporadically, surfacing only now and then. You know how frustrating and disappointing that can be. You want to do something, and you just can't seem to get in the mood, or the mood won't last—and you've got a deadline and other things to do. So meditation is meant to make contact with this marvelous haven called the unconscious in order that the unconscious be now linked with your steady awareness.

Most of our mind is not under direct control in an easy and efficient way, and that is why life is neither as steady nor as spontaneously cheerful as we would like it to be. Every now and then a "devil" pops up, and we're thrown by that feeling, or image, or fantasy. But by steadily working with the practice of meditation we are creating an inner atmosphere whereby our depth of awareness begins to enlarge its self-imposed boundaries, exposing these "devils" for the fiction that they are.

These boundaries are there because most of the power of your awareness is directed through your senses, so you depend upon the senses because you have been pretty successful in life by doing so. In traveling, for instance, you need your senses to tell you how to get there; you followed the right road, you made preparations, you notified the people where you were going to be staying. These actions required a certain amount of sensory knowledge which you apprehended and communicated to others. Similarly, you travel through life during your waking hours, depending on what you receive through the senses—those five major avenues which connect you to the outside world. This dependency is not bad; it is necessary. How else could you fulfill your job opportunities and raise your family?

But you suspect that there are deeper levels within. You are not just a sense being, emotionally reacting to life. There are subtleties within you that can't be reduced to sensation. The fact that you can use words like *friendship, love,* and *justice* indicate that there are experiences that cannot be resolved back to the sense level. Animals normally don't talk about justice and friendship and truth, but you and I do because we are more than our bodies, more than just a reflection of the unpleasant or pleasant moods at our sense levels. True, we like the excitement that's engendered by being in contact with that which is tangible, but after a while it begins to pale. Most of us could not spend all day in a movie theater; it's not stimulating enough. Our nature provides us with certain signals that say, "Come on, let's go deeper. There are other levels you need to attend to in order to be satisfied, to understand life."

This doesn't mean repressing what is apprehended by the senses. The practice of meditation aids one here by slowly expanding one's awareness of how to integrate all the levels of our personalities while understanding their limitations. Then you can live out the truth that's already in you at that level. When you understand what constitutes sensations and emotions, and how they affect the mind, then you're much freer to deal with the situations that provoke these levels of awareness.

A human person is a multi-leveled being. Your nature not only shares sensations with the animal level, but you also share something with the vegetable and mineral kingdoms. In other words, you already comprise all the levels that constitute the realm of nature. You are a microcosm within the macrocosm. All the principles and elements that are in nature and the universe are contained in you. But being human implies something unique because, in spite of those elements, you have an additional quality, one which sets you light-years away from the universe—that is, you can be conscious of yourself and of all those elements of which you are comprised. You know when you're feeling joyful; you know when you are bruised; you can discern when a situation is disturbing to somebody else. You have this remarkable ability to apprehend life around you in a nonmaterial way so that you literally become one with it in understanding it. True understanding requires this spiritual unity.

But a caution is needed here. In learning about life, by using the mind to deepen your comprehension of nature and the cosmos, you can unify with something and be trapped by that knowledge, for when you cling to your knowledge you make it more than what it is in itself. You have set up a new "devil." You are positing from your mind something that's really not there, and you're thinking that the mixture is reality. When it disappoints you, pain and sadness result, along with frustration and anger. Frequently this happens because we invest more value in the object, the person, the event or the activity than is really warranted. Our hopes are built up, but the future doesn't unfold as we expected. We feel that life lets us down because we haven't learned discrimination. This is where meditation clarifies the situation.

The mind pursues life because its very nature is to know the totality of the universe; that's its inherent proclivity. Man's soul is a miniature cosmos, and man's destiny is to bring that cosmos into reflective understanding. You are born into a flight toward that understanding. You have a nature which must obey certain laws, and those laws are thrusting you towards reality. The inner dynamism to experience life and conceive meaning constitutes a law of your being. You are by nature meant to comprehend the ultimate meaning of life.

Some truths of life will not endure—they're not meant to last. These truths reside at the relative level of understanding. We strike a match or go jogging. True acts, but how long do they last? How long is the food you ate for breakfast going to remain as food? Through the day we experience reality in different ways. Some things remain with us longer than others. Some things, by their nature, are only passing. All affect us in some way. When something touches our spirit, there's perhaps no discernible change; we don't weigh more or grow taller. We seem to look the same as we did before, even though we may be learning magnificent truths about life. But the experience enlarges our spirit. A strange paradox. If I give you something material your personal quantity increases, and you can only accept so much and then you say, as at a meal, "That's enough, I don't want any more. I'm filled. Come back tomorrow; today I'm filled." But do you ever say, "No, I don't want you to love me anymore. I don't want our friendship to deepen. I don't want to know more about the truth of the mystery of life." We rarely reject these truths. We feel compelled to know more. We can't stop wanting more, and the more we obtain, the more we want. The thirst of the spirit is unquenchable. Bodily matter, on the other hand, is very definitely limited. Sensation is very definitely limited.

But spirit is of another order of reality. The truth of the reality of the human spirit can't corrode, become stale, or wear out; it's just the opposite to the body's entropy. This doesn't mean that the body is bad; it means that the body is limited, subject to time and space. The body isn't evil, it's just that its truth is limited. You can only do so much with the matter of the body by itself. In spite of its marvelous agility and dexterity, its natural truth is quite relative. But if I ignore the basic, common-sense laws of taking care of my living body, thinking that somehow my spirit is superior to its needs or that I'm somehow holier, more balanced, because I disregard my health, that again is confusion.

The key to human fulfillment, spiritual realization, is first integration. If you want to reach the spirit, you don't ignore the body. Instead, you find out how the body and the spirit relate. What are the laws that guard and preserve that marvelous relationship? You don't just jump out of your body when you decide to become spiritual. Genuine sages—if you examine their personal lives—never tell you to abuse your body. In one ancient tradition, in fact, the body is understood to be a temple: it's something sacred. Why? Because within it dwells the supreme spirit. But it doesn't just contain the spirit; there's an organic relationship, a living relationship, between the two.

What makes matter a human body is the presence of the spirit. What makes matter in you alive, and not like stone, is the fact that a life force presides there. In a way, to neglect the body is to neglect the spirit as it exists in the body. Your spirit is giving life to your mind as well as to every cell of your body. Therefore, you have to understand and acknowledge the laws at each level of your being. If you don't, then it's not possible to integrate that level of our person in a coordinated, intelligent, peaceful way. What ought to be cared for becomes suppressed, and your suppressions and misconceptions inhabit the subconscious, become the brooding "devils" that interfere with your discovering the truth of life.

Repression can occur when the mind refuses to acknowledge certain basic laws in the mind/body relationship. These laws need to be attended to; bypassing them only provokes pain. Closing the door on natural promptings doesn't send them away for good. Their presence within the subconscious disturbs one's feelings and thoughts. Depression, excitability, and fatigue can be agitating from their source in the unconscious, but the mind won't allow them to come up in order for you to deal with them intelligently, to resolve them, and be free.

You are a unity. The body/mind complex is so intimately related that thought and feeling, intellection and emotion, mutually affect one another. If I think a certain way, gland secretion prepares the body to assist the direction of my thought. An obvious example is the act of dwelling on a thought of anger or sadness. The entire body is affected through the nervous system. In the magnificent psychosomatic relationship there is not a thought you can think that will not provoke an emotion. Under the influence of thought the body changes; under the influence of emotion the mind changes. To find the real amidst the changes of life, to find the stability amidst the flux of matter, to find security of mind amidst the misfortunes of history, a different kind of experience from what the body and mind can provide is required. We are talking here of an experience of spirit alone, without the body and mind being directly involved. We are talking of finding a reality within that unifies all levels of our being.

In meditation an inner tranquility is sought through the calm experience of integrating body, mind, and breath by means of the harmonious rhythms of breathing. Subconscious memories then surface before the mind's eye, and in this way the old repressions are dissolved gradually through the experience of expanding one's awareness of them. In meditation you meet the inner obstacles, those self-defeating attitudes which prevent you from knowing your own nature as it truly exists. The emotionally tinged thoughts of fear and anger subside over periods of meditative practice, because the act of meditation reconstitutes the body/mind complex into its natural state of peace.

From the vantage point of tranquility, then, you can measure life more accurately. Your former tendencies to imposition become less and less as you sustain the clarity of mind derived from meditation in your daily activities. A growing sense of tranquil integration is recognized and preserved longer during the day. You know how to recover its presence and prefer more and more to judge life from its perspective. Instead of being a haunted house, you can draw upon the power of the subconscious for creative insight into the world at large, and through this creative awareness you are becoming your own nature and fulfilling your destiny.

The Gazes That Renew

CONTEMPLATIO

Reach back into your memory to that solitary autumn walk some time ago. Recall that stroll through the woods where you became enthralled with the colors shimmering around you in the cool wind and the fallen, rustling leaves flying outward as your feet kicked delightfully at them. Or recall walking through the snow-filled paths as the white flakes swirled about your feet. Perhaps somewhere along the way there were moments that you would not have traded to be anywhere else.

How different are those moments from the rules of hurry and worry, the impatient wait for traffic lights to alter, the tense search at the customer lines along the grocer counters for the shortest exit.

There was nothing prearranged about your nature walks, no effort at control. You just came along unannounced and there it happened; your eyes met nature. You gazed and a revelation occurred.

Intangible but real, the truth of nature's beauty showed itself to you. In that enduring exposure, you awakened to an ancient echo. Bearing that experience you cannot depart from the woods feeling the same as before.

How intangible, almost impractical, this conscious, physical delight in the beauty of nature! Effortlessly, it stirs us.

When you listen to Mozart's 33rd Symphony, peer at Rembrandt's portraits in Amsterdam, read a favorite scripture passage, marvel at your children's dexterity on the monkey bars, or become transfixed by the shuttling, colorful sweep of the Aurora Borealis in the evening northern sky, your consciousness engages the power of life in a special way that exceeds sheer reasoning. Some days you pause amidst your busy schedule, get caught off guard by a thought, a phrase, a remembrance of someone you love dearly. You ponder a topic in the quiet of your mind. And suddenly, after persistent reflection, a new inference emerges as an unexpected gift. You see the issue in a new light. For those brief seconds the march of time halts. Your attention is willingly widened, lifted from its routine cares: you reminisce, weigh, savor the seen. Are you less human for this intrusion?

Human consciousness, in addition to its everyday exertion of reasoning to earn a living, pay bills, and pursue dozens of mental activities, possesses an innate capacity of simply sustaining its gaze in an act of appreciation for the intrinsic non-utilitarian values of life. We call this conscious embrace of beauty and truth, *contemplatio*, Latin for contemplation.

MEDITATIO

The versatility of your mind shares another route to reality when it is sufficiently invited to do so. Instead of being enthralled by the world about you, your mind can withdraw into its own source of life and light. Without moving the body, one can journey to the inner galaxies of memory and creativity and beyond.

Most of our daily efforts with material things produce eventual entropy. Things lose their use over time because they wear out. A strange reversal occurs, however, when we close off our senses to the outside world, quiet down, and systematically slip into the stream of our consciousness. There is no weariness inside. The mind, unlike matter, doesn't diminish with use. Instead, by this inner dwelling, the mind increases its power of refreshment that affects even its body. In our ordinary world of diminishing returns, the mind is unique: a self-renewing reality.

The journey inward is full of surprises. Although your eyes are closed, you still gaze upon the horizon of your mind and become aware of its active inhabitants: feelings, images, ideas, and their variations. But your excursion is not merely to take an inventory; rather it searches out the life source within. You want to find that fountain of love, truth, and peace that occasionally emits snatches of its presence. You want to meet your soul in its pristine existence. Cast among all the roles you've already played in your life, you want to answer that irresistible question: Who am I really? The bewildering mystery of meditation, *meditatio,* is that sitting quietly over time can bring about the stupendous marvel of disclosure.

Whether to practice contemplation or meditation or both, we are all drawn to these artful paths of self-knowledge. How far we proceed is the question of how free we want to be.

Yoga: The Impossible Dream

Translations of the classical text, *Yoga Sutras*, are easily available in the West. From the scholarly compositions of Harvard's James Woods and our tradition's Swami Veda Bharati to I.K. Taimni's clear presentation for Westerners, Americans can now read this transcribed wellspring of yoga. Interestingly, Swami Rama helped the latter two authors compile their research.

The *Yoga Sutras* contain 196 aphorisms, or distillations, of the centuries-old oral tradition that Patanjali redacted: but it's not his creation. In fact, Patanjali may be the name of a group of yogis. This is, however, the classical textbook of *ashtanga*, or *raja* yoga, the mother of all yogas.

The first four sutras describe yoga's purpose, its goal, its finality. Chapter two depicts the aspirant's obstacles on the path to enlightenment, which is a fascinating tour of human psychology, even if most of my readers have hardly any obstacle! In chapter three we discover the bonuses, namely the emerging powers hidden in consciousness. Chapter four is the crescendo of the ultimate state of existence.

Swami Rama, the scientist and mystic who showed researchers the powers of yoga at the Menninger Foundation of Kansas City, emphasized that the entire essence of yoga is borne in the first four sutras. The first sutra presupposes a certain maturity in the practitioner when it says, "Now you are ready."

The second aphorism also has a special allure, for it underscores the central responsibility of a practitioner: "Yoga is the self-control of the powers of the mind." In reading various translators, a variety of words like "cessation," "repression," "stoppage," "restraint," "restriction," "stilling," are used for the Sanskrit word *narodha*. Those selections of words have long puzzled me.

Swami Rama mentioned that over the many centuries, certain nuances in the Sanskrit tongue have emerged among the Himalayan masters, not necessarily found by delving into the etymology of the language, but arising from a scrutiny of the human mind's dynamics. One day, he casually said that the *Yoga Sutras* are not a handbook for students at all, but actually a textbook for experienced teachers. He smiled and went on to say that some of the Sanskrit meanings spoken among these rare yogis won't be found in any classroom. The meanings are not about scholars parsing words from a dictionary, but closer to "on the job training" while deftly exploring the mental terrain that yields these pertinent insights.

The difference in the wording used in various texts of the sutras is near radical. If "restriction" or "repression" is the meaning of the code word narodha, where does that leave a person? If, on the other hand, one could adroitly orchestrate every single modification that the mind generates in its conjunction with the body, who's to say what could not be done? Swami Rama's shocking experiments at Menninger can then make sense!

Among the budding practitioners, who hasn't at times abdicated responsibility and just capitulated to a stressful situation? Who doesn't love to commiserate with close friends, shrugging shoulders and noting how tough and unfair life is, how the mind just won't slow down? We have all been there. "Control" for us seems the impossible dream.

The yoga masters shrugged with that dream too. Just so we don't keep pondering in the dark, wondering why all the fuss is about "control," the masters added the telling sequence. It is the third sutra: "Then the person abides in his or her own essential nature."

Unbelievable, but the incessant question finally gets nailed down: I now know who I am. The weary hunt's over. Free at last.

"So what?" you say, or "Sounds idyllic!" you might reply. "What's so special about knowing your nature?" Your hesitation is incorrigibly confused if for one moment you assume that abiding in self-knowledge is like reviewing your credit report.

Since you are measuring yoga from a safe and blasé outlook, let's set up a contrast to bring the issue home. If you had the audacity to trace and face all your conflicted problems with life, every misgiving, regret, and complaint about stolen opportunities and false starts, every suppressed shame of personal failure and infidelity, along with wounds received or perpetrated (need the litany go on?), what would this colossal mess come down to? Wrong genes? Neglected inner child? Rigid authority figures? Those suspicions are your desperate rationalizations.

Or does your mind suspect that something is missing in your life? Now you are getting closer. When we cease whining, look hard at ourselves, and stare at the abusive hollowness of our lives, the moment of truth looms. Accompanying your abject plight, underneath all the lurking excuses and sympathetic evasions, the common denominator for your endless sorrows remains: your reluctant lack of establishing your true identity.

While some psychiatrists would dash off prescriptions for an anesthetized escape from mediocre living, the true yogi master won't let a student off the hook. He or she quietly points out that your list of typical self-incriminations just embodied the fourth sutra: "Otherwise, there is an identification of the person with his or her thoughts."

You think you are your thoughts? Then the joke's on you! As long you cling to them, Grasshopper, you can't miss suffering. Henceforth, on those scintillating terms, how could you not encourage eventual failure? It's your shadow.

As for evading reality, Bernie Siegel, M.D., once remarked that most of his heart patients would rather endure a by-pass operation than alter their diet. Oh, how we love to intoxicate our energy with every ersatz substitution available in society. How hard can life be? As hard as I want it to be. Ouch!

If, after reading and pondering these four sutras, we still don't get it, Swami Rama hurls his famous punch line: "You are the architect of your life; you decide your destiny." Add his proclamation to the four sutras and you will have exposed the ultimate conundrum of human existence.

This is just too much reality all at once for a lot of people. The crowds have just scattered. But that yogi master has not abandoned you; he's got another surprise. You'd better sit down though when you hear it. It is: "Your implacable suffering becomes the admission ticket to paradise lost." Surprise! You brought yourself to a crossroads and your pain becomes the presumption that makes you eligible for the path of yoga. If you want to continue with the verdict of your past, then exit, for you are wasting Patanjali's time. On the other hand, your past, however you care to appraise it, is over. Chapter closed. Now a new chapter starts. You can begin again. Don't think of your failures as falls, but as spirals. You come back to start again, bruised, but a little smarter. Take credit for your mistakes and glean from them.

Swami Rama, like Patanjali, poses that the appeal of yoga is less a dogma than an injunctive. That saves a lot of empty discussions. You have to try it to find out what it's about. In its performance lies the revelation. Action first, then speculation. If you haven't been up in a hot air balloon, how can you judge the thrill? In other words, take the sutra text for a test drive. Prove it to yourself. No threats, no saviors. You do it and decide. Patanjali even offers you a lifetime warranty!

All that yoga wants to propose is that in the gradual understanding of yourself resides the potential liberty to transcend your pitiful sorrows for good. It's been done before. Your self-forgetfulness is not a permanent malady. But be careful here. This "yourself" has little to do with the ways you have already dissipated your liberty. Rather, you launch a fresh look upon a familiar landscape, using a lot of your everyday experience of life, but now from a perennial perspective. Simply and accurately, "yourself" comprises a body, emotions, breath, mind, and a lot of demanding desires. Obviously. And it's all taking place in time and space in a local community. Inescapably, you are in a cultural labyrinth.

But that's not all. Arguably, your best tack is to utilize not authorities, but your brains. Trust your cognitive and emotional powers. You've given them enough abuse. Now respect them. Amidst your busy schedule, insert a little more order into your lifestyle, if for no other reason than to keep things toned up. Some gentle yoga, a spot of hatha, a breath break.

The singular reason that yoga is neither an imposition nor a new product is that it arises from its perennial origin, your nature. Inscrutable as it seems, the model for yoga and the design of the sutras came right out of the personal, cognitive investigation of conscious living. They anticipated the Greeks. There is no other way to remove the amnesia of not knowing who you are. Life itself serves as the resource. In your reading of the four chapters, you are thrown again and again back into a studied experience of daily existence.

Swami Rama tells the story of his brief stay in a Tibetan monastery where he noticed the bowing reverence paid to an auspicious-appearing tome placed high upon a shrouded altar and surrounded with burning oil lamps, aromatic incense, and silken drapes. When he inquired if he could read it, the shocked and solemn refrain came back that these revered pages were a divine revelation much too holy for him or the eyes of lowly monks to peruse. Any impure person who dared to cast his sight upon those words would be immediately blinded and struck dead. That's all the young swami needed to hear.

Late one night, a certain slender guest entered the shrine, stealthily reached up, and carefully paged through the forbidden volume. To his astonishment, he was reading a few pages of one of the Vedic scriptures. His laughter was heard by a sentinel who shouted that the sacred text was being horribly desecrated. The enraged monastery rose to defend their heirloom with swords and spears. Our curious guest, however, was fleet of foot.

Yoga is not a doctrine for belief, but a charter for self-exploration. The sutras are less a sacred scripture to be worshipped on an altar than a motorcycle manual for self-maintenance. We don't genuflect to the texts; we personally authenticate their insights. Imagine how those undaunted investigators of the embodied human spirit searched and tested within themselves until they hit gold. Imagine the irrepressible joy that our ancestors must have felt when they validated those non-cultural, universal, operational guidelines that pave the way to an immortal adventure.

A parent beams when her child tests his strength and creative ability learning about his unsuspected powers with their impact on society. Likewise the expedition by those ancient pioneers of consciousness into the marvel that we are, gradually led them to cross the imposing borders of conventional expectations of health, longevity, and rationality to arrive finally at the awesome fountainhead of life, love, and wisdom. Home at last. They then walked among their fellow citizens while radiating their boundless freedom.

Stay the grand course, Swami Rama exhorts, and you may elude your mortality.

Notes on Yoga

Every student that finds the Eastern tradition called classical yoga eventually reads the famous 196 aphorisms attributed to Patanjali. Centuries ago yoga's oral tradition was collated into four chapters. To be critical for the moment, we often refer to Patanjali as the author. But like many ancient documents, apparent authors are seldom for real. The disclaimer, for example, for the Christian gospels shows up at the beginning, "The gospel according to Matthew, Luke, Mark, and John." In the context of those days, it was more pertinent for the followers to keep alive and redact the stories, impressions, and varying remembrances than cite the precise authors of the words. The gospel name lends a general flavor to each compilation as distinctly different from the others in the way its handles both unique and common oral sources.

Likewise, Patanjali didn't invent the 196 aphorisms; he—or more likely a group under the name—compiled them over time in script. While they are not complete, they are an intriguing, robust launch to self-discovery.

THE UNIVERSALITY OF YOGA'S INSIGHTS

Now the authorship contention is not primary for students. More at issue is to note that the dynamics of yoga, although compiled from the regions of the Himalayas, loom larger than the Indian continent. When the British physician, William Harvey, in the seventeenth century, proved the circulation of the blood, admirers did not anglicize human blood as essentially English. When Nikola Tesla discovered AC current systems, engineers didn't refer to electricity as Croatian. Likewise, the geographical origin of the *Yoga Sutras* does not make followers of the text Indian or Eastern. Harvey, Patanjali, and Tesla sought a similar goal: explain the intricacies of the subject matter at hand.

Patanjali's methodology, however, follows a systematic progress that fits a more practical human quest. Unlike Harvey, who wanted to understand and explicate the body's circulation, the *Yoga Sutras* offer a pragmatic program for understanding human nature for the purpose of changing it. The four chapters proceed with the subsequent questions: what is the nature and goal of this subject matter; how to reduce the obstacles to the subject matter; what are some of its properties that are found along the way; and a further explanation of the goal.

Patanjali is not interested in explaining how someone becomes a better butcher, baker, or candlestick maker, but how to fulfill the human potential precisely as a human being. First, for him, put body, mind, and spirit in order, then we can talk about your career. Being goal-oriented creatures, human beings are always on the move toward some type of fulfillment. With that in mind, the ambition of the *Sutras* proposes a sober schema, not just for Easterners, but for achieving ultimate self-understanding on any continent.

What gives the *Sutras* their perennial viability is neither their original language nor any cultural bias, but rather their point of departure: the examination and utilization of the universal, operative characteristics of all of human nature. The *Sutras* are not a product of ethnicity nor of religion but an intriguing disclosure of those effective steps for self-actualization under all times and climes.

What catches people off guard is the simplicity with which Yoga explains itself. Sutra two defines yoga as the control of the mind's modifications. All the remainder stems from and expands on that principle.

At a first reading that flat statement seems naïve. To appreciate that concise definition, ponder for a moment. What if you could go through your day with a deftness of awareness and self-control that no feeling, image, bodily movement, or concept could escape the ease of their management and direction by you, under all circumstances? Typically, we assert at times, "I can't stop my thinking. My emotions drive me crazy. I can't handle my appetites. I sit down and my mind goes a mile a minute. I'm moody and can't figure out how to move on." If recoverable self-control seems insufficient to enrich personal freedom, then sutra three justifies the definition: now you are rooted in full awareness of your nature.

YOGA MEETS THE ULTIMATE QUESTION: WHO AM I?

Here is the unconventional hypothesis. The experience of gradually gaining body-mind self-control, what psychologists call psycho-somatic integration, not only brings more order into my hectic lifestyle but affects, in stages, the simultaneous, conscious, inner revelation of my essence. To put it differently, instead of being only the marketable conclusion to my resume, acquiring the art of self-regulating my physical and mental faculties surprisingly awakens and broadens, as it were, new ranges of awareness that enable me to perform new personal possibilities. New choices become evident in more ways than just what society presents.

Psychologists would concur that sufficient inner reflection on one's behavior brings increasing self-knowledge. One can improve upon and expand that rational knowledge. No doubt. But the *Sutras* take a giant step. The emergence of sutra three, at its early stages, is more comparable to being born color-blind and one day awaking to the flickering of Nature's colors. As this sensory awakening grows, the power of my discernment leads to penetrating the surface at hand, perceiving the inner structures and dynamics behind the sensory inputs.

Curiously, ordinary human consciousness, state the *Sutras*, contains within itself the indispensable tools for achieving this integration and the resulting cognitive expansion.

Occasionally, when we meet reality at an unexpected turn, such as taking an evening walk under a moonless sky, we accidentally gaze upwards and become enthralled, arrested by the beauty for some moments. Our evening saunter evokes a contemplative gaze upon the splendor of the night sky. We expand past our preoccupation with mundane reality. We slip past our work-a-day worries. We didn't labor for this night of insight; it bestowed itself as an epiphany of knowledge. However brief, the act of uniting our awareness to the ambiance of the star-filled sky widens our appreciation for being alive as a knower. And often new questions about life and my potential arise spontaneously from that encompassing experience. Who is to say how far one can increase the capacity for knowing life with expanding perception and comprehension?

It takes a long while before one steps past the normal constraints of viewing life bred by society and our self-imposed, educational limitations. That we have an unrestricted desire to know anything and everything about the entire universe, not just on the surface but with full comprehension of everything's inner nature may seem a bit too much. To know Nature's inner secrets in this manner would yield us the hidden key to orchestrate its operational conduct. When we boost knowing Nature and the Cosmos beyond conventional science, we near, as proposed by Patanjali, the hallmark of our destiny.

How far-fetched that sounds, like something out of fairy tales, *fabulae mirabiles*. Yet in the myths and legends that fascinate our attention as children, where we read about the abode of the gods and heroic adventures, these metaphoric stories may be symbolic of the hidden ambiance of our own supernatural forces that stir in our hearts. While these tales may bear cultural overlays, yet their meaning speaks to everyone.

In Patanjali's proposal one grows, as it were, into the fullest disclosure of one's awesome nature. We are not talking about gaining academic excellence or IQ status. A better word would be a transformation of conscious awareness that includes but spreads beyond the normal rational boundaries. Unprecedented powers of discernment unite knower and reality in such cognitive intimacy that the performance of matter is at my disposal. Nothing in this universe remains strangely distant anymore. There are no unanswerable questions. If that's not freedom and wisdom, then what is?

In this era, we speak of striving for the elusive control of our lives, eliminating the consequences of our ignorance. So Patanjali proposes that we start on an experimental path, not to theory, but to useable self-knowledge. The proof resides in the pudding. Treating the *Sutras* as a sacred text misses the point. The manual is for use not for its preservation on an altar. It has gaps that can be filled in with the perennial wisdom of the West. The investigation, say, of the Cardinal virtues would enrich Patanjali's codes of conduct for the modern times, while the findings of biofeedback and the contributions of Neuro-Linguistic Programming supply healthy nuances for self-care practices.

What escapes sincere students is that fullness of knowledge that the *Sutras* point towards. At first, the student tends to place the knowing of the essences of things in its ordinary rational mode. We can say that in principle the human spirit can learn everything it desires. But there is so much more to learning than the rational mode suspects. What follows shows the implications of our suspicion.

All experience is knowledge by identity. For the human spirit to know anything, it must become that which it knows. How mysterious that the object in itself is also now existing in the knower exactly for what it is in itself. Otherwise, no knowledge. The material being of the object exists in the knower in an immaterial manner, some may call it a spiritual mode of being. That innate capacity is what makes the knower unique in Nature. The knower knows another without losing itself in the process. The knower keeps its identity while assimilating the identity of something else exactly. This is not a photo but a living experience. That experience is what sets spirit apart.

A comparison with matter would show the radical difference. To chop down a pine tree for the lumber achieves its end but at the cost of the living pine tree. The pine tree can yield to the change but loses its original being in the process. One started out knowing a living pine tree. Now the end result is a batch of lifeless lumber.

To know the pine tree simply in an act of knowledge with no ulterior agenda for lumber leaves the existence of the tree intact yet it exists in the being of the knower as it does in the forest. Same tree—one identity—with two modes of being. The union of the known and the knower means knowledge by identity.

Of course the knower's material body launched the encounter. The use of the senses—sight, touch, smell, even the hearing of the wind through the branches—are indispensable for the tree to become known. After all, humans are embodied spirits. The more I perceive the tree over time the more my spirit, through my senses, learns about the individual being of the tree. The union affects an increase in knowledge.

Again, what makes the human spirit unlike anything on the material plane is that there are no holds barred in increasing experience with the existing world. No one ever says that his spirit is so full that he can't learn about another reality.

The reason that some knowers know more than others about the same reality is that identifying with our pine tree, for example, demands attention. We pass through many events of the day with hardly a glimpse to detect what is taking place. When a world-famous violinist played a classic piece in the Boston subway during rush hour, no one paused to unite himself to the player in the action of playing. They may have faintly recalled some guy fiddling away as they rapidly walked to their train entrance. But only a few small children lingered and kept peering and listening to our artist playing the same piece that he later played before his evening audience in the orchestra hall. Without attention, knowledge and joy flee.

Through the proper preparation, the knower eventually comes to the insight that the union between him and the known can reach a depth, as it were, where the state of their identity yields all the power of the known to the knower. The very dynamism of the known is in the hands of the knower. Optimally, the knower identifies with the entire Cosmos and lo the power of the Cosmos is his in perfect identification. This is the final mystery of identity. As the yogis put it, self-realization turns out to be self-identity with all being.

For those reluctant to explore a systematic, self-confirming path then sutra four prevails. We get stuck in our moods, united only to our mental quandaries and disturbing imaginings about life. At best, we may gain cultural success on the societal plane to some extent but not fulfillment on the precipice set for us by the *Sutras*. Without a counterpoise of self-knowledge, one roams, like it or not, within the whims and fashions of the day.

In examining the human patrimony of wisdom literature, the wellsprings of the *Sutras* present a unique, holistic enterprise that is coherent, testable in everyday life, and fully acknowledges human beings as embodied spirits working out their destiny with relations to the world. Even the Angels envy this course of study.

Prana and Listening

Any pursuer of yoga philosophy today will come upon the Sanskrit term *prana*. What is it? There is no better contemporary way to translate that word than to call it energy.

A question immediately looms. Is prana akin to modern energy concepts, like horse-power, electrical amperage, or nuclear energy? Not exactly. Prana's essence exceeds in subtlety the physical forces that would be the province of study for the sciences of physics, chemistry, or electrical engineering. Prana exerts its primary presence as the animating life force that permeates nature. It keeps organic beings alive and thriving. It is the life force, the vital energy, of the entire universe.

A famous yogi claimed that physical matter is also a derivative of this universal force. "It is the prana that is manifesting as motion; it is the prana that is manifesting as gravitation, as magnetism. It is the prana that is manifesting as the actions of the body, as the nerve currents, as thought force. From thought, down to the lowest physical force, everything is but the manifestation of prana. The sum total of all force in the universe, mental or physical, when resolved back to its original state is prana." With these words, Swami Vivekananda shared his assessment of prana in the last decade of the nineteenth century with American scientists, including Nikola Tesla, the inventor of alternating current. Tesla was so impressed with the yogi's concept of prana that he gradually utilized yogic terms to explain his research into electricity.

In analyzing the principle of prana, the power of life, as it affects our lives, the ancients discovered that there are at least five major resources of prana available. Some are less evident than others, but let's take a look at all five.

The sun is a source of prana for nature. Can you imagine a world without diaphanous sunlight and all its properties without sun? No flora, no fauna. The greenery of the forest would vanish; the life of animals, the coloration of flowers, the flow of water would all be gone. Prana enables things to grow, to flow, to flourish.

Together with the sun, other planets in our solar system are supplementary pranic forces, distinguished by their vivid presence in the colors of nature. Contemplate a red rose, and you meet the pranic force of Mars. Notice the blue in a chicory plant, and realize Saturn has made its prana felt. The yellow and white are accountable to Jupiter. Green is essentially from the sun of Earth.

The second source of prana is food. The recognition that we get prana from food has captivated the yogi's attention for analysis and probing. The natural flavors, the vitamins, the enzymes, the protein and carbohydrates are all products of the pranic presence. While the quality of food determines the impact of the prana, its energy does not always stay permanently in food. When we expose perishable foods to the elements, like a salad left overnight on the kitchen sink, there occurs an evident change in its appearance. The vitality has tangibly dissipated. The taste has altered. The prana has departed.

The third source is breathing. Parading through the Schumann resonance field of energy, Earth creatures walk about in an invisible ocean of prana. Polluted at times, Earth's atmosphere is always available. It's interesting that recent medical studies are beginning to emphasize the importance of proper breathing. They are looking at the dynamic functional use of the lungs, and noting that the respiratory process is a major factor in determining longevity and the quality of living. When you feel out of breath, nothing else matters until that depletion replenishes. Catching your breath means catching your prana. The ancient meditators metaphorically taught that the chemicals in breath, such as oxygen, carry a rider, prana, into the body. As the *Kaushitaki Upanishad* asserts: "The breath of life is the consciousness of life, and the consciousness of life is the breath of life."

There is another resource of prana; it is ideas. Can you recall how excited you become when some promising news is finally confirmed, or when a stimulating conversation bursts forth with new, enticing ideas? Experiencing the intellectual concepts spreads, engaging your feelings. A definite flush of enthusiasm pervades your person. That also is a source of prana. Negative ideas, of course, would have the contrary effect.

The fifth resource is unique. Each individual bears a radiance of vitality, an aura, which acts like a living signature. Your ideals, ambitions, distinctive characteristics and idiosyncrasies, virtues and vices, your very persona emits an irrepressive energy field. That total composite, subject to change, is the prana of human presence.

When we meet and attend to someone, the encounter always leaves an impression. We gain a sense of the measure of that person. Often we have, at the initial encounter, an immediate, abundant reaction either positive or negative. Sometimes it is borne out, sometimes not. Indispensable for life, of course, are the other pranic resources, yet when we come to human communication, presence takes the lead.

The detection of the energy of presence is due less to rational cognition than to another power. As you look at a person, you notice his or her height, weight, the clothes worn, the demeanor of the face, the tone of conversation, the movement of the body. These empirical impressions feed the rational mind and you draw certain inferences about the person, however speculative they may be. But more than a sensory and rational contact, a certain tacit discernment about the individual occurs. This non-discursive knowledge, a kind of immediate apprehension, cannot be strictly abstracted from the sense data regarding the individual. Because our reliance upon the evidence of our senses and rational analysis is so normal, customary, and civil, we dismiss these tacit impressions as dubious. Yet they return.

Everyone has episodes of sudden knowledge with little or no logical evidence to support the uninvited disclosure. It emerges as a feeling as we attempt to articulate it in rational terms as best we can. A friend was driving through a northern area, enjoying the winding roads through the autumn forest. Suddenly he became cognizant of a strong, pervading sense of sadness. It took him by complete surprise. His rational mind reflected on the lingering episode and could not find any empirical data or hints of what could be accountable for the sudden change in his feeling. He knew it was not hallucinatory nor sheer imagination. Some minutes passed before he read a large sign on the roadside. He had entered a poverty region of an Indian reservation. Now he understood. As he changed course and drove off the reservation, he shed that mood, keeping the information and feelings to himself. Later that evening, his travel companion mentioned over dinner that earlier that afternoon she was unexplainably filled with an uncomfortable morose mood while traveling. While it lasted only a few minutes, she pondered how strange that such feelings would occur in complete contrast with the enthralling beauty of the woods.

This special mode of cognitive apprehension, what we might call intuition, or second sight, accompanies our normal hours and our other senses. The subtler depth of prana is stirring, however. It never takes a day off, and it comes with the territory of being human. While there is more to seeing and hearing than meets the rational eye and ear, one has to stake a claim on it.

We meet life with our whole being, and when we meet someone, we communicate with our whole being. With some people, we feel refreshed after being with them; with others this is the contrary. With them we just know that something is discernibly askew.

Optimally, what makes human communication so valuable is that like the sun, food, breath, and ideas, the encounter enlivens us. Somehow the prana pervading you is enriched by the pranic radiance of that other individual, and hopefully it's mutual. That kind of communication is profoundly found in the intimacy of friendship. You want to connect, share, unite at more levels than the obvious.

Without that tacit, intuitional knowledge, however, friendship is impossible.

One of the Greek masters, Aristotle, points out that people usually relate to each other in one or more of three ways. They establish an association based on pleasure, utility, or kinship of spirit. Usually the first two are easy to secure, but the latter is genuine friendship. He was not implying that you should strive to be friends with everybody. No, he just noticed how society ran itself.

How would one enhance an appreciation for life, foster a friendship, become skilled in art and science? One way is to be truly receptive to the reality, the pranic field at hand, or the unique expression of that person. How do I do that? In its broadest context, this way is called contemplation or the act of listening. In silent awareness we allow the other to disclose its presence. No tinkering, no modifications. That demands a tremendous honesty upon the part of the listener.

J.M.W. Turner, so the story goes, paid a captain of a cargo ship to take him along during the crossing of the English Channel. He deliberately picked a day when the sea was violently stormy. Then he refused a cabin. He preferred, instead, to be lashed to the ship's mast and ride out the storm. So powerful was the experience that he went home and conveyed the storm to canvas.

Listening means to be able to perceive the truth of the reality in its act of revelation. The truth of another person demands that the listener hold himself accountable to that task. Friendship requires revelation and responsibility. Coming into contact with reality, the being of that person, produces a transformation. Because the act of listening reaches past the head to the heart.

When we listen from the heart, it changes the very communication, not by interference but by expansion. When head and heart join together, we have the finest listener because the whole pranic awareness is present and a recognition of spirit ensues. The act of listening in the broadest sense becomes an act of contemplation. Contemplation attends the pranic field of the universe.

In meditation we volunteer to listen to the journey inwards and let it take us where it will. We are not blind; we stay attentive. Gradually there's a profound change that starts to come about. When we come out of meditation, our presence is different and our energy signature can be sensed by others. Over time our acquaintances will also begin to recognize that something is different about us.

Among the Western sages, Plotinus says, "Goodness is diffusive of itself." It is just like a mother who can't wait to share the bountifulness of her cooking with her eager children. She can't hold back. No way. Impossible.

The yogis discovered that the very essence of being has that same characteristic. When we sit, and listen in the act of meditation, we can never be vacant or empty. The being of our essence is going to render its revelation in and through that silence, through that solitary stillness. There portends a law of reciprocity. If you want to improve your listening skills with people, improve your skill of listening in meditation and vice versa. Will that your meditation in action be congruent with your meditation in silence. Can you listen to life? Can you listen to people? Can you get the story straight? Are you aware of what's going on? Do you clearly see things for what they are? That has to be first before you respond. Then do you respond to what's there or are you simply imposing again? Are you operating out of fear? Fear always constricts our listening. So, in meditation you get the opportunity to expand your listening. Nothing is coerced; it's merely a recognition, because in the act of listening, you'll learn that the music has always been playing.

Fulfillment to Samadhi

Q: How does one unite with the known?

A: You raise the vexing, inviting question: how to unite further. We can thank the senses and reason for setting up the union in the first place. That's why the body is so important; woe to anyone who puts it down. The rational mode of consciousness, in conjunction with the senses, puts us on the track and we can keep drawing more and more with its application to the subject at hand. Let's call it rational discernment which leads to the contemplation of the tree; they seem to work together, i.e., the more I investigate with my senses and reason the more evidence to contemplate, which in turn may raise questions for more rational investigation, and so on. I am already in union, but I can't experience the full impact of that identity yet. So I keep going. This seems to be the way one obtains increasing union with the reality, a natural process that demands attention. Here is a possible sneaker: the more I focus my attention and ponder over time, the more my consciousness penetrates the reality and perceives the levels of its being. Our consciousness moves naturally into more and more subtle union until it's complete.

Q: Is the expansion of discernment through the expansion of one's senses? Are the immaterial, the energy, and the spirit more of an extension of, not separate from, the material realm?

A: Obviously the more anyone applies himself sensorial to his task over time, the better his perception gets. I'm waxing back and forth: does the ability to see auras come from the spirit directly or is it an enhancement of sight? I'm inclined to the former because of meeting a blind yogi who could see everything as he served me tea, and likewise Swami Rama telling me what's going on at the moment hundreds of miles away. I think the empirical, scientific habit of investigation, weighing and pondering the data is important if for no other reason than you probably can explain the new insights from the contemplation better, at least by analogy, comparing and contrasting. The pine tree is more than just blunt matter. Its living dimension is more in tune with spirit, which is always involved with our senses in some way. And both the acuteness of the senses, and the expanding presence of the discerning spirit are what maturing in knowledge is all about.

Q: What is the proper preparation and are virtues one of the key elements?

A: Preparation is meditation, breathing, and contemplation practices that sharpen and make you more interiorly aware. As you gain more control over your inner powers, new insights, sensitivity, perception, and empathy arise spontaneously as these powers get stronger. But also these powers need indispensably the virtues, so that your life of action and relationships stay in harmony with the practices. Hence a holistic lifestyle and of being in the world and yet transcending it.

Q: Is the spiritual path to sharpen one's discernment and discover for oneself?

A: You have to let go of a lot of selfish thinking, and of course you think you are losing something worthwhile in the process, which still shows your naivete. The scales of naivete take so long especially when you hold on to a way of appreciating life that is relatively good, restrictively speaking, but immature. You don't see the immaturity; in fact you find it insulting to think that you could be wrong in your limitations. You keep making wrong judgments but don't discern the twist in yourself that accounts for these mistakes. Of course you treat them lightly when they show up occasionally, which again shows how you are not facing up to the obvious facts.

I think a lot of people treat truth as a mood when it suits them. Of course it almost hurts to admit that. In a way they get glimpses of objectivity but decide to color it over, touch it up here and there. I think their immaturity is a kind of cowardice; they are afraid to lose, to be embarrassed, to go against the crowd, to appear odd, and so on. It's hard to stand alone even when you know indisputably that you have truth on your side and are not flaunting it.

Finally dawns the day when you start to admit to yourself that things are only what they are, and you unpretentiously strive to nourish that appetite and surprisingly discover that you actually enjoy life more. Sometimes you lose even though you know you stand in the truth. You are releasing your selfish boundaries on your thinking and emotions. To me, this is the key to liberation. Waking up can be such a shock. Concurrently you realize that any cynicism or romantic glow is strictly your own way of still trying to color the facts, again turning objective reality into an immature personal issue to suit yourself.

Q: In your view, what does Swami Rama mean by expanding one's personality?

A: Swami Rama said about personality expansion: "As your self-expansion develops, you become less self-conscious, less worrisome about your status in life." That remark floored me! It sent me reeling. Again, the simplicity of it. How ironic: as the self expands, pettiness contracts. The hang-ups, the anxieties about your role and acceptance by others, clusters of preoccupations, anticipations of problems, keeping yourself busy to cover the worries, the self-pity, all begin to dwindle. As these issues recede, just imagine what happens now about your awareness of living. The newfound freedom can't help but awaken spontaneous enjoyment about existing.

One more surprise. He says, "There is no maya. It's all your self-made delusions about life that hold you captive." Then he told the story of how his Master said that he would reveal maya to him. The next day they went walking through the woods and suddenly his Master ran ahead and leaped onto a large tree trunk. As he held on, he screamed that he was caught, the tree had him. Swami Rama ran over and stood perplexed. "What do you mean you're caught, just let go."

"Can't you see, the tree has me, it won't let me go." Swami Rama just stared at his powerful Master and when he tried to pull his arms off the tree, his Master held on stronger: "It has me, it has me!" He kept repeating how the tree held him tighter. Young Swami became exhausted attempting to release his arms. Finally, he sat down wearily and told his Master that he couldn't free him. With that, the Master smiled, sprung loose from the trunk, and with a chipper remark said, "Of course you can't; only I can free myself." And they continued on their walk.

Q: What prevents ordinary, solidly honest, good people from advancing to fulfillment?

A: I suppose it is how one defines fulfillment and which groups of people one is talking about. For example, there are religious people who would view it as a utopia or heavenly existence after death. Yogis may phrase it as self-realization, of knowing the essence of life and oneself, of knowing Truth and establishing union with nature and all of life and reality during one's earthly existence. Religious fulfillment may be impeded by immoral acts, lack of good works, false beliefs, wavering faith or lack of grace. But lack of fulfillment for yogis is another matter. My simple and broad response to the original inquiry is ignorance and fear. Christians are generally ignorant of the yogic concept of fulfillment outside of a heavenly obtainment and if they are familiar with it, they are hesitant to pursue it for fear of damnation.

Q: But what prevents yogis from advancing to fulfillment?

A: Also we may lack mental and physical purification, knowledge, and determination. We are laden with doubt, laziness, and a deep uncertainty of whether this thing called Enlightenment really exists and is possible. It is like shooting in the dark at an unknown target. So students do the practice, consistencies vary, life's mundane affairs interfere, frustrations arise (expectations not met), distracting infatuations surface, etc. Those who have progressed and experienced positive results can still be consumed by what they lack. We seem to be fixated on our inadequacies, not on the prize. We keep circling the mountain instead of heading upward.

Maybe we lack confidence, fear the unknown, or feel undeserving. Possibly we are unprepared, lacking the necessary equipment to journey further. Ignorance is an obstacle for us as well. This stymies many. What do we need to do to polish and smooth our distortions and what qualifications are we lacking? Do we lack the discipline, the virtues, the longing, the hope, the strength, the mental capabilities, the emotional stability, the right character, the faith, and the proper attitude? Do we need to lessen egotistical pride, vanity, impartiality, moods, sentiments, illusions, biases, superstitions, fears, and false beliefs? Do we need to uncover our unconscious prejudice, false motives, emotional distortions, and dishonesty? Do we need to sharpen our discrimination, enhance our sovereignty, ponder, reflect, meditate, philosophize, to fully engage life, to love, to question?

We question whether we are pursuing a fantasy, a conjecture. We may feel caught in an endless maze. We keep plodding along. But what is needed? All of the aforementioned is needed! But what is most needed and pertinent for one's advancement more than anything else? To me that is a key to further one's progress. What does one specifically need at this moment and this juncture in their journey? How can one lessen the load that one unnecessarily carries? The maze can be perplexing. Which door should one chose? We can talk of simplicity like Ramana Maharshi, asking one to inquire about who is asking the question—know that and one will be fulfilled. But there is much complexity within that simple question. The inner workings of oneself, the variety of choices, and the apparent qualities needed for advancement are complex.

Q: Now how does one envision higher states of consciousness from this waking state?

A: Your everyday awareness of life is the awake state but it's unfulfilled. By living an intelligent lifestyle, you continually enrich your awareness of reality, drawing closer to fulfillment. It's the human path called skillful living through virtuous conduct, which explains self-realization. You are becoming wiser about daily existence. Your appreciation for living and your personal conduct continue to mature, and this keen perspective expands your self-understanding and increases your freedom. We can't exactly "envision" higher states, but we get genuine clues and glimmers, as it were, through some of the peak experiences in our life. As we strive to hold the intent by desiring to know and love life and act on this awareness, then we are becoming as humanly fulfilled as possible. We are ripening into, name it as you will, perfection or enlightenment. You are, as it goes, lighting your own lamp.

One of the most admired Catholic mystics, John of the Cross, admitted that the only mode of description that could begin to describe his experiences was poetry. I think poetry, folk stories, nature experiences, even ancient legends, fables, and fairy tales, including literature from all continents, for example the *Upanishads*, can all be used analogously to affect some insight. They are inspiring. Again, how do you ground their descriptions? These fabulous writings can almost compete with peak experiences. In fact, a certain peak episode may ring an association with some past tale that adds a fragment of clarification or depth. The constant danger is to take these texts as literal, without proof. I want as much data as possible about any "mystic" episode so I can then ponder the intelligibility in the data. Unfortunately, the written descriptions are rarely described in a commonsense fashion. Many of the earlier biographical statements about the catholic French saint, Therese of Lisieux, including her pictures, were redacted—enhanced, as it were—to make her appear more appealing and pious.

Given the fact we have a definite nature, it seems that a genuine transformation can be not only explained naturally but reveals certain characteristics that are facts. If we want credible truth, then we have to produce sufficient evidence that verifies our judgments. In my readings of saints, their usual explanation is that a higher force did it to them—a gift of grace, from a deity, always beyond their competency. They could not avoid this kind of explanation given the context of their indoctrination and current life. For my quick suspicion, it may be akin to or even a peak experience, along the lines of an expansion of consciousness or even an aesthetic arrest. Interestingly, religious mystics are indoctrinated in believing that it's all up to the deity. So they have a natural block to suspecting they could elicit it by themselves. So when it happens episodically, these events confirm to them that it is only a special grace freely disposed from the deity. I don't like to use the term "mystic" or "mysticism" since it is laden with religious connotations. With that assumption, people won't accept or entertain a natural explanation.

Q: What is the fastest way to samadhi?

A: Whoa! What an enticing question! How to pursue the quickest way to enlightenment. For our readers I will call upon some astute researchers who can offer their auspicious opinions. If we put that question to Ramana Maharshi, he may retort: "Who wants to know?" He is not asking for the name on your credit rating or your driver's license; he pushes past those superficialities. Nor is he dodging the reply, but urging us to pause and probe: "Who is the 'who' asking this question?"

Leave your surface reply aside for the moment. Instead, get at the real source of your rejoinder and find out if it's worth an answer. Right now all you think of yourself is mostly displayed on your resume with a few anecdotes from your kids who spy on you in the early morning. No problems at that level except that Ramana wants you to uncover who is the "I" holding your changeable life—past or future—together. Who is the "I" undergirding all your aspirations and flights of fancy? Are you ready to venture into that kind of self-interrogation? And if you are indeed ready, then you might discover who is the "I" on the fast track to samadhi.

Another consultant on life, Swami Rama of the Himalayas, offers a few pointers on this issue. Taking a different perspective, he might suggest standing before a lengthy mirror and taking it all in. There you stand upright as a bodily, breathing, observing being. But that's all the mirror can reflect. Turn around and you behold a householder, in a society, surrounded by nature and a gaggle of daily responsibilities. Turn inside and you host unkempt ideas, images, and habits. Immediately you ponder: "What is this inner ensemble all about?" The questions arise almost interminably: "What's my purpose? Of what am I capable? What's life up to? What makes me truly different from other creatures?"

Gradually it dawns on us that for personal safety and other benefits, we'd better know our nature, its capacities, and how best to use them. If we don't learn to appreciate this inheritance, how will we ever learn to explore its advantages? Knowledge, love, and action are partners in our ongoing quest. And through that investigation, we discover a major benefit: increased freedom. The study of the world can take us far, but self-study invites us ever further. Who would have ever thought that the inner sanctum to samadhi was there before the mirror? Simply go inside what you see. Then you'll enter the fast lane.

Four | Lessons for Modern Living

Are You a Risk Taker?

To laugh is to risk appearing foolish.
To weep is to risk appearing sentimental.
To reach out for another is to risk involvement.
To place your ideas, your dreams, before the crowd is to risk rejection.
To venture forth is to risk occasional danger.
To hope is to risk disappointment.
To do is to risk failure.
To love is to risk refusal.
To meditate risks solitude.
Who risks nothing, forfeits liberty.
Who risks little gains little, so fettered to his anxiety for security.
Only a person who boldly ventures tastes freedom.

Why Ethics in a Maddening World?

Amidst the ambiguities and complications of living in today's maddening world, people still ponder in their minds and hearts the ethical question and its quest: how best to live as a human being? We are not talking about career advancement or economic opportunities or national treaties, but what characterizes and fulfills citizens qua human beings.

On this topic, what comes to mind are interchangeable notions like humane, morals, trustworthy, altruistic, benevolent, integrity, humanitarian, and, of course, ethics. The last word is derived from the Greek *ethos*, meaning character, and from the Latin *mores*, meaning customs. Many people are skilled in certain arts, sciences, and crafts but their competency doesn't guarantee that they have character—i.e., adept at being trustworthy humans.

Looking upon this contemporary world, we are confronted with an unending array of opportunities for the clarification of that opening question. All sorts of venues, from neighborly chats to religious institutions, from political gatherings and military recruitment to self-improvement courses, provide an abundance of suggestions, propaganda, and mandates for compliance.

For those who would askew, however, the social pressure for being told what to follow, a nearly-forgotten tradition in the West that's never mentioned in common parlance nor high schools and hardly in colleges, may yet connote an appeal. For individuals who think that taking primary responsibility for their life offers special benefits than just rallying with the crowd, there exists an eminent tradition, a humane way to conduct our lives, a natural perspective, if you will, that's right around the corner.

PROSPECTING FOR NATURE'S LAWS

We are panning for a tradition of knowledge that derives its sustenance not from ancient myths, authority figures, or religious texts, but from delving firsthand into Nature herself. Sometimes this approach has been shaped as an inquiry into a natural law ethic. Law is not meant in a legal sense here but more akin to the consistent regularities noted in Nature's ambiance, such as the successive way things grow, the detectable effects of gravity, the appearance of rainbows and the aurora borealis, the emergence of frost under the due weather conditions and, of course, annual harvests. In other words, with sufficient, ordinary exposure to Nature and her wares, one can ascertain that she demonstrates operational orderliness, recognizable tendencies, and familiar performances in and out of seasons. And so we use the common term the "laws of Nature." As unorthodox as those notions seem, let us explore how they may be connected to our maddening world in its competition with an ethical search for a meaningful life today.

Out of the ethical mists of the ancient West, there echoes the familiar endorsement: know thyself. Some would opt to start our search from this aphorism. Yet this indispensable admonishment may be better appreciated by pursuing a prior line of investigation and then returning.

As a preface to our investigation, recall that self-understanding does not arise at the beginning of one's awakening to life. What looms, first and foremost, is the awareness of the Cosmos at large. Life about us beckons. With an irresistible curiosity, we are impelled to reach out and touch reality, to puzzle out daily existence. Later, we catch up to personal self-reflection.

SAUNTERING UPON THE TERRAIN

We commence with the obvious: the sensible realm of Nature that surrounds us. We are not talking here of statistical analysis. Instead, let us deploy something old-fashioned that still works. We are insisting on a rationale that acknowledges the sensible real world. We probe that realm with the commonsense awareness of daily existence in which we live and move and have our being.

Walking about the forest in the spring, one doesn't expect the bees to become trees, or squirrels butterflies. As the days continue, we note certain consistencies of expression throughout the forest varieties that prevail, depart, and change in relation to the seasons. The inhabitants of the territory, from animals to rooted entities, behave, maneuver, and conduct themselves in recognizable, characteristic ways that typify and lead to their fulfillment. From the evidence of their behavior and operations, one garners the insight that there is an inherent constancy that enables these creatures to be and act as they do. Otherwise how could they get from spring to the verdant summer? Our familiarity with these expressions even enables us to judge their status in terms of development and fulfillment. Some make it to fruition, some don't. Some buds blossom, some don't. Overall, creatures in nature display actions and changes throughout their careers in sufficient orderly ways that lead to their fulfillment, which is another way of saying the perfect good of their nature.

RECONFIRMING NATURE'S WARES

Moving from a general picture, we apply our senses and intelligence to examine more closely some of Nature's inhabitants. We note in their make-up, for example, structural differences, color variations, texture, dimension, attraction to other creatures, flexibility, frailness, odor, resistance to disease, even longevity. Panning with our senses discerns variation in their common properties and conduct throughout the days. All are sensible qualities, verifiable by interested onlookers. In summary, we may say that natural things exhibit in their growth cycle a conatus—a vital, innate striving in a discernable, orderly process toward perfection, i.e., fulfillment of itself. The acorn strives through the seasons to become, unless thwarted, a perfect oak tree. Natural entities have an impetus for fulfilling themselves irrespective of my observations. From our continual experience with the forest, we arrive increasingly at an understanding of the being of Nature.

Likewise, rationally prospecting in the nearby cultivated fields shows the spring seedlings as the inception of life that leads to the late summer harvest. These stages of growth Nature repeats, for better or worse, again and again, throughout the years. Perceiving the tangible progression of ripening, the farmer judges when to harvest. There is an objective value to the status of the harvest. Would he not give up his vocation if the planted fields grew helter skelter? As long as most of the crop reaches term, the farm stays in business.

As in the forest, so in the farmer's fields, the inner dynamism—the conatus—of nature's species functions in sufficient consistency over time that gives them their being, which we learn to recognize and cite. Whence it may be said that Nature is full of natures ready to be discovered. And those are objective facts.

NATURE MEETS CULTURE

The pressing question remains: what has the study of Nature's natures got to do with ethics?

First of all, as human entities we share a living inter-dependence with Nature at large. Although not as seasonal-dependent for our existence as the latter, nevertheless, we feel and endure seasonal changes. Just live in Minnesota for a while.

The most dramatic difference, one could say, that differentiates humans from the forest dwellers is the evidence of the former's much greater facility in maneuvering themselves as well as enacting selective changes in the environment. The result is more than survival; it is the making of a living, a lifestyle, a culture, lo, the human community. And while we share a great deal of corporeality and dependence with the critters of Nature, humans attribute a special ability exclusively to themselves: the inherent power of intelligence. The exercise of rationality gives us the defining resource that makes us human.

Culture, unlike Nature, is not something that just occurs spontaneously, like weeds in the corn field. Our orientation to reality is more than biological maturity and physical health. We need but seek more than bodily self-preservation. We are ambitious visionaries. Our rationality constructs, invents, legislates, and shapes society. We plan for the future, deliberate about our behavior, affirm or reject actions, even in mid-stream. We demonstrate a wider latitude in engaging with life than the forest inhabitants. We have a range of possibilities undreamt of by pinecones and badgers. Yet along with them, we have our corporeal limits. With the power of choice, we can set our agenda. We implement goals. We communicate in a myriad of ways unique to our nature. We take action, for better or worse, toward our aim's fulfillment. And those are facts.

THE HEART OF HUMAN NATURE

Overseeing and guiding the aforesaid is the constant prevalence of intelligence. We act unlike machines but as responsible agents of discernment. We know what we are doing and respond to the consequences. To utilize this capacity, this inherent power, for leading an intelligent life underscores our birthright. Its deliberate actualization, not for the moment in any professional or occupational capacity, but simply for the sake of becoming a wholesome human, is due to nothing less than the disposition of virtue. When it's all said and done, it all comes back to the determination: what kind of human have you become?

We deploy virtue—*vir,* or power, as the Latin puts it—in two ways. One, as the means for a nature to fulfill itself. The other, as the emphasis of the various powers inherent in our nature for the good of the task at hand. Examples would be for the power of the eye to see color, the physical power of the body to exercise, and the mind's power to design a business plan.

Our nature is not arbitrary. We are consigned to become, voluntarily, an integrated, fulfilled existence or pay the price. However, the use of the natural powers is another story. We can knowingly disturb ourselves and society. We may act in harmful ways. The irony is that we deploy reason to act unreasonably. Unfortunately, humans are the only inhabitants that can violate their natural tendency toward good. Unlike the forest critters, we can foul our nests. We choose vice, but only because we are getting something out of it.

Now we are getting closer to ethics. Again, by analogy, just as Nature has her proper way of acting to achieve her ends so, likewise, humans. In both instances, we are talking about what is the good for the nature itself. In this vast world of ineluctable change and stability, growth and decay, success and failure, things go from potency to actuality. The acorn is the potential oak tree; the oak tree is the actual fulfillment of the acorn. Our stance, from the common sense experiencing of Nature and ourselves, is that the good of a nature is its fulfillment. The child matures into the adult; the adult progresses in humane skills called virtues or constrains development by choosing vices. These co-dependent principles of act and potency inexorably transfuse everything that exists. All is objective.

Our commonsense approach to appreciating the significance of human life views our efforts as endeavors for the sake of good. An ancient maxim goes: good is to be sought and done; evil is to be avoided. Along these lines, then, Socrates' profound axiom about self-knowledge remains insufficient without the rational actions that confirm the point. We are not good by speculating about it's essence but by proving it through decisive actions that are in harmony with our nature. Overcoming ignorance is not the main issue. Pondering the good, however satisfying, still keeps one in potentiality. Initiating the right actions is paramount. It's the pudding, not the excitement over the recipe, that counts. When right thought and right action come together daily, then we have the ongoing self-realization of our nature. A virtuous person is upon the scene.

At this juncture, led analogously by our brief study of Nature, let us draft a common-sense proposal of ethics: the study of the principles and causes that constitute the self-fulfillment of human nature.

BACK TO THE MADDENING PRESENT

The most stringent opponents that would dismiss our proposal as archaic are modern governments and corporations whose vision of social and entrepreneurial success hardly includes common sense moral tenets but rather fosters the expansion of monopolistic strategies and commercial policies of expediency.

Internationally, millions go to sleep at night in fear and trembling. Even though there are beneficial actions and creative enterprises each day, societies as a whole are not as peaceful as they desire. In our country a lot of fear and pain exist in communities, hardly pacified by dubious assertions from political officials.

In our struggling efforts to make ethical sense of our "maddening world," one could search the halls of politics and find what journalist Ron Suskind recounted, not too long ago, in a discussion with a top White House official:

> The aide said that guys like me were 'in what we call the reality-based community,' which he defined as people who 'believe that solutions emerge from your judicious study of discernible reality.' I nodded and murmured something about enlightenment principles and empiricism. He cut me off. 'That's not the way the world really works anymore,' he continued. 'We're an empire now, and when we act, we create our own reality. And while you're studying that reality—judiciously, as you will—we'll act again, creating other new realities, which you can study too, and that's how things will sort out. We're history's actors . . . and you, all of you, will be left to just study what we do.

What is surprising is not that policy statements about inventing reality are a new political gambit, rather the articulate description seems delivered with an insouciant flair, worthy of an Empire. Anyone overhearing would no doubt get the idea that this is the way it is now, and the public better believe it. It goes with the territory that with civil officials and CEOs, fiats are not hard to come by especially when coercive power and enormous wealth are at your beck and call.

Nor is it any wonder then that there eventuates, concurrently, an entourage of public statements by favored institutions whether civil, military, or religious, as well as society's esteemed personages, that are of the utmost importance for shaping your individual destiny. Conveniently, ethical solutions to vexing questions are issued by decree. Equally supporting that propaganda is the implication that one's inner resources alone are too scant or weak to take seriously on their own terms. In other words, self-understanding and cultivating your nature in body, mind, and spirit is seriously defective at best. On those terms, citizen intelligence lies in a state of default.

EVEN SCIENCE MAKES IT SO

Along with this curious stance on human destiny, there are some important scientists who, by their professional view of the world at large, would vouch for creative policy making. Professor Jacques Monod declared in his BBC interview that, unequivocally, human life on this prodigious planet appears but randomly: ". . . man knows at last that he is alone in the indifferent immensity of the universe whence he has emerged by chance." On that cheerful note, when he was awarded the Nobel Prize perhaps that honor confirmed his declaration. As a postscript, when Monod was asked in the interview how he arrived at his chance-filled universe, he calmly replied that he ignored any evidence for order and causal connections. How convenient for him.

Lest Americans feel this curiosity only applies to foreigners, shortly ago in his renowned TV series *Cosmos*, a famous scientist admitted that: "I am a collection of water, calcium, and organic molecules called Carl Sagan."

From politics to science, our list of these surreal pronouncements would place them in what may be called the ethics school of no rhyme nor reason. As the Bard might say, what can be gratuitously affirmed, can be gratuitously denied. When reason is disparaged, it's an admission that someone is cutting off his nose to spite his face. Once rational common sense is abandoned, there is no way to argue; then it's time to fold and go home.

To continue on our gamboling with human nature, there is an issue that captivates humankind and all the famous Masters and philosophers offer their recommendation. Simply, is there an ultimate purpose to human nature? And what would this have to do with ethics?

LIFE'S POT OF GOLD AWAITS

Commonly, as we acquire various goods of nature and culture, there is always more available, from better products, easier devices, and evermore attractive items, to Nobel awards and TV appearances. The pursuit of knowledge itself knows no bounds. From these experiences, sooner or later, another question emerges: we ponder about what might be the ultimate good of life. To rephrase it critically: is the admission that while we rationally attempt goals and projects from health to wealth, and prestige to property, are not these enticing acquisitions only penultimate?

Although ancient teachers claimed life certainly offered bundles of possibilities, nonetheless, there was a special good beyond all else for which human life exists.

In our era, the fields of psychology and psychiatry sent some representatives to make claim the meaning of the purpose of life. For Freud, it was the power to pleasure; for Adler, it was the power to superiority; for Frankl, it was the power to meaning. There were others who each touched a part of the elephant. In each of their proposals, a ring of truth sounded. Yet common sense would be wary of thrusting the exclusive meaning of humankind into one aspect of human ingenuity.

In the face of these contributions to self-understanding, let our bid in playing for the top prize be the holistic perfection of one's nature through a lifestyle of intelligent living. This means that the world is ours to use and enjoy through rational desires. Our sovereign dignity is our self-determination and a matter of character.

Moreover, we venture that happiness is less the goal of life then the fruition of virtuous maturity. A holistic striving for intelligent living on all fronts is funded by choosing a path of intellectual and moral virtues. Without them one joins the maddening crowd. The action of virtue is what explains the good of self-realization. Through virtuous conduct alone one gains on-the-job training for self-realization. Unless you render what is due to others, how can you enjoy justice? If you don't manage your sensory proclivities, how can temperance emerge? If you don't meet adversity with a certain aplomb, how can courage be? Finally without the experience of mistakes, how can you choose the right means, at the right time, in the right way, and thus learn prudence? For what could be more in accord with our nature than that which fulfills it—a flourishing life of virtue from which freedom and happiness ensue.

Now add the virtues of mediation and contemplation and savor the final frontier of wisdom.

And that, Grasshopper, is how we side-step the maddening-hatters of this marvelous world.

Marriage: Path to Self-Realization, Part I

To write on marriage is to write about a very practical experience and one that is completely holistic. It is a profound relationship of physical, mental, and spiritual unity. But perhaps the most sacred thing that can be said about marriage is that it is a mystery. This means that it is a relationship that cannot be explained merely by human reason. It is beyond our complete understanding. Marriage opens up reality with such richness that it baffles the rational mind. This is because love is greater than reason.

When two people come together in love and choose to become one in marriage, they are embarking upon a unique adventure. It is an adventure full of surprises and unlimited possibilities for growth. It is a path that can lead to fulfillment and self-realization.

The very essence of marriage is friendship. Thomas Aquinas, the great medieval philosopher and mystic, said if we wanted to find phenomenon in the world that expressed the highest form of friendship, we could look no farther than marriage. Thus, if we want to study marriage, we can to some extent study the nature of friendship as well.

When we set marriage within the context of friendship, we have to accept certain requirements. First of all, friendship must be developed. It does not happen of itself; there must be a give and take between the individuals involved. I must go out of my way occasionally, and so must you, if we wish to develop a friendship. In friendship, as in marriage, there is a certain sense of responsibility that we take upon ourselves in order to nourish the relationship. But here is one of the first surprises of friendship: that act of being drawn out of ourselves reveals who we are.

How do we know people? We know them through their disclosures of speech, movement, activity, the way they look, the way they dress, what they share in conversation. This whole composite somehow brings home to us who this person is. That is where marriage comes in.

As we grow up, we have a strong tendency to be very selfish. We are interested only in ourselves. Much of this is fostered by the world community in which we live, but much of it is our way of developing an individual personality. We have to dress well; we have to impress others; we have to have a good car, an apartment, a stereo. We have to start a career and impress more people there. We enjoy this image-building as well as the acclaim of our acquaintances. Of course we sometimes entertain friends and colleagues selflessly, but our first real interest is ourselves. There is nothing wrong in this except its incompleteness.

Then love and marriage become new goals for us and we allow another person into our life. We might think we know what life is up until then, but we do not really know ourselves yet. Acquisitions do not tell you about yourself or your potential. They cannot reveal the self; they only reveal the surface. So another person comes into our life and shakes us up, really upsets us in a loving way, to begin the process of self-knowledge.

There are three kinds of friendship. First is a friendship built primarily upon pleasure. This is not bad, but it is not the highest motive. These friendships are not deep, but rather superficial. They are with people whom you meet only for enjoyment, at parties, or sports, or other gatherings. We choose these friends merely for the enjoyment we get from them. "I like you because you are fun to be with." We are by nature pleasure-built and cannot escape our desire for pleasure. Without it we would be terribly obsessed. We need pleasure because it is like spice. We must merely remember that it is only a spice and not the main meal.

The second type of friendship is the friendship of utility or need. We ask others in choosing a friend, "What can you do for me?" We wish to manipulate others to be of help to us and select those who are most useful to our needs. There is then a tendency to take advantage of these friends, and to take them for granted. Friendship sometimes goes this route, although often it will be a mixture of pleasure and utility.

The third type of friendship is rare. This is the friendship where we meet ourself in the form of another person. The hidden self in you is revealed in that person. Those qualities, those aspects that you are hungering for, that you would like to see in yourself, you suddenly recognize in this other person. When you meet as equals and have this response, something stirs within that is absolutely essential for spiritual growth. That is self-esteem.

Loving for pleasure or utility does not expand us, but when you meet yourself in another, you are expanded. If I recognize the qualities in this person that I am astonished with, that I take profound satisfaction in, those qualities will come to me. That is the essence of love—love unites in order to expand. Love brings two incompletenesses together so that they become totally developed. When there is real friendship, real love, one does not snuff out his individuality, but expands it. When there is an affirmation of another's existence, as assuredly as you would affirm your own, when that affirmation can grow and be nourished, then you do not lose your personality—you find it.

Love gives a security that no other phenomenon can possibly supply. You can be the best genius in the world, you can be a Nobel Prize winner, but if you are not loved, you will always be insecure. There will be a hunger, a restlessness, a kind of anxiety that destroys you from within. You could be admired by the world and be known by many, but if you do not have the experience of being loved, you will feel a failure even though you have all the world's acclaim. When there is real trust in vulnerability, it leads to security.

We are not only rational beings. There is an affective dimension to us. We have feelings, we have emotions, we have a will. We are born a bundle of potential. Our first exposure to life is basically through our mother, the woman who gives everything. Because she can identify with her child, her self is expanded. That is why motherhood is never a hardship. The child needs constant reassurance over and over again, because he is growing up in a world that is too strong, too large for him as yet. A child does not know the world, and not knowing what one has to face causes fear. The essence of fear is lack of confidence to face the unknown. So where does the child get the courage to face the unknown? From the two adults behind him who in their own love supply to the child that necessary substance, that intangible, powerful ingredient we call love. Because love is a response to value, when parents affirm the goodness of the child, the child says, "I am worth something." When I finally see some person touch me at the deepest level, I am given the most profound value I can ever have—my own self-esteem.

And so love confirms our self and in the act of confirming it, we grow. That is why the only thing that can transform a person profoundly is love. You can actually change a human being by loving him, if he is open to that love.

One marries for many motives: sexual attraction, ambition, prestige, family ties, career advancement, and so on. One's motives are usually mixed. A man and woman may not even realize that they are coming together in order to know themselves, but that is the basic underlying reason behind marriage.

The first year or so of marriage two people test each other. They want to find out their partner's limits. Sometimes all those marvelous qualities I find in my spouse are eclipsed by the fact that he squeezes the toothpaste tube in the middle! These two people are like diamonds in the rough, unpolished and uncut. That rubbing together of daily problems smoothes out the edges and gives them a brilliant shine.

Married people share a great secret, namely, that they are becoming one. Love draws and pulls us out of our narrowness. It makes us broaden our horizons. But sometimes it is painful to share with another person. We learned this as children. "I like this piece of cake and do not want to share it with my brother." Thus we realize that love is sometimes difficult. But that is the challenge of love. Love is giving, and in giving there is no loss, no depletion. At the tangible surface there may well be a loss—I no longer have my piece of cake—but at an intangible level I have gained something that cannot be obtained without that little pain. I have learned something about myself; I have grown. In love and in marriage one will have to give without expecting any return. To me that is the sign of growth.

As married love matures, the exuberance and excitement of finding yourself in another will be superseded by something that emerges out of that. It is a very deep love, very unique, that grows between spouses. No one else can understand the great love that two people have, nor how it is expressed. I was raised by my grandparents, who were like parents to me. They were older people, married a long time. My grandfather was a simple, hardworking man; my grandmother had no formal education. I was always baffled because they had very little money or possessions and yet were always satisfied. They were not cultured people but were very wholesome. I would watch the two of them sometimes when we went for a walk together. My grandfather always reached for my grandmother's hand. You could feel something strong between them. There was a certain understanding, intangible, but very evident. They really knew each other's moods. Grandma used to say to me, "Do it this way because Pop would like that today." And of course he did. And Pop would praise my thoughtfulness, which was really my grandmother's. He would do the same thing for her.

It is difficult to speak about things that are so fundamentally real. It is very easy to talk about superficial things, things that will not matter in a short time. But how do we define love or friendship or spirituality? When we speak of experiences that involve the total person, it is very difficult to grab on to something that completely describes it. So one has to use poetry, analogies, and metaphors. We must create an atmosphere instead of words. So it is with love and marriage. The kind of relationship that you have when you live with another human being at such close range creates an atmosphere. It should be completely without defenses. It should make you feel totally at ease. You must have a spot in this world that you can come home to and say, "Here I can be myself. I know I will not be hurt here. I know that my spouse loves me." This is marriage.

I remember an incident that happened many years ago. I was visiting a very close friend of mine in his sprawling house. He had a large, happy family and many pets. Among the animals was a beautiful golden retriever with one terrible defect: the dog was born with his hips half-developed. The front half of the dog was normal, but because his hips were deformed, the dog would move by using his powerful chest and forelegs to drag along his crippled hips. One evening my friend and I were sitting together when the youngest son entered the room. He pointed to the dog, sleeping before the fireplace, and said, "Dad, why do we keep that crippled dog anyway? Why don't we just get rid of it?"

The father thought for a moment and gently answered, "Son, has the dog ever hurt you?"

"No," answered the boy.

"Is he a good watch dog?"

"Yes. He always barks if there is a noise."

"Do you think he would protect you if you were in danger?"

"Oh yes, I think so, Dad."

"Then in his own way, the dog loves you. Why would you want to get rid of someone who loves you?"

I well recall the expression on the boy's face. He suddenly realized how selfish he was. He was willing to discard a faithful animal because of its deformity. Why should he let the body be a measure of his acceptance or rejection? Real love meant complete acceptance in spite of defects or inadequacies.

This sense of acceptance and freedom and comfortableness is what love should try to induce between two people. Then your spouse becomes not only your wife or your husband, but the most personable friend you could ever have. You could hand your heart over and say, "Do with it what you will" and have the firm conviction that it would never be harmed. Marriage is such a profound reality that often we cannot put our finger on the precise impetus that leads to unity. The daily growth and maturity of the partners leads to this oneness of spirit. Little things bring treasured moments. Pain and confusion are shared. The toleration of each other in difficult days leads to the joy of deep friendship.

Marriage: Path to Self-Realization, Part II

Whenever a crisis comes in a marriage, it is a sign that growth is about to take place. Sometimes it requires a little ingeniousness to recognize this fact. Crisis is not a sign of failure, but rather a sign of growth. If you want to turn it into a failure, then you have failed that opportunity. Crises come from every direction, but whenever or wherever they come, it means that the spouses are ripe for it. Nature treats us with great respect and will not force difficulties on us that we cannot bear. When you have a partner who loves you and is by your side, then together you can turn any crisis into another stage of growth.

The one overall most important aspect for a happy marriage is the need for the spouses to decide together what is the goal of their life. As I was growing up, I witnessed seven divorces in my family. These involved all my aunts and uncles who lived together in our large house. I did not know exactly what divorce meant. I cried because I was losing an aunt or an uncle each time a new divorce was announced, but I could not understand why they were doing this. Gradually I began to see something missing in all of the marriages. All of the couples shared a life that had no common goal. Nothing had an ultimate meaning to them. I realized that two people must first sit down to talk to each other and share their thoughts and desires. They should try to see what the meaning of life is and how they fit into it. They should decide how they can achieve the goal. They must try to understand the ultimate significance of their existence. There must be some kind of coming together of heart and minds in agreement about what they wish to accomplish together while going through life.

When the marriage goes through a rough period—a disaster, a sickness, a death—what will hold them together? The pain and frustration are often very great in life. There must be something ultimate that they can bank on, so that they can take the temporary cross and fit it into the meaning of the goal of life. If this goal is rich enough, then even suffering takes on a value, so that the marriage can grow through it. Otherwise suffering becomes an enormous stumbling block.

This is where yoga philosophy comes in. In yoga we realize that we are an entire human being, not just a body or mind, or memory or nervous system. We are all of these things plus much more. There is something endurable in us, something imperishable, something that cannot be weakened, cannot lose its vitality, something that is more than time itself. That is the very heart of the person. We call it the Atman, the Purusha, the Self.

In marriage, what we are doing is peeling away all these coverings of habits, defenses, ego, memories, body, and even the mind itself. We are discarding these outer garments that conceal the soul, the Self. We are penetrating behind all the veils that we think are so important to hide behind in order to be a person. We keep opening up and revealing more and more of ourselves and discarding layer and layer of concealing garments until we finally see that through this union with another person, we have found what we really are. We have found our real nature. This is what marriage should do.

We are thus involved in a marvelous opportunity to find the meaning of life. A companion, someone whom you can joke with, be intimate with, someone whom you never have to question in terms of loyalty, is helping you to discover yourself in the ultimate meaning of life. When you live with someone very closely, where love is the foundation, and support the constant nourishment, your intuition grows. You begin to read between the lines. You can tell moods; you can anticipate thoughts. As these inner dynamics develop in you, one more step must be taken toward further growth. You must recognize that the self that you share with your partner must be shared with the world. Your love is not meant just for each other, because your self is more than just each other. You must recognize that you are to become a sign to the world. In some way, your union must show others what the meaning of life is all about. You have a universal career, not just a personal one. When people look at you, they should see something of what they would like to be, because of the love that exists between you and your spouse.

Sometimes young people are drawn to a married couple and have a desire to duplicate that marriage. Why? Because in that marriage they see this richness, this sense of maturity and fulfillment and sharing that is instinctively drawing the young person because he is meet-ing his real self again. Marriage is like a mirror. We reflect each other always. As we develop in love, we brush the dust off the surface of the mirror, we repair tiny cracks that mar the image, we polish the shine so that gradually we mirror each other's self properly. But then we must turn the mirror outwards to shine for others. We have an obliga-tion by love itself to reach out, following the lead of love, to become the universal sign of divinity.

To a great extent, we are the person we are because others have loved us. It often takes a long time before I realize that the qualities that are attracting others to me are the result of the love that my partner has given me.

There are two factors always working together in marriage. I need your love and you need my love. In some way we will not grow without it. In the beginning when I love you, there is a certain dependency, but if the love is properly given, I gradually become independent. You do not stop receiving love, you only mature with it. When a parent nour-ishes the child, the child is utterly dependent on that love. But what is the end result? A mature adult. There is a paradox here. The child does not discard the parent; he changes the love from that of a child to that of an adult. The quality of the love changes. The essence is still there, but the quality changes. A man and a woman loving each other as adults become more and more what they are meant to be as they accept the responsibility of their love.

If you begin to affirm each other as loving equal beings, then you can discover your total self. There are many people who will never grow because they don't know how to love. One cannot be selfish and arrogant if he wants to love. Love and selfishness are incompatible— one eventually destroys the other.

A child is not meant to be forever tied to his parents, but is meant to go out to express his creative love in his own way. Thus the parents are giving their love to the world in and through that child. Couples without children, however, have the same obligation. They must give their love to others in terms of themselves and their activities. Love cannot be hoarded, or it will die. It must be given away in order to increase it. Love is a puzzle; the more you give away, the more you have left. That is the whole meaning of Christ's miracle of the loaves and fishes. The food was a gift of love from Christ to the multitudes. The more the disciples gave away, the more they had in their baskets, until finally after thousands had been fed, Jesus said, "Gather up what is left." Amazingly, there were twelve bushelsful.

When you love properly, you become independent. You free yourself from the bondage of your actions. There is no more bondage because the love of the act burned up the bondage. If I refuse to love, then I am caught in the bondage created by my selfishness, my narrow-mindedness, my inability to appreciate others. When I hold back love and try to keep it for myself, it becomes a weight that retards my progress. If I give my love away, I am giving the highest value I have, yet I am not losing or depleting or lessening; I am enlarging. When I give love, I have no fears. I am free. I can develop in whatever direction I wish. So those who love for pleasure or for utility are merely burdening themselves. They are hemming in all of their potentials.

Through meditation and self-study we gradually learn that the basic self within each one of us is the same as the self you face in your daily life. We are all at different levels. We all come from different backgrounds. We all carry different responsibilities. Yes, there is nothing you can do for me or that I can do for you that we both cannot benefit from. If you get a flat tire and I take time out to help you, then you can get back on the road quicker, but I have also gained. I have learned that assisting another human being is more important than the value I put on time.

For most people, one of the most interesting activities of life is, of course, finding out more about themselves. All of our basic questions are summed up with one: "Who am I?" All questions lead to it. Everything we do explains, confirms, fulfills, or realizes that question. Any time our curiosity is peaked, we are really hoping to find out something about ourselves. It is our most secret desire. In marriage, we share the same fundamental thirst for self-knowledge. But now we allow that interest to incorporate another person. We become a Sherlock Holmes and Dr. Watson for each other. We seek clues to our own real identity in each other and together reveal, and seek clues from, the world. Whenever I share deeply with another person, I learn about myself. And the more deeply I share myself, the deeper the truth I discover.

Sometimes in marriage you must say you are sorry. The trick of learning to say "I'm sorry" is an art. You have to learn to be patient. You have hurt this other person; you have let him down. You may have shown an unpleasant side of yourself that he did not know you had. You must give him time to adjust to that. Perhaps you have hidden a weakness from that person, fearful that he would not love you if he knew about it. Perhaps you were so arrogant that you did not think you should let him know your weaknesses. Then you must be wise to recognize that you have been unfair. Remember, by the very act of marriage you are saying, "Here I am—all of me. I want to be your companion. We live together, we sleep together, we eat together, we plan our future together." So why should I hold back any of myself? Why don't I trust?

At times you will love your partner more than he loves you. At times it will be reversed. This is part of the joy, the surprise of love. But never, never be afraid to say you are sorry. And never, never be afraid to say, "I forgive you."

The highest sign in spiritual growth is forgiveness. When you can accept someone's apology, however awkward it is, you are becoming a sage. There is a story in the *Vedas* where the sage is compared to a mango tree. A group of rough-neck kids come up and hurl rocks at the tree. What happens? The tree drops fruit into their hands! You must be that way with your partner. Even if your spouse causes you pain, you must give of your fruits. You will grow and you will become a saint. You will become the man or woman that you want to be. You must learn to forgive again and again, because that is the nature of love.

You know there is something within you that is eternal. You know that the confusions and the disagreements can never be about what is eternal. They can only be about what is in time. Therefore they are very insignificant. Learn to keep the context in any disagreement. You will see that an argument is always about something relative. Recognize where these things fit into the context of life with its flux and change. Problems are meant to be steps to development; they are not eternal barriers. There is no such thing as an eternal problem; there is only eternal joy.

Sri Swami Rama speaks of husband and wife as the two wheels on the chariot of life, rushing forward to its goal of happiness. When a married couple keeps in mind this goal that they share, their love will bring joy to themselves and to others. Marriage is the road to self-realization and ultimate bliss. And if the road is sometimes rough, the goal can be reached even faster, because rough roads are often shortcuts. The reality of marriage is a reflection of the eternal quest of consciousness for itself. The love of spouses is a reflection of the love of divinity for humanity. The joy of marriage is a reflection of the complete eternal bliss of the self of all.

One Mountain, Many Paths

The mountain that modern man needs to climb is not as well-known as those scaled by members of mountaineer clubs. It is a secret mountain, a hidden mountain that few wish to scale, or even prepare to ascend. The mountain is the reality of man's own consciousness; the climb is a journey upward to the inner peaks without moving from place.

To scale these heights man must first slow down, for if he tries to assault this inner mountain he will only find himself breathless and discouraged. But modern man rushes through life. He sees hurry as a way of living, and his hurry with himself is reflected sadly in his daily habits—the way he drives his car, the way he eats and drinks, walks down the street, faces another weekend. Instead of experiencing life, all he experiences is his hurry. The task of living intelligently, with peace of mind and concern for others, seems to him a foolish wish from a bygone era. Now is a different time, he is told, an uneasy period in history. The solutions to his problems are always just around the corner—a better job, a promotion, moving to another section of the city, new technology, lower prices, another self-improvement book on the market. These dreams are indulged in year after year until he finally realizes that yesterday's dreams of promise, with all their vigor and excitement, have dissipated, to be replaced by fearful "insuring" against old age.

Where has the chase led? Even if the dreams were to be fulfilled, and more, would they make one immune from their consequences?

Has the rush been worth the price? Am I healthier for it? Because of my struggle, do struggling people find in me a welcome refuge of trust and wisdom? Have I touched the lives of men and women who have earnestly hoped that I would linger more in their vicinity?

A sign of today's confusion is that people complain about the right things for the wrong reasons. They expect their health to improve as soon as the new drug is discovered; they expect the hours after dark to be safer when there are more laws and a stronger police force; they expect not to buy on credit as soon as they make more money. They cannot understand why health, virtue, and happiness are not the result of scientific discoveries, merchandising, or legislation.

Hurry and confusion use energy, and the consumptive expenditure of energy, including human, proliferating on our planet today far exceeds the accumulated sum of entire Western civilizations of the past. The competitive demand upon natural resources is incredible. Almost without realizing it people, in their endorsement of material values, become more and more impersonal in their relationship with society. Their unthinking acceptance of quantitative goals expends their emotional and intellectual resources. A question may be asked here: Could the depletion of man's energies and the strain of modern life have a relationship to the startling increase of degenerative diseases in contemporary society? Our unbalanced, hurried living reflects the lack of an all-embracing perspective that would enable us to evaluate various lifestyles as well as the proper use of nature.

Man's spirit has requirements that may not be entirely satisfied by his unthinking hurry. The failure to appreciate this fact of life prolongs the hurry and worry. Change exists, but man's constant searching for change and "new experiences" reflects a wish to escape, almost a refusal to be in touch with his spirit. To exploit the potentialities of matter without understanding the spiritual side of his nature, modern man undermines himself and confuses material progress with personal growth.

The pursuit of newness has become a dominant theme of our era. Yet people today are often overwhelmed by the unexpected changes that occur in every strata of society, for too much change evokes anxiety. People then start to question the values of continuity and preservation. If man lives by change alone, then the future looks foreboding, for not knowing what to expect, man panics into trying to make the present last as long as possible. But matter and its forms cannot last; entropy is its law. Clinging to the present newness or escaping into nostalgia only hastens the deterioration of man's hopes and plans. Why work and save for a future that guarantees its own obsolescence? People sense the need for some kind of permanence, but where can they find it amidst all the pressures for change?

The ancient traditions teach that man is more than matter. According to them, his home is essentially spirit. External changes are not enough to satisfy him, for humane living involves more than merely adjusting to society. These traditions teach that man can rediscover the purpose of his being, and it may be a restoring change for modern man to learn that ancient truths are ever fresh. Unlike matter, they do not deteriorate—they are only forgotten. In fact, the incredible age of their truths testifies to their indepletable vitality.

The more man earnestly recognizes them for himself, the more he experiences their quickening effect upon him. Their reliability has been proven even if modern man does not have time to appreciate them. They attest to the value of permanence and restoration, and since others have successfully traveled these routes to the mountain peak, they provide an added incentive to the traveler.

Resolutions with Wellness

One of the major lessons of each year is that we don't have to repeat it unless we want to. The tangible circumstances that comprised those twelve months are irretrievably gone and cannot be recalled except in memory. But that is also the catch: we who have engaged in last year's episodes still have memories of those events. When we embark on resolutions for the New Year, we have, ultimately, two choices. We can either attempt to extend last year into the coming months or we can truly fashion the year anew.

HATSUMODE

Choosing to make a truly new year does not mean that one must abandon one's lifestyle and career; it means to freshen one's outlook on life. This can be done in many different ways. I witnessed one of the more intriguing traditions when I lived in Japan and participated in the Hatsumode celebration. At the close of each year the Japanese faithful ignite huge bonfires in the courtyards of their neighborhood Shinto temples and stoke the flames with piles of personal items from the ending year—clothing and furniture, letters and reports, desk and house decorations. The Hatsumode symbolism reminds us that to move ahead in life requires ridding ourselves of attachments that are no longer helping us to grow but are beginning to hinder our development. Releasing the material items signifies that certain choices and selections in life are finished. The New Year's conflagration is carried out not so much with an attitude of destroying the past, but of purifying it for the future. Whether the past months have rendered well or ill doesn't matter. The point is that last year is over; it is tallied up and consumed in the fire of time. The ashes say it all. The New Year awaits your endeavors.

In casting away the attachments to last year, there lurks the danger that, in the hope of constructive change, we will nevertheless continue to do what we have always done and thus always get what we have always gotten. In measuring our future, we often see ourselves merely repeating our yesterdays. It's like looking at life through a rearview mirror. We want our old thoughts, emotions, and actions to support our new dreams and plans. We want to change but we get caught in duplicating the past. Our New Year's resolutions stay on paper and never see the daylight.

With a wellness approach to New Year's resolutions, we remember that when the full person—body, mind, and spirit—engages our intent, then we have an abundance of energy at our disposal. Our entire self makes the resolution, not just our mental faculty. To bring home the importance of resolved changes for the next twelve months, our entire person needs to become engaged in the process, not just our mind. We need our emotional and physical self to be as involved as our mental self. An intellectual commitment uses only a part of our life energy for the resolutions, and so the likelihood of their completion diminishes with time.

Over the years I have kept a tally sheet on many acquaintances who have pursued their list of resolutions as the year passed and then scrutinized their list at the end of the year. By estimate, fewer than 80% of their resolutions were satisfied. The key for the success of the other 20% was the fact that those changes were embraced in a holistic fashion.

CREATING AS EMBODIED RESOLUTION

One way to begin the fresh approach of an embodied resolution is to reconsider how the brain and body affect behavioral change. If you were to consider taking a summer holiday, no action would be forthcoming if your mind had only those two words—summer holiday. Your words have insufficient content and no specifics to move your body to prepare for the trip. With only those simple two words, your imagination remains blank. Many empty New Year resolutions are made the same way. They are merely positive statements about a possible future.

You want your resolution to be not an abstract idea, however, but a motivating force for the year. Research on creativity and body/mind medicine points to the nexus between the brain, its images, and their communication to bodily emotions. What mobilizes the body to take action is images. The more the sensual imagination can be brought into play, the easier and quicker the body can respond. Since a resolution is a course of action, an imaged plan engages the emotions necessary for the action.

To bolster the success of your resolutions for the New Year, explore the following procedure.

1. In your imagination generate a vision of exactly what you want. Then sit down and take a few minutes to write out your intentions. You could make a list divided into categories, such as personal, family, career, and community, or you may want just one major category.

2. After reading your list, sit down and settle into diaphragmatic breathing. Then close your eyes and begin to visualize yourself doing your resolution. Gently guide your imagination to include all the sensory details that belong to your resolution—the scenery, colors, sounds, odors, textures, and movements that pertain to it. In this way, you allow the scenario to manifest in your mind, imagination, and bodily feelings. Of course, place yourself amidst the sensed scenes in their dynamic unfoldment. Imagine it happening before you.

3. Dwell interiorly upon the scenes. This is the key to success. Let your body *feel* the reverie.
4. Bring ideas and imagination, and embrace the energy levels of your whole person. You will then direct your life force to its optimal performance and move into the New Year with an embodied awareness to guide your actions. In this way, you will change your mind about the New Year and, of course, always keep the change.

The Two Birds

Imagine sitting near someone who speaks insights that touch your everyday world and, at the same time, opens a vista onto a transcendental universe. That's what the Upanishadic experience was for the student. The student is privileged to sit near a teacher who has arrived, someone who knows the score on both sides of life. The actual word *Upanishad* conveys the nearness to listen and the liberating knowledge conveyed. Very down-to-earth and very extraordinary knowledge being rendered for those who care.

The *Upanishad* authors are those remarkable people who have achieved enlightenment and are expounding from that experience in a way that entices their audience. That's all they want to do—get you there. Each of the *Upanishads* unfolds a theme, an aspect of that universal reality, and invites your attention. There are hundreds of these fascinating writings. Are there certain classical ones? Yes. Scholars index about ten.

Let's examine a portion of the *Mundaka*. In chapter three there is a brief episode about two birds. They are companions, perched on the same tree, the same branch. The one repeatedly snares and relishes sweet fruit, while his lifelong companion looks on in silence. End of story.

Okay, what's the point? Before replying, let's consider the challenge the teacher embarks on with an audience that is interested but still enthralled with lesser truths about life. To speak of available realities above and beyond their current capacity means to resort to some kind of connection that makes sense at their level, yet bespeaks more reality than at hand. The possibilities for the student to perceive the author's intention come from the latter's careful selection of connectors, in this case, a little story with a metaphor. When composed by a gifted artist, metaphor has the symbolic power to arouse the mind to new vistas of understanding.

The point of the story is that we are not one or the other of the birds, we are both. The first bird is you, that resourceful person who enjoys the world, engaging in all its complexities. The second bird is along for the ride, just observing. The *Upanishad* indicates that the second bird has an advantage unseen by the first. Now we're talking from a universal point of view, not just the context of everyday life.

Everything being equal, the second bird has the advantage and it doesn't mean a disparagement of the first bird at all. It simply means that the first bird is preoccupied with the first world because you have to be.

But you are also going to be subject to sorrow and all of its forms. Can you relieve yourself of that sorrow? You have to discover your second pair of wings and learn to fly with them. One pair of wings enables you to fly around the world with all its desires and occupation. Wonderful! But you also have a second bird that enables you to soar even higher. Your job is to put those two soarings together. If you don't learn to stretch the wings of the second bird you can get trapped in the sorrows of life. The rest of the *Upanishad* elaborates on how to bridge both worlds so that you can soar.

The *Mundaka Upanishad* suggests that you have a tool for building the bridge, called yoga. To bridge a holistic life gradually prepares you to exercise your second wings. Along the way of your preparation certain treasures open up, like an increase in peace of mind—more profound than the pleasure you could find with the first bird. It's the second bird that is to lead you to wisdom, not the first bird. The first bird will make you shrewd and competent in the world at large; you need that kind of flying. But that's not the ultimate stratosphere; you're not soaring high enough.

The second bird is there to take you upon its wings and show you that there is a higher wisdom in life. You need experience in low-level altitude flying first. Then, with your practice of meditation, you gain the strength for the higher altitudes of life. You have your life in the world at large earning a living, eating the fruits. You must have a career and you have to know that there is more to you than your career. So nothing is a waste of time, nothing gets demeaned. You are raised in an atmosphere that is basically worldly. That's the way it is meant to be; it's your experience of first-bird flying.

Sooner or later you will raise questions that the world cannot answer. That's the beginning of the fluttering of the second bird. And hopefully, you can find a practice that strengthens your wings to a deeper sense of what it means to experience the silence within. You can also do it through contemplation, the silence of contemplation.

My favorite example is a walk in the woods. To be aware of the woods requires silence. It's a contemplation of the reality, but from a silent point of view—not being engaged in a utilitarian manner. In this preparation, the act of contemplation can also awaken you to the presence of the second bird. Usually we do one or the other or sometimes combine them, depending on our preferences of life.

A question often arises: When you discover the second bird do you then have trouble flying at low levels? The importance here is to examine the nature of the first bird. How does it relate to the world? If the world is getting to you, then you don't understand it. Often yoga students pull back and fear flying. They rationalize that by refusing to fly at low levels they are becoming very spiritual and holy. All they're doing is escaping. We all go through that. You have to be able to fly freely, fearlessly, when you discover your second wings.

Interfacing with life does not mean escaping and going beyond or transcending. We are not here to evade life. Interfacing means that I understand life now and I recognize its pleasures and its limitations. When I'm okay with that, the second bird is at hand.

Some of you may be thinking, "I realize you have to grow into it, but I think growth is so slow." "Oh my god, I have to go to school, but it takes years." Yes, that's the way it is.

It's that exposure through the very stages of your biological and sociological growth that helps you become more and more competent as a human being. Leave aside your career skills, just expand as a human being, so that you can enjoy the freedom of being in the world. Then it's much easier for the second bird to come into your life.

Because you're not using your wings as an escape, you're embracing them as a completion. Then you're free to use both sets of wings. There is a special word for this in yoga; it's called *jiva mukta*. *Jiva* means the individual soul, *mukta* means liberation. You fly now as a liberated spirit among those who are caught in low altitudes. And you can see exactly where and how these birds leveled off.

One night Swami Rama replied to a student who inquired, "Where's your mind?" Swami answered, "One part is with you here in this room, another part is with my master, and the third part is with the divine—all at once."

Swami Rama flew barrel rolls in all altitudes. He was a pilot of the skies. He flew with such freedom that he became a *jiva mukta*—a free spirit that signals to us to rise into the sky of freedom. That's what the *Upanishads* are for: to inspire our aspirations to let our spirit soar.

Love

Q: Love stories abound throughout history. One's heart clings to such stories. But it all seems like a fantasy.

A: No doubt a lot of love is more fantasy than real. Yet there are plenty of instances of love that endure and perfect one's nature. In fact, unless one can love with unending endurance, there is no perfecting of one's nature.

Q: Love falls short in real life. There is heartache, betrayal, and infidelity. Are we setting the bar too high? Do we have an unrealistic idea of love? Or is complete, unconditional love an unrealistic expectation in the real world?

A: Love can fall short, obviously. Love stories are just literature, fascinating at times. They may approximate the real or not. They are never a substitute for the real thing. In this day and age, why not set the bar higher. The word "unconditional" sounds romantic at best, almost childish, and unrealistic in fact. My preference is to foster a discerning love. One strives for, as you say, a "complete" love (not sure what exactly is meant here). Now I would take it as a striving that endures, that grows stronger and more perceptive in its vitality. I know what I love and love what I know. Hardships, circumstances, so what? Betrayal is tricky. In my experience, this happens due to lack of discernment, primarily, and perhaps expecting too much and not detecting the limitations of the loved object or person. On the other hand, nothing can stop you from loving life and being realistic about it. I keep an affable, unobtrusive manner with a tacit, critical awareness. I strive to be the architect of my life and forge my destiny, which means that I love on my own terms.

Q: We learn from lessons and try to love again, eternally hopeful, but hope and effort never seem enough.

A: Says who? Hopeless individuals, in my experience, misunderstand life; they get caught in their view of hardships. Frankly, without hope life isn't worth living. Make a determination to shape love as an attitude, a fundamental deportment. That insight will one day make it self-evident to you that this deportment belongs to the essence of your nature. What amazes me is how long it takes before you realize that you can't help but love reality. Then life becomes the art of possibilities.

Q: When we discover another way to experience love, loving without an object, love then can be expressed more fully in the world. Otherwise we all seem to be bouncing off the walls with no guiding light, no direction. Only trial and error.

A: As for your last sentence, "trial and error" is how we start; like most things we pick up the clues as we stumble along. "Love without an object" is an oxymoron. Almost facetious. That's like declaring you can see more clearly in pitch darkness. The source of love is within oneself, or it doesn't exist. There is no source "out there" to experience. By its nature, love is "pure," which means it is what it is. However, it can be malformed, twisted out of shape by deviousness such as overt selfishness. But those aberrations do not change its nature, just its direction.

Ah, the art of love is a different story. Most people are naïvely in denial when it comes to admitting their need for training in the latter. Like any virtue, it needs cultivation. Genuine love without ulterior motives often can have a profound impact. On the other hand, sometimes people finally wake up when enough pain results from their unloving ways.

Q: Love seems to reach toward its potentiality only by discovering some fragments of its purity within first.

A: Love actualizes its potential when the other virtues mature with it. We flounder when we refuse to live an intelligent life, which includes loving the right way. Love cannot stand by itself. It needs the other virtues, especially courage in times of strife and opposition. It's hard to keep your own integrity when loved ones betray you. Another reason we flounder: love is not a cognitive power. It only knows what reason presents to it. The will and emotion of love are stronger than reason, yet without the latter's insight, love easily goes astray. When intelligence becomes keener, then love can expand with it and the application to life reaches a "higher degree of fulfillment." What sustains you is the courage of your convictions in the face of adversity. This stance takes real self-love.

Q: Can one truly love without ever having an inner experience of love or experiencing the source of love?

A: The source is within your nature. What hastens this source experience is the cultivation of the range of virtues including, indispensably of course, meditation and contemplation. To say it another way, after being around in the world as an adult you realize, sooner or later, that the world is not necessarily going to love you for who you are. Neither your good efforts nor your creativity, your unselfish acts and devotion to causes, your willingness to go out of your way without regard for reward, your wealth or poverty. No, everyone in the world has their busy, important agendas and they may not include you even when you think they should. Through no fault of your own, events may occur that seem so unfair and which you can't walk away from. How does one respond? Some students of spirituality will jump up and readily state that the proper response is contemptuous detachment to these unimportant, temporal matters. Their self-satisfied incredulity blinds them to their moral apathy. This is obviously not someone you want with you in a tight spot.

According to some Ancients, we live and love on a battlefield and your vocation, whatever turn it takes, includes your meeting the challenges of the day. This maddening world will force itself upon you at times and that is when everyone finds out who you are. There is a medieval saying: "When you stand in the truth of your convictions, you can face the Divine in the eye." But the battlefield is not all there is to this astonishing cosmos. Amidst the havoc, you walk in fearless readiness for the incomparable beauty that awaits your gaze, your ear, your touch. As you rise above and beyond the frenzied stimuli of culture, true friends will come your way. You can get through it all by refusing to surrender your dignity, not unbloodied but unbowed! Your journey to happiness is meant for nothing less than the noblest possession of all; to experience the eternal love and truth and freedom that emanates from you as a wise human being.

Q: And how does one truly love thyself, love existence, love life?

A: It's got to do with your sense of personal identity and its extension into how you view life, the Muses whispered as they laughed at the simplicity of it all. Learning to love yourself usually comes from a combination of the offer of friendship (including family affection) and learning to be competent, self-reliant, and independent, while fostering an intelligent lifestyle that includes concern for others and being untroubled by the havoc around you. These characteristics show that you naturally love yourself without calling attention to it. You know, self-consciously, that you can choose the direction of your future.

Five | Know Thyself

The Mist

Sitting in a garden one day at dusk,
A student contemplated upon the divine origin of the cosmos.
A luminous mist formed by the pine trees and the student began an
inquiry.

I asked the Divine to take away my annoying habit.
The Divine said, "No.
It is not for me to take away, but for you to relinquish."

I asked the Divine to make my handicapped child whole.
The Divine said, "No.
His spirit is whole; his body is only temporary."

I asked the Divine to grant me patience.
The Divine said, "No.
Patience is a byproduct of tribulations; not granted but learned."

I asked the Divine to give me happiness.
The Divine said, "No.
I give you blessings; happiness is up to you."

I asked the Divine to spare me pain.
The Divine said, "No.
Suffering draws you apart from too worldly cares and enables you to become considerate of others."

I asked the Divine to make my spirit grow.
The Divine said, "No.
You must grow on your own, but life will prune you to make you fruitful."

I asked the Divine for all things that I might enjoy life.
The Divine said, "No.
I will give you life instead so that you may enjoy all things."

I asked the Divine to help me love others, as much as the Divine loves me.
The Divine said, "Ahhh.
Finally you are getting the idea."

The mist vanished and the stars all appeared.

The Human Being: A Never-Ending Question

Aristotle once remarked that man, by nature, desires to know. What an understatement. Just ask any parent. From the moment of birth the early stirrings in the child vigorously affirm the desire to taste life. For a growing child the questioning never ends, although the parent at times wishes their darling's inquisitiveness would not be so persistent. Later we pursue the questioning into fields of art, science, or commerce, organizing our life energies around a career within which the questioning endures. We are beings who question, reflect, and act.

While we may abound in knowledge, our appetite for reality seems boundless, arousing more questions as we touch down in our encounters with life. Our multi-directional pursuit portends no closure. The dynamism of living, however, surreptitiously draws us out to suspicions beyond the immediate satisfaction of daily needs. How curious.

Stimulated by these encounters with life, the horizon of our questioning, sooner or later, broadens into a showdown with itself. Unexpectedly, my daily engagements with life turn out to be the prelude that startles me to the brink of a new reflection. Here the practical immediacy of life is temporarily put on hold. Before, I went about my days directing my questioning energy to the tasks at hand, occupying my energy with bodily survival and career preservation. Now I am caught up in raising unavoidable questions that are not derived from my immediate experience of the empirical world and yet connected to it. It is like being thrown back to view the whole terrain of life. In these moments, the questioning mind changes its stance radically. Like Scrooge, my mind widens to all points of my embodied history, and I have the inner experience of stepping outside its borders. There I mirror myself with a different brand of questions. Who is this questioner, who is this knower, who is this doer, who is this experiencer of life? Whence does this seemingly unrestricted inner power to know, reflect, and act come from? What is my significance in life? No longer the simple matter of daily questions and responsibilities, now it's a matter of radical identity, a question of ultimate concern.

My questioning has led me to the matter of definition—self-definition —clarifying one's being beyond the obvious. Unfortunately this type of questioning can be smothered, brushed aside amidst the busy cares of the day, postponed with the excuse that no one really knows the answers. Do the best you can.

The refusal to answer is an answer. Not to consider the question, to put it down without a fair examination, declining to wrestle with its implications, only points to a certain skepticism that has overtaken personal growth. The child-like desire to know, the inherent thrust towards exploring life, that pursuit of knowledge that feeds the life of the soul halts. A certain calcification sets in. A plateau awaits. Yet an unexplainable restlessness persists, an inner loneliness is felt in spite of the satisfactions of the tangible world. Now and then a book, a lecture, something someone says, resonates within and gives a momentary flash of insight that briefly throws light on the problem. For a moment there really is more to life than its immediate demands. A slight awakening has stirred. Will it survive?

REALITY AWAKENS

The awakening, however slight, puts the person in the frame of mind that can listen to what the ancient travelers have been saying for centuries. As a questioning being, one is not merely finding information, but attempting to find ultimate meaning in life. My nature seems to bear a restlessness that will not let up until it experiences ultimate meaning for itself. "Our hearts are restless," Augustine Aurelius reminds us, "until they find rest in Thee." We are searching to complete ourselves absolutely.

The question and the quest of ultimate meaning take different forms throughout history. To survey the whole terrain with all its pathways is beyond the scope of this essay. Yet there are certain broad markings that may be found in the development of those embarking on this quest. In the tradition of perennial philosophy, one finds three broad levels of integration that comprise the evolution of the individual. These levels are not meant to stereotype the person, diminishing the personal idiosyncrasies and potentials to a rigid pattern of conformity. A healthy, self-training, sadhana, on the contrary, does not devitalize the person but demonstrates new energies and a sense of controlled freedom. People have a clearer sense of what they ought to do with their lives.

PURIFICATION: GATEWAY TO ULTIMATE KNOWLEDGE

In examining the steps in the perennial tradition towards achieving ultimate meaning, one finds that the first part of the journey is engaged with self-discovery at the tangible levels of daily existence. The body, the passions, the social relations, the various sensual appetites for life itself, need adjustment and modifying. The aspirant struggles with building new habits and remolding old ones. Caution is urged because the passions are the strongest forces that the body employs for its contact with life. Commandeering the passions as such is not the hallmark of development. Instead, one slowly modifies them by first understanding their nature in the concrete operations of daily living. One brings them more and more under the directing action of reasonable living, letting the notion of the good guide the feeling of pain and pleasure, in no way underestimating the continuing fact that human nature involves bodily aspects. The purpose of asceticism then is not to restrain the passions but to coordinate them with a creative control so that their expressions are productive on humanistic terms. This coordination of body and spirit is called "virtue." *Vir* is the Latin word for power. By bringing one's powers under reasonable guidance, one develops the life force into the freedom of maturity, a life that remains open to further questions about the ultimate significance of things.

By establishing a functional balance among the various powers or appetites, one can pursue the challenges of living with less self-imposed obstacles. In the schema of yoga, the purgative phase holds first place in similar fashion. The first two rungs treat the same areas in the personal and social dimensions that are found even in Christian asceticism. The common ground is the basic human nature that both traditions are concerned with for development. From the gross aspects of bodily existence one goes on to examine the more refined areas of the human personality. The yamas and niyamas offer the gradual integration of character, the "virtue" that is striven for in the West.

MEDITATION: DAWN OF SELF-UNDERSTANDING

The practice of virtue, the practice of the early rungs of yoga, are not meant as ends in themselves. These activities are means for preparing one to apprehend life more deeply. The refurbishing of body and mind rids the person of the discouraging tediousness of life. Self-training enhances sensitivity to life. The purgative phase enters now into levels of self-illumination. The combination of inner exploration and outer order provide the kind of environment for enriching self-knowledge. We see ourselves and life around us with fewer pretenses. Our vision is clearing. Our judgments are sounder. We waste less time and energy. Richard of St. Victor, a twelfth century aspirant wrote that the "whole essence of purgation is simplification." As our life simplifies, we are prepared to enter more into the journey of acquiring natural insight.

The inward practice of meditation expands this insight. Intuition dawns. Life is faced more honestly. There is less dependence upon outer things for self-satisfaction. The recognition of one's duties to life takes on a freer reevaluation. A holistic integration of mind and body, along with breathing and diet, sleep and exercise, are understood more and more against the background on meditation. The Spanish mystic Teresa of Avila cautioned that, however advanced in spiritual progress, one should never give up meditation in the quest of the ultimate.

Like an athlete who finally begins to round into condition and thus only then discovers what the movements of her body are all about, we have entered the phase of self-development known as the illuminative stage. One is evolving, as it were, through training, affecting a continuing series of self-discoveries, gradually seeing that the inner life force, the sense of self-awareness, is behind all life experiences. Through my self-training I keep revising my self-understanding. How I view myself is the determining factor in my outlook upon life's adventures. Am I a tense person, a frightened person, a suspicious person? Do I mistrust others and myself, or am I aware of the limitations of myself and others, coping with these realities without sweeping condemnations of our mutual efforts? These are the questions with which life challenges us as we go about our business. A change of environment can give temporary relief, but the quest of the meaning of our lives haunts us for an answer. The purpose of these ascetic practices is to clear the air of the congestion from negativity, depression, fears. The more I understand the natures of things, their temporality as well as their enjoyment, the more I am free to be enriched by involvement with them. I "see" what they are and are not. Meditation enables a calming of bodily energies, the imagination, and mental flow, letting the inner force reestablish its equilibrium between body and mind, producing a wholesomeness within that guides my judgments in life.

Classically, the Christian tradition places meditation within the context of prayer. Often one cannot tell the difference between the way the writers explain these two practices. Frequently, meditation is described as a two-stage process. The first level involves the thinking faculty. An image or abstract quality is chosen for pondering, allowing the mind to ruminate and analyze the contents with the eventual purpose to bring the penetrating results into application to daily life. Meditation in this manner is really a discursive process. Teresa points out that while this type of inner exploration yields truths and insight, yet the aspirant needs to go beyond the discursive level. One must enter farther into the very center of the consciousness, that level of serene awareness which is non-discursive. Here is where the more profound stages of Christian meditation and yogic meditation converge. A medieval text on meditation, *The Book of Privy Counseling*, explains it:

> *I know you want to see God; I know you have been offering prayers and singing psalms and doing many other things. But now I want you to reject all thoughts whether they are good or evil. I want you to see that nothing remains in your mind save a naked intent stretching out. I only want you to keep a simple awareness that you are as you are. Do not fill your mind with content or images . . . I want you to leave your thoughts quite naked, your affections and emotions uninvolved, and yourself simply as you are, so that the grace may touch and nourish you with the experiential knowledge of God as God really is.*

All traditions both recognize that the outer world only supplies incomplete answers to the meaning of life. If one was only a body and emotions then the external world could provide the comfortable resolution to the mystery of life. One would then be part of the animal kingdom satisfied with the environment. But the inner restlessness and questioning beckon to search within. How strange that the inner search, which at first seems so empty and intangible, should be the indispensable means to self-discovery. There is no rushing this investigation. One makes progress by calmness. Teresa echoes the yogis when she indicates that progress in self-knowledge is signified by tranquility. An inner peace abides throughout the work-a-day world. One unites to peace, which in turn generates more energy for tasks. Her busy career was a dynamic example of the union of opposites:

unruffled peace amidst the pressures of reforming an entire congregation of nuns throughout Inquisitorial Spain.

THE FINAL CONCLUSION: THE QUESTION IS ANSWERED

One's final destiny is to experience the ultimate meaning of our nature. Yoga describes this state of experience as *samadhi*; Christian writers speak of the mystical union, often choosing marital metaphors whereby the soul is wedded to the divine spouse. Again the terminology reflects the cultural and poetic milieu, but the meaning conveys a state of completion, a freedom from suffering and ignorance, the end of the questions. This third level of consummation remains shrouded in mystery. Mystery here means more intelligibility then the rational mind can comprehend. The brightness of this wisdom blinds the mind, which is too weak and limited to view it. The total regime prepares the inner eye to experience the inherent dignity that is our nature. The further one enters into the self, the more awareness opens to unify with all of life. The last barrier is overcome. We cleanse the egotism, increasing our compassion to embrace the universe. Every tradition speaks of this rebirth. The aspirant is born into the inheritance that is shared with all, an inheritance to know and love without reserve.

Ahimsa's Pact with Satya

Who could ever suppose, let alone believe, that humans have the capacity to know everything about this expanding cosmos? Who would not view this assertion as preposterous in the face of the geographical complexities of everyday events and the enormity of other galaxies? The truths of reality, personal as well as cultural, are too vast and complicated. However ignored by modern times, the ancient tradition of *philosophia perennis* yet upholds a universal principle: *vincit omnia veritas*—truth conquers all things.

From that perspective, to which classical yoga belongs, the very nature of your soul is to penetrate to the essences of all reality, seen and unseen. In the face of amnesia and ignorance, we are born with an unrestricted desire to know the truth of things, to embrace reality. Children's behavior renders indisputable evidence that it's unquenchable. What healthy child needs encouragement to engage life? More than nutrition for bodily existence, the human spirit thrives upon its just desserts: satya. We hunger for genuine knowledge. The pursuit of various interests, projects, particular hobbies, a chosen career, illustrate continuously that irrepressible desire to grasp and seek the meaning of life. Whether we pronounce it in Eastern or Western terms, the joy of being alive flows from our rendezvous with truth. How confusing and listless existence would be without satya, without *veritas*.

*Yet the truth that dwells in the core of all things none but
the few do contemplate.*
— Anselm of Canterbury

When we think about it, our practical achievements in life are built upon the truths that inspire them. We dream of sharing a life. One day opportunity knocks and we answer. What could be more fascinating, especially at the personal level, than the truth of knowing someone you love? How precious to experience the excitement and enjoyment of watching your children mature, sharing events with them, sympathizing with their struggles and play, embracing all the mix of activities that draw you into knowing them. Yet we also know the truth of living on a planet with many serious conflicts.

Given our indisputable reliance upon truth and its consequences, it appears puzzling, at first glance, that classical yoga's manual, the *Sutras*, slates truth as the second disposition to assist in one's journey to self-discovery. With our irrepressible propensity to know how things work and communicate our knowledge, not choosing truth as primary seems impertinent, if not unnatural. So why is *ahimsa*—the attitude of non-harming—given precedence?

Some time ago, a renowned French scientist, Jacques Monod, proudly announced that the world was basically a chance filled universe. Simply put, there was neither rhyme nor reason for its existence. Everything—from Malibu and monkeys to mushrooms and moonbeams—was aggregations of random molecules. Nature is terribly overrated because her wares possess no consistent natures. Plant your garden, and what comes up is wholly by chance. The presence of intelligent life on these terms is an aberrant incident, an accidental evolution.

When the scientist was pressed on how he reached his staggering conclusion about life, he blithefully replied that he excluded in his examination of reality any evidence for order, stability, coherence, and purpose. How liberal of him.

By dismissing those inconvenient clues that, in other words, would resist his predetermined thesis that life endures as essentially chaotic configurations, he betrays truth for his personal agenda. To get us to agree with him, just avoid any facts in evidence that preclude a sense of recurring order. Quick to reply to our professor is Aldous Huxley: "Facts do not cease to exist because they are ignored."

Thinking about these professional assertions, clues emerge why ahimsa rises first in dispositions toward reality. Most people, including scientists, would prefer to guide their lives with truth rather than deliberately delude themselves, no matter how comforting the latter. If for no other reason, factual truth tends to be safer and more profitable in the long run. Just ask mortgage investors.

In this context of remaining in touch with reality, the wanting of the truth implies, first and foremost, a primary non-interference regard for things as they truly exist, warts et al. That may seem obvious but it's importance cannot be emphasized enough. It's so easy to abuse the truth to my advantage. To step into a scene of life and immediately select what facts to line up as predetermined may obtain results, but truth is not one of them. Rather, what the truth seeker intends to respect is the scene, the situation, and the story with its full report. Commentary comes later. To achieve this kind of demeanor toward the reality requires a receptive attitude, so to speak, that must accompany the entire pursuit of knowledge. It is more fundamental than memorizing rules of engagement. Otherwise truth is warped amidst subjective fancies.

> In our doing and acting everything depends on this, that
> we comprehend objects clearly and treat them according
> to their nature.
> — Goethe

Truth, the vibrant fruit of knowing, flourishes when the learner allows reality to be itself. For me to know you, I must let you be. How could it be otherwise? To insist that you dance to my drummer may please me to no end but the truth of you stays obscured. For then whom am I actually loving?

The only indispensable, irrefutable way to know the nature of truth is to pursue being as it exists, as a lover would stand before his beloved. Being neutral misses the point. To discern truth means to express the exclusive demeanor of the respectful inquirer. One initiates, keeping all due respect, a courtesy call upon reality. Unless the seeker sustains this tacit sense of fairness as he learns, the opportunity for the full-ness of truth diminishes. Thus, we would remain in our chaotic world endorsed by Dr. Monod.

Are you strong enough to let things reveal themselves? A neighbor, instead of beholding the requirements of one of nature's marvels, once cut off the bottom of a cocoon in order to expedite the caterpillar's shedding its cover. A deformed butterfly emerged unable to open its crippled wings.

Ahimsa emphasizes that facts are respected as they are. Could you possibly understand anything, let alone a person for whom you profess affection, on the pre-condition that they first meet your terms? You may not necessarily approve of what you detect traveling down the byways of cities, but the truth of the matter is that even slum dogs can become millionaires.

A receptive bonding invites the learner. Ahimsa implicates satya in avoiding the tempting penchant for enforcing subjective agendas contrary to the facts. To demure to reality keeps your love for truth unspoiled.

If this premise is too high then life remains mediocre and manipu-lative. How to achieve such a humane standard? First, cultivate perception without pretensions. When you step out of your home on a wintry day, the weather does not await your approval. When you arrive at your employment, the blustering work situation, without your presence, is already in play. Like it or not, neither the climate nor the office environment are there with your permission. Who says any factors must suit your expectations before you acknowledge their significance? Recognition of truth does not demand condoning, only deciphering the facts. What you do with this unpretentious view of life is another issue.

When you ponder the truth of a person, for example, you recognize something uniquely real—an embodied spirit. Fostering friendship, you embark on an investigation of a complex being whose revelation ever increases. Only careful attention, however, with an abiding receptivity enables discovery. What cautions you from trying to manipulate personal truth, using it for your own utilitarian devices? What pauses one from slyly speaking and acting toward others from hidden agendas? What else but ahimsa wedded with fairness to the pursuance and communication of truth.

> *A wise person is one who savors all things as they are.*
> — Bernard of Clairvaux

How long before we learn that deliberate ignorance can be costly as well as bruising. Yet some resist any arduous way that proves knowledge liberates. Instead, we isolate ahimsa from satya. We exploit learning without the regard due to things and people. We observe calculative abuses in politics, relationships, even religions. A measure of the ingenious ways one can subvert truth and offend others in the process is portrayed by a recent investigator for banking irregularities, William K. Black, who published *The Best Way to Rob a Bank Is to Own One*. Unless the practice of truth shares the journey's leadership with its companion, ahimsa, freedom remains an elusive dream.

When one practices truth from a disposition of love, unexpected—even amazing—things can occur. Some years ago, when Swami Rama was walking along the shore with his master, a station manager approached them and implored Swami to give him a practice to do.

His master replied: "From this day on, don't lie. Practice this rule faithfully for the next three months."

Our aspirant went away determined not to lie nor do anything unlawful.

Shortly thereafter, a railroad supervisor came to investigate rumors of thievery at the station. Our new truth teller answered candidly that he and the staff were involved in accepting bribes. Everyone was rounded up to jail. You can imagine the reaction among his coworkers when word got out that he had exposed them.

Well, they decided to set things straight by colluding a story that Mr. Informer was the sole ringleader. Our aspiring truth discloser was indicted and while he was waiting in jail, the others were released. Abandoned by wife and family, who withdrew all his finances, he became a *persona non grata* and the laughingstock to his friends and associates.

A month later his case came before the court. As he stood in the docket, he must have pondered, "This is what I get for telling the truth."

The judge inquired about his situation. Undeterred, he calmly explained to the magistrate the whole story, was willing to accept whatever the court decided, and asserted that he was most interested in what the next two months of following the truth would bring.

Something about his story intrigued the judge enough to call a recess.

He interrogated the accused and recognized the mentioned Sage as his own Gurudeva. Now the real story came out and the others were indicted and our accused received a brief sentence.

On day ninety, a telegram arrived for our penniless, but truthful vagabond. The government was awarding him one million rupees for some land that belonged to his family in another province.

Once his wife heard the astounding news, she insisted that her divorce from him was an unfortunate misunderstanding. He smiled knowingly, gave her and the children his compensation. Departing for the mountains, never to be seen from again, he was heard muttering that after speaking only the truth for three months, what would happen if he didn't lie for the rest of his life?

Perhaps Swamiji's master was insinuating that something much greater awaits when one determines to be a lover of truth by piercing the compelling temptations to short-circuit life.

I wonder what would happen if more people spoke the truth for ninety days?

On Studying Oneself

How many people among your relatives, neighbors, and colleagues, would acknowledge themselves as budding scientists? That they are is easily evident.

From childhood onward, do we not spontaneously inquire why nature exhibits her wares and performs her ways? Why so many stars? Why do seasons alter? What keeps our heart beating? What makes moss grow on rocks? Why are hummingbirds attracted to red flowers? The questions are a never-ending spiral of surprise. In fact, the more we journey down that intriguing road of life, the more we persist in the pursuit of further knowledge. It's an irresistible quest to know the reason why. It's an innate, natural propensity that beckons the scientific curiosity in all of us. It's the echo of the love of wisdom, the urge to philosophize inner rumblings.

Formal sciences take their cue from this tacit font. Professional scientists sequester their investigation and analysis to some aspect or region of the external world. As they probe the pertinent facts, examine the evidence, collect and test the data, and arrange the findings in order to perceive their causal connections that reveal the make-up of their subject matter, they arrive through their methodology at the sophisticated goal of scientific knowledge.

For discussion, let us propose a study of human life that would concur with this natural methodology but focuses less on the external and more on the internal. Here the subject of choice, strangely enough, is the investigator himself. But we will investigate ourselves not as a statistical abstraction, which occupies anthropologists and sociologists, but as a living being subject to change and development. In other words, our natural propensity to reach out to the knowable world at large and enrich ourselves from that forage now drastically alters course from looking out to looking in. Attention, as it were, reverses itself. The goal is nothing less than the explication of the make-up of the investigator as a natural entity. Caution here. We are not after cultural and subjective idiosyncrasies, abundant and fascinating as these traits may be. Rather, our focus of interest probes further beneath the personality to spy those universal principles and characteristic features that compose that most elusive of subject matters: human nature.

Obviously, this same common ground can be depicted from many valid viewpoints—from studying it, say, as a biological species or as a consumer in society—all of these viewpoints revealing valid knowledge about the human reality. On the other hand, let us take a radical stance and examine the entire subject matter of body, mind, and consciousness from the perspective of self-consciousness. Let's investigate the very premise that enables us as investigators to gain knowledge and live our lives. One becomes not a CSI but more an LSI—a Life Scene Investigator.

What is amazing, at least for this writer, is that one's mind can monitor one's mind in all its living operations as they occur in society as well as in memory and imagination. With the widening of one's human experience as a natural physical being in various environments, a certain self-knowledge develops in tandem with self-perception. One becomes notably cognizant of the follies and rewards of playing out a human existence which eventually constitutes the basis for a science of humane living. It doesn't take long to realize that self-knowledge and self-development join, thus making this science most practical. In fact, its guiding postulate poses that the very heart of human nature is self-consciousness.

Just as physical scientists seek the truth of their subject matter, so our science would demand nothing less while yet eliciting an additional obligation. This science seeks not only to know the universal truths of human nature, as any other reputable science would from its selective approach, but it uniquely requires of its investigator to participate in that universal knowledge and thereby affect more than an upgrade in intellectual ideas. As the saying goes, she builds the plane as she flies it.

Our secular sciences derive from an intellectual habit that can be skillfully displayed in research, lectures, and reports. An astronomer or physicist bears that habit as part of his professional portfolio. Not untypically, his scientific acumen hardly affects his lifestyle. It's just another important role that occupies part of his valuable daily life. Not so with the enterprise of our life science.

Simply, we propose adjunctive knowledge: one learns only through performance. Understanding dawns when actor and action join. Only deliberate engagement by the investigator into his living subject matter—mind and body in its environment—can yield its fruit, namely, a new knowledge that affects the investigator as a kind of self-transformation. This approach is not knowledge for knowledge's sake, as our customary scientist would conclude, but knowledge for one's being's sake. As a participative investigator one is not after information alone, but rejuvenation. In other words, one experiences and acquires the vital actualization of one's innate potentials.

One knows oneself anew by exerting the action that produces the self-knowledge. The status of one's nature alters. Like a portrait artist in the midst of painting, one who knows himself in and through the conscious act of painting transforms himself into his artistry. In this way, self-knowledge emerges in and through self-expression. Being an artist takes on new life.

In building the science of life, I conduct on-site experiments with the components of my nature, always in relationship to the environment. One could say that I am dabbling with my life force. These experiments may take shape in various ways, such as probing what happens when I breathe in this or that fashion. How does the exercise of bodily postures affect my flexibility and the tonality of my internal organs? What occurs mentally when I enter inward to quiet my senses and dwell in interior silence? How do I advance my understanding toward career and family?

In this manner, my nature and its environment becomes the vast field for living investigations. In the ongoing analysis of my manifesting lifestyle, certain insights arise comparing before and after as I experiment with and modify my natural powers and their behaviors. This monitoring of learning illumines as it affects, say, improved health status, emotional stability, mental concentration without stress complications, or even a more palpable sense of peace and freedom. Based upon the facts in evidence from these experiments *in vivo*, I can gradually establish a verifiable, practical, philosophy of life. We have here a performance-based science. The ancient axiom, "Know Thyself" would be its calling card. Self-discovery would be its constant theme.

By now you readers know where we are heading. If one were to search history for a fundamental approach to life that espouses an unconditional endorsement of human nature as we have briefly outlined, one could do a lot worse than the accumulated tradition of classical yoga. While some of its scientific insights are codified in the ancient text, *The Yoga Sutras of Patanjali,* its importance is not on its pages but in living its subject matter. Even this irreplaceable manual may be enriched from the font of perennial philosophy. Readers of the scientific knowledge from the sutras may satisfy intellectual curiosity, but the actual power of the science derives only from the living participation in those actions which vindicate the text. *Prius vita, quam doctrinam:* first experience life, then codify it.

The art and science of yoga is hardly a series of Eastern dogmas from an enshrined past, but rather an invitation to discover for oneself the implicit art of living and dying. The sutras are unlike religious myths. They provide ascertainable guidelines and testable exercises for critical implementation. From where did these codified insights originate? From probing the act of living in varying circumstances and noting the results.

When forging a manual, one keeps what works. Whether living as a hermit in a Himalayan cave or raising a family in Minnesota, one applies what fits. The proof is where else but in the pudding. Like any tradition that purports to show a way to fulfillment, yoga takes on the same task but maps it out differently based entirely upon the self-revelation of one's conscious being.

As a practical science, yoga has a *telos,* an end, in mind. This navigable goal derives from the progressive, personal fulfillment of one's nature, often referred to as *samadhi* or enlightenment. These curious terms are not meant to be esoteric. They insinuate that the optimal fulfillment of humane living, the *totum bonum*, is a state of immortal consciousness in which all the secrets of the universe are beheld. Ignorance and death are forever banned; sorrows are forgotten memories. One's new status means one's arrival at the impervious realm where, as the ancients put it, "the gods roam in freedom." Thus by following Truth, you discover your nature. No saviors are required, no beliefs are necessary. By your own sweat and scars you found and grasped the helm of your nature's destiny and steered it into an eternal port.

Crafting Common Sense: Knowledge and Reality

Facts do not cease to exist because they are ignored.
— Aldous Huxley

ENCOUNTER

You walk into a favorite forest. Obviously, it is not the only forest near your home. Yet this territory of the woods, like many others, is commonly referred to as Nature. On this planet, there are sundry more woods that comprise the vastness of Nature. While we may not always go to these particular woods, there is little doubt what we mean by saying we are heading into Nature, in contrast to taking a walk in the city.

In our walk we sense the vast array of Nature's inhabitants—trees, underbrush, flowers, weeds, dirt, insects, wind, birds, along with all the colors, contours, sounds, odors, etc. The surrounding atmosphere constantly occupies our senses as we walk. As we saunter, gaze, smell, and listen to Nature about us, a distinctly sensual pleasure swells within us.

LET US ANALYZE THIS EXCURSION

We have the capacity to sense the natural world. We make contact with its inhabitants and know it. That contact is simply called sense knowledge. My mind goes from a potential state of knowing to one of actual knowing. To refine this process more: my senses contact Nature, and this interaction enables my intellect to assimilate Nature about me. From this brief experience, I gain some knowledge of Nature.

KNOWABLE REALITY AND THE KNOWING AGENT

How this change from unknowing to knowing is possible requires two factors: one from Nature and one from the knower. First, Nature is progressing through her seasons as I walk through the woods and view this procession. It did not start with my entrance, nor will it cease when I depart. Nature is a power onto herself, independent of my presence. Her manifesting stages of growth and decay do not depend upon my presence or anyone else's for that matter. Nature is not statically real, as a statue in the town square but dynamically real—full of surprises. This power to exist and undergo tangible changes means that Nature's inhabitants exhibit their reality. If Nature lacked this power, then she would be unknown. Moreover, this power to exist demonstrates that natural things are capable of being known; they are, in a word, intelligible. The real equals intelligibility.

The second factor for my knowing is my innate apparatus: mind and senses. Just as Nature has the power to reveal or manifest, I have the power to perceive and apprehend. Although Nature exists and can be known, she remains unknown unless I apply my powers to her. I must desire to change from potentially knowing Nature to actually knowing her. When the receptive power of intellect, by way of the senses, meets the expository power of Nature, we have the interaction called knowledge. Knowledge means that I apprehend and become the reality. Now Nature exists in two spheres, as it were, on her own and equally in my intellect.

A curious feature of knowing is that the more I apply my mind and senses to Nature, the more she seems to reveal about herself. Was she holding back? Hardly. My knowledge of the real is my responsibility. By my attentive presence over time, learning occurs.

INCREASING KNOWLEDGE

As I delve into Nature and study it through the seasons, certain know-able aspects emerge. These aspects in the real were always there but could not be immediately discerned until I took the time to become more familiar with her ways. In studying Nature, my mind is in the act of discernment; the implicit becomes explicit. As time goes on, the exposure of my mind and senses to Nature apprehends more and more of the subtle aspects and their associations. My personal growth in knowledge about Nature depends less on Nature's power to reveal herself than my power to discover and discern what is existing before me. It is the nature of Nature to reveal herself—but only to those who have a discerning attentiveness. Nature always speaks, as it were, and I have to listen—or miss the message.

PAYING ATTENTION

To my attentive eye, I gradually discern that Nature is not haphazard. Both in general and in exquisite detail, I apprehend through continuous exposure, say, to pine trees, certain orderly processes, recurring alterations, patterns of growth, size, cycles, interdependence, quality and quantity, aberrations, symbiotic connections, and more. These insights or ideas are not invented out of thin air; rather these empirical descriptions are the intelligible aspects of the complexity of real pine trees. These descriptive words are my verifiable attempt to explain the reality of pine trees. When I compare and contrast pines, say, with other woody plants of the forest, my knowledge broadens more to apprehend and distinguish their similarities and their differences. A science of forestry is burgeoning.

All of this growth in knowledge occurs over time because I have an innate capacity or potential for knowing the real. It is the objective real that reveals its truth, not the knower that would impose or presume. But I must assiduously apply myself to the subject matter, become an attentive discerner, or my knowledge stays superficial. In this way, the various sciences emerge as I explore Nature's variety.

My mind and senses derive their knowledge of the real from the real; they don't make it up. No doubt, I can forget, make mistakes, misjudge, impose, overlook aspects, but the combination of continual exposure to the facts and my vigilant attention helps in correcting, clarifying, and confirming the truth of the matter. The joy of knowing comes from knowing reality not as I would like it to be, but as it truly exists.

As the Ancients put it, *veritas sequitur esse re*. Truth follows upon reality.

THE UTILITY OF KNOWLEDGE

Given my state of knowledge regarding pine trees, I can reach out and apply that knowledge to other spheres of human activities. I can distill the resin, for example, and use it; I can chop down the tree for a Christmas decoration; I can slice the tree for building structures; I can use the needles for various concoctions, etc. In other words, my mind can discern the possible utility between the pine tree and practical enterprises.

The knowledge of the utility of pine trees does not come from the discernment of the pine tree as an object of knowledge, but as a possible intervention from my creative imagination. It's not the tree that inspires utility so much as the practical bent of my desires. My imagination plays with the potential usefulness. Notable is the observation that the practical in some way depends upon the speculative. Unless I have sufficient familiarity with the nature of the tree and its inherent properties, there isn't much to imagine. Knowledge precedes utility.

Reflecting on this wondrous experience of knowing, one can discern that amidst the variety and diversified abundance of Nature and culture some enterprises would reveal a richer reality, as it were, than others. Even though one could spend a lifetime examining, say, the realm of snowflakes with their crystalline structures, the application of my mind and senses to other realities—family life, commerce, law, fine arts, etc.—would enrich me more in terms of both personal knowledge and human fulfillment.

A COSMIC QUEST

Finally, one might venture upon the study of human nature and its implications for existence.

Raising the question of "why" about human existence pertains to all cultures. We phrase this "why" in different ways, such as: What is the purpose of life? What is my origin? Where is my destiny? How best to get there? How can I be certain what is the right course for me? What's the best lifestyle?

Then, or course, the correlative questions: What impedes my purpose? How can I eliminate these impediments? Why do people differ over human destiny? How can I prove these assertions? Why is there so much conflict between societies? Can what I don't know hurt me?

In response to these perennial questions classical yoga proffers at least two scriptures regarding this urgent matter: the *Karikas*, a collection of philosophical poetry, and the *Yoga Sutras*.

LIFE'S PREDICAMENT

In short, the heart of the vexing problem of life, for yoga, is the survey that human existence across the board exhibits a profound state of unknowing—ignorance or *avidya*. What's tragically more in evidence, you are unaware that you are in that predicament. Double jeopardy! You don't truly grasp your full nature and you don't know that it is your predicament. Thus, you suffer in innumerable ways.

To put it another way: our lack of self-knowledge means we are less real than we can be, less creative than possible, less interested in life's abundance.

This also implies that our discernment of the world is less than what it can be. For all the enjoyment, sorrow, comfort, pain, thrills, distress, beauty, disappointments, and discount benefits that we can and do experience, we are light-years from the unalloyed enrichment of our natural heritage. Hence, we stumble along.

The good news, however, is that our ignorance is not a total absence of reality and truth. Rather, may I suggest, we are more akin to near-sighted and partially color blind individuals, with diminished hearing, slightly uncoordinated, with a little malnutrition thrown in, subject to moodiness, and easily prejudicial. Hey, things could be worse. And what makes this plight even more interesting for many persons is the conviction, for the most part, that this fine state of affairs is the way things should be. And so we put up with it as best we can. We tolerate our discontent.

This kind of thinking is fostered variously by the array of culture, which includes institutional religions.

Decision

You are the architect of your life; you decide your destiny.
— Swami Rama

Above the mantel in our residential ashram in St. Paul is a portrait of Swami Rama with the above words. You may have heard this quotation of his before. It sounds nice. We say it blithely. We agree with it. It's inspirational. But to actually feel its import can be somewhat shocking because of the implications. It is one of the hardest (I mean hardest!) ideas to get into your system.

We have been brought up in a culture where we have, to a great extent, yielded our power to other people. When you were a child, you counted on your parents, or with great trepidation an older brother or sister. You knew they loved you and, if it didn't embarrass them, they wanted you to succeed. You often went to them for counsel and, for the most part, followed their advice.

Then you moved into education. You believed your teachers. If you went to church or synagogue you had Bible school or the mass or service. You likewise listened to the clergy or the rabbi. You assumed that they were acting in your best interest and so your mind was filled with their impeccable advice and mandated directions which you were told you should follow in life.

Then you entered a career. You went to work. Again, you had to believe your boss, your superior, the system itself.

In an amazing amount of our life we're told what to do. Interestingly, in following the recommendations of others we get a certain compensation, not only monetarily, but also emotionally and intellectually. We feel safe, wanted, tolerably well off.

Then there's that opening quotation. It rubs against our background. It doesn't mean, of course, that everything you've been told should just be put aside and you should start all over from scratch. No, it simply means there has to be a reflective moment in your life—like an awakening—when you have to truly sit down and reflect, "My choices are the only ones that really count in terms of where I'm going in life."

The world out there will tell you all kinds of things to do with your life. It will even try to make you feel guilty for not complying, because it has agendas for you. However, you have to decide: are those the agendas you want?

The main key here is the experience of choice. You must realize that your powers—your will, your intellect, your emotions, your body, and your behavior—are within the grasp of your own hands. The day you begin to assert personal choice for all your powers, instead of going through the ropes, is the major moment that your life becomes a path that really starts to work for you.

Still, there are people who will embrace a path; they'll follow the advice, say, of a spiritual director or a mentor, and they will never arrive at this insight of choice. There's the story of a group of students who listened attentively to their spiritual master for months on end, basking in his presence, boasting to others how high he was in the hierarchy of saints and what good karma they had to receive his *darshan.* One of the students got tired of sitting around, just chanting and asking the same weekly questions. He decided to go off on his own to the forest and test for himself the validity of the master's teachings. Some years later, having embodied the teachings into his lifestyle, he returned to find his old friends still admiring the teacher, still consoling themselves that they were graced to be at the master's feet, still reminding others of his degrees and honors, and still asking the same questions. Nothing had changed except for the student who chose to change his life.

Choice is dangerous; it fosters self-reliance. It gives you new eyes, new ears. You see and hear things differently. The commitment to the fact that you choose your destiny gives you, by that very self-evident choice, a better perspective on reality. And in that perception, you now have greater options from which to select. In other words, your freedom is starting to grow—real freedom now. Real freedom cannot be given by other people; it has to be claimed. There can be changes made in laws so that you don't have to pay as much tax or can be given a reduction in the speed limit. But in terms of real human freedom only you, by being willing to exercise the choices you make, can arrive at the plane of freedom.

This endeavor is a kind of paradox for choice. It's a determination. It's not arbitrary. Freedom is not just doing anything you want—that's a teenager's dream! Freedom is getting used to discovering what is true about yourself and embracing it, embodying it, living from it, and gradually becoming unafraid of taking it as far as it will go.

Along the way, there are many truths you're going to need in life that are only temporary. That's fine. There's nothing wrong with short-lived truths. We shouldn't be sad if we need a truth that only goes so far and can't be taken further. We were told things as a child that only befit a child. By necessity we have to outgrow some ideas. The child's ideas have fulfilled their responsibility.

Likewise, you're going to meet people based on the choices made. They'll be friends for a while and then maybe you'll have to part. You move to a different neighborhood; your job assignment takes you to another state.

Our whole evolution through life is a series of choices that bring us into new circumstances. In those circumstances, with your perception, you begin to see that you have to make additional choices. You can't get away from choosing. Not to choose is a choice.

You are not alone in your choices. Nature's dynamism, reality's purpose, is to come to your assistance. In Yoga philosophy there's a distinction between nature or *prakriti,* and the individual soul or the *purusha.* The purpose of *prakriti* is to support *purusha.* Life does not oppose you, but is to be your ally. Another way to put it: opportunities galore for those who have the eyes and ears to perceive.

But first there is a premium to pay. It's contained in the ancient axiom, "Know thyself," posted over the Delphi temple. In knowing yourself—and here's the magic—you'll find out about the Universe. The energy of reality is there for you; self-discovery occurs by exercising choice.

Physically speaking, the composition of nature is your legacy. A friend of mine, past chairman of the astronomy department of the University of Texas, detected one day as he was examining the stars through a color scan, that the galaxy abounds with amino acids. Everything in it resides in you! So he theorized that at one time we chose to experience ourselves as stars.

As you make the choice to decide your destiny, you're not going to know the full impact all at once. That's part of the mystery and surprise: to discover consequences as you go. The very fact that you're willing to put yourself into that practical perspective will bring forth a new kind of resolve to cope with the random chaos and unpredictability of life.

The whole path of Yoga is learning how to live and be in harmony with the dynamism of the world, not by pulling away, but by entering into its complexities. It's quite simple: unless you know yourself, it's hard to trust yourself. The word "confidence" comes from the Latin, meaning "with trust." So the more I know, the more I can trust myself as well as life. And that's the basis of my freedom because I know the truth of who I am.

Eventually, our pursuit leads beyond the obvious. But it shows up in all of the variations and all of the themes that make up our individuality.

You want to be able to walk with ease in your neighborhood, in your city. That doesn't mean being naive and denying the darker sides of life. It's not casting concern aside and saying, "Here goes!" with no thought about safety. Not at all. It means that you stay in touch—examining, tasting, comparing, observing, poking here and there, asking questions of yourself, of reality, even taking risks at times, until you become, in everyday parlance, "street smart." Then your self-confidence grows. Then you stand poised for your choices in your freedom.

Your destiny is more than just this planet. The earth is not the final real estate for your residence, but here is where you get your grounding. Here is where you determine the architecture of what you want to do with your life force. You have been in the land of choices in time and space in order to understand its potential power.

We're here to explore and create anew the kind of world that will allow us to understand ourselves more. To rid the world of the fears and the horrors—the unfair discrepancies and the insolent prejudices that exist because people choose not to know—is all part of the drama that awaits our contribution.

Why me? When we choose to re-examine the borders that we grew up in, hope shifts its perspective. Instead of replaying verbatim the roles of the past, a wider range of possibilities looms. Your willingness to supersede your past determinations by others, however useful for keeping you just the way you are, serves as a proof for the innate freedom of the human spirit. Now you act from the echoes of your inner Self whose presence has more power than any other single factor.

When you walk into people's lives, they pick up on you with their subconscious. Not just on what you say, but also on the radiation of the integrity you bear. Everything you pursue—your understanding, your desires, your ambitions—everything you have chosen for your direction, all that is radiating from you. It's communicating. And that's how we touch people's lives—mainly by presence. A path integrating body, mind, and spirit radiates presence when you meet someone. People will sense a wholeness about you, perhaps even a core of honesty and peace. Inside yourself the cultural anxieties that overwhelm others will not be hiding.

As you continue on your path, you'll be reshaping the architecture of your life, your lifestyle. There'll be changes in how you use your leisure hours. There'll be changes perhaps in the way you appreciate food. Certain new ideas will suddenly become interesting to you.

Businesspeople who are highly successful in their area of expertise sooner or later realize that "more" isn't the answer. When we arrive at certain stages of life new questions start to arise beyond our accomplishments and dreams for our career and family.

Why do these questions arise? They emerge from you. They echo from your soul. Whispers. You have to search, probe, discuss, read, and explore. You have to go to this seminar and that seminar. Each event adds a little piece here and a little more excitement there, as the choiceful journey starts.

And then pretty soon the "wows" hit, and the big ones emerge. "What's it all about?" One day it occurs to you that the answers are not out there; there are only stimulations out there that provoke the questions. The answers are inside.

The most important architecture you build is the one inside yourself. It's not fate; it's explorative. You pose hypotheses. Try them out. You question their efficacy: "Well, what is this doing to me? How does this affect my relationships with people? What does it do to my attitude toward myself, my loved ones?" You lose your fear of measuring how you are doing.

In that way we choose our destiny. As Swami Rama used to say, "You're complete, but unfinished." You're starting to finish the job. You want to bring forth all the majesty that's in your spirit. You want to know and be and live with utter freedom so that you can give of yourself if the circumstances call for it. You want to be available to your friends so they know you are someone they can trust. Through your choices, grounded in reality, you are at last finding out what it means to be human.

Bon voyage.

Ego

Q: What is ego and is it necessary to rid oneself of it?

A: We start out in life with a vague sense of self-understanding. At first, our small sense of identity is referenced mostly to our parents and siblings, the world about us. Our parents name us and thus a distinguishing mark is given to us. My "I-ness" is now known by that name. Everything I conceive, assert, or do is a search for myself. This individual task that sets me apart incrementally declares my identity, my ego-ness. My appetite for life is awakened.

When psyche meets flesh, the result is an individual, an ego—one's indispensable presence in time and space. A corporeal manifestation, if you will, of the spirit. You are lodged in embodied existence. That total ensemble is collectively an ego, a corporeal self, an existing individual with all his/her idiosyncrasies. To rid oneself of ego is like blinding oneself then expecting to see well.

Just as no two magpies are the same, so ego, not your nature, makes you different from other selves of your species. As each day changes, so do your responses. Yet you don't reinvent yourself daily. There is a perduring substance of awareness. Regardless of occurrences that you sense, perform, and reflect upon, you know that you are still the same ego throughout these experiences. Your ego is the self-conscious, cohesive principle that unifies your distinguishing choices, various considerations, and multiple actions by which you give meaning to yourself. Like in an orchestra, the ego is the conductor that holds the performance together. In the act of living, you gradually come to know who you are, and others know you then for what you are.

Meanwhile, we assume a collective harshness toward what we refer to as the ego. We imply derogatory statements like, "He's full of ego." We accuse some of being egotistical, meaning arrogant. Often we assume that the ego is something to abhor, to resist, to denigrate, to abolish, even to consider villainous. Yet can anything meritorious be accomplished without a colossal ego? The attempt to rid ourselves of the naughty ego makes as much sense as to sever a child's fingers for raiding the cookie jar. Try as you may, one can't exile the ego. Another tack would be to explore: what constitutes its ultimate purpose? Do you seek self-preservation and self-importance more than truth?

Think of Planet Life as a grand stage which requires individual thespians who don various roles to enact the drama of human existence. The performers sashay upon life's stage in order to perform their roles for the sake of the unfolding drama. They are identified as characters in the play because they assume roles. The Bard reminds us that all of life is a stage, and so we in our individuality, attracted to the stage, cannot help but assume a persona, a mask of individual performance.

At first, we can't help but presume, since we are born amnesiac, that we are our masks. As we establish relations with the world at large, we keep the drama unfolding. Both necessary and, at times, cumbersome. Yet in the drama of life, an inadvertent confusion prevails for a long time. There is no hired stage director to assign the script and guide our roles. Instead, we stumble upon the scenes of life and create our roles ad hoc. I, the ego, me, enact myself as I perform in reference to the scenes already in play. I build my ship, as they say, as I sail it.

All the human performers obviously presume they are their developing roles even though their scripts are malleable. Does this feature of life make the ego bad? Not at all. It shows our normal perplexity at times about trying to figure out who we are and what the drama is all about. We are ushered into the world without a manual that explains ourselves. We become butcher, baker, and candlestick maker. There is no drama without them. We are compelled, for playing out my sundry roles is indispensable for my growth and continuance in life's adventures. Accolades or not, where would I be without my roles? They fill my appetite for life. The show, painful or joyful, must go on.

The years go by. One day it partially dawns: could my shopworn ego be more than its bodily persona?

More queries arise: could the force for enacting my performances be not rooted in the energy of the persona but lie behind the mask, as it were, poised offstage? Unknown to most players, a radical difference exists for some few surreptitious performers who know that all of their temporary ego is within self-consciousness, yet not all of their self-consciousness is necessarily within their ego. They finally pierce the drama and discern that they are actors only wearing a mask.

However important their ego may be for conducting civil life, these subtle individuals draw upon something more than revised scripts; the ever-sustaining wellspring of their power, the immortal Self. They have shed their mask to recognize in self-awareness that the ego is not the pretender to the throne of life, as most proclaim, but the vicar of the Self.

In that liberating acknowledgment, their amnesia fades spontaneously away. For now they walk the face of the planet in wisdom, with invincible freedom, undisturbed but utterly aware, and compassionately involved in the significance of the times.

Q: Is ego a modality of mind or spirit?

A: This is truly subtle. I may repeat myself in different ways. Methinks the ego is the subtlest mode of spirit. And ego observes its functioning by simultaneous reflection. Ego is the same as an individual person or embodied spirit. It simply means just plain me, I, this living entity. Ego is an identity word for the whole living being. Our mental and physical powers cannot run themselves; they need a director to coordinate them with the task at hand. Hence, ego (meaning me) functions less as one of many mental functions than as the controller of all functions, the superintendent of what's going on for this individual. Ego moves the body, focuses attention, chooses, judges, decides how to run the show given all the powers it has at hand. Thus, we say, "I intended it and did it and I take responsibility."

Ego is aware of its essential relationship to all the powers, all the time, and yet can resort to any one of them at will. The sense of ego can remain "easy in the saddle" with full awareness, until it decides to go into action. For me it's just the commonsense way we humans operate. Ego is the individual spirit: limitless.

Q: I am trying to understand the egoless state from the writings of Ramana Maharshi: "We need not to acquire anything new, only give up false ideas and useless accretions."

A: Egolessness, like selflessness, is strictly speaking an impossible state, for then you would not exist. As colloquial words, they are used ordinarily to convey unselfishness. Whether saint, sinner, or sage, your fundamental identity is being someone, which simply means an ego. Call your identity a self, if you will, but it amounts to the same reality. My I-ness, my ego, is always involved in everything I do. Otherwise nothing occurs.

It's what you or ego does, how you or ego use yourself, that warrants scrutiny. The word comes from the Latin *ego*, which means simply "this human individual." There is no moral overtone connected or implied as such. Psychologists and spiritual writers, including Vedantists, invariably expound on it and misconstrue its meaning. Their confusion, it seems to me, lies in imposing gratuitously an opposition or essential difference between ego and self. In ordinary conversation, or upon personal reflection on the facts of living, I find no experiential support for this division.

Q: Can we say that one's ego is, and always will be, maintained on all levels of consciousness and in all material and non-material realms?

A: That I am—I am That—without my Thatness I would be Thatless. What is this That which of which I no longer would be That I am not human, but That—a That can only be a That. I can be no more or less than That. That is That—how can it be anything else?

If you followed That—you are definitely That.

I sense that I have lifted one foot off the illusionary world and am stepping towards Nature and Life. I have dipped my toes in the waters of Nature, testing and assessing my experience. So while one foot resides in illusions and fantasy, the other will hopefully, in the future, become planted firmly in Nature and Life. So I then can begin the process of lifting and removing my foot from the land that, at one time, served a purpose and was satisfying, but is so very limited and small. This last foot, however, seems more stuck than the first one. Lifting the back foot interestingly has different dynamics. I know now I must lean forward and release the pressure off the back foot, to focus on going toward something, not on what I am leaving behind.

As I lean toward life and wisdom, I notice my back foot frees a little in the cement-like substance. It loses some of its grip. I sense I need to focus on establishing both feet in Nature and Life and less on trying to remove the other foot. I suspect that I will fully realize that the hold on my foot was of my own doing, similar to Swami Rama's master being "held" by a tree. I simply have to lift my foot, placing my awareness and purpose on what I am stepping towards, with confidence and love, and not on what I am stepping from! Such a fascinating journey!

Goals and Destiny

Q: "You are the architect of your life and you decide your destiny" is a quote by Swami Rama. What gets in the way when you're trying to create something and other things happen?

A: On the route to your destiny, which is your fulfillment, there are two things that are going to move you: your aim and your goals. They're not the same. Goals are time stamped: I want to raise a family, I want to take additional courses and get my MBA. Those are goals. Now hopefully the goals are in harmony with the aim. When they don't get in harmony, then the problems start.

Our aim comes out of our nature if we rise to it with sufficient reflection and intuition. Are you a human being searching for religious experiences or are you a spiritual being evolving through human experiences? Swami Rama used to say, "You have everything you need but you don't know what that means." So you are perfect but you're unfinished. Our goals help us complete the unfinishedness, so that we can realize our nature. And your nature is to be free, to be wise, to enjoy the bliss of existence.

In your struggle in life you're constantly setting up goals. Some goals take you so far. Fine, you've accomplished it and you say, "What's next?" Okay, you start a new one. Some goals don't really lead you toward your nature, then you've got problems. The struggle between these two is something that each of us have to work out for ourselves.

Oh we get help, we get inspiration, we get friendship, we get support—or we don't. But the point is that each of us has to do it in a somewhat solitary way. It's not meant to be punishment, because no one can do your practice—no one can get you there except yourself. You do it basically by making choices and then observing the consequences.

We can't always anticipate every consequence, so we learn from our experiences. Now, we have built into our nature to always know if this is the right path we're traveling. Are these the right goals? Because we have an intuition, we have a conscience, we have a certain resonance with things and we often ignore it. Then we find out what happens. But it's in you and you can call upon it. And it gets better as you pay attention to it. It's a law of the universe that if I want to increase my awareness, I have to attend to it. If you want to learn a new art you have to pay attention to it. You may still make mistakes simply because you're a greenhorn. That's fine because you'll learn from those mistakes because you paid attention to them. So that struggle is just part of becoming acclimated to understanding what life is about.

You have built into you a certain sense of what's right, what's wrong, what's correct, what's proper here and now. And you have to just wrestle with that until you begin to get a sixth sense of things. You see that with people in all arts. Eventually you're willing to go to certain people because the advice, the possible suggestions of this person, will probably be more accurate than anyone else you could go to. Why? Because they have gone through their own experience. They understand you, they understand the situation, and they can make a proposal to you—try this out and see what you think.

Along the way as we fulfill our goals, there are little traps. They're not essentially bad, they're not evil. They are just things that hold us back us and keep us from enjoying freedom. We often associate so much of our sense of control, especially our sense of being really safe, with things around us. Then we realize that it has to come from within. This body is always vulnerable, but the spirit isn't, the spirit is invincible. But, again, we don't know that; we think it can be controlled. We assume if something is missing at this earth plane, that's somehow going to be an encumbrance for the spirit. We don't realize, no it's not. In the fulfillment of our goals we have to realize that there is no immediate goal that guarantees the destiny. All of you are discovering what humanity is about in your own way. Each of you are becoming human.

Swamiji's master once told him, "Your job is not to become divine, you're already divine. Your job is to become human." That's a different take on things. You would think, "Oh I've got to be holy, I've got to be sacred, I've got to be divine." Here's the master saying no, no, no. You already are. Your job is to become human. And I think there is a little irony there because it's only in the act of becoming human that you discover your divineness. You can't bypass the human dimensions and factors and aspects of what constitutes your humanness in order to discover how holy and divine you are. It's in the act of realizing your humanity that you know what divineness is all about. And this takes a while.

It's your kindness, your ability to forgive, your ability to overlook your desires, sometimes for the sake of somebody else. It's the encouragement you give to others. It's the very presence you bring to people that they feel and are touched by, even though you may not know it. Just walking in a room sometimes, just sitting down and starting a conversation. That act may have removed that person from their worries and problems because you gave their minds something else to concentrate on. The very fact that you were courteous—don't underestimate that.

It took me a long time to realize something about Swami Rama. He used to constantly emphasize be kind to people in life, be kind. Over the years I began to realize what he was talking about—that the kindness oils things. It takes away the possibility of being a threat. I didn't discover until after his death in the body that there were over twenty-six people he put through college out of his own pocket. He took it upon himself to get room, board, tuition. They were on a full scholarship he arranged for them and he kept it quiet. So I began to understand what he meant by kindness. The action of kindness opens you up to seeing things and receiving things that you never suspected would come into your life.

As you move towards your destiny, you're going to get signals. You're going to get clues. If you're alert, you'll see them. Many of them go by and you won't see them. Somehow you will get a tip-off when you're about to venture something, to engage life in something that's bigger than you—especially if it's bigger than you. And those are very comforting at times; it's really fun to see exactly how that's working out and when that occurs. I am more and more convinced that life is constantly sending us these signals, but we miss these clues.

In our tradition we want you to enjoy the whole trip, not just the destination. Because everything that is happening to you is in some way a glimmer of the final destiny. The joys you're experiencing now, the breakthroughs in awareness, the insights into truths. That's all a glimmer of what is waiting for you when you make the final crossover in the fullness of destiny. You really are the architect of your life. You decide the goals on your terms. You must choose whether they're consistent with what you really ultimately want in life, which is your aim. And as a result you learn more about yourself. The turning point is when you are really convinced, not on faith, but with conviction, "I am the architect of my life." Then you look at life differently and you will see things that you never saw before.

Six | Swami Rama and the Himalayan Tradition

A Far-Away Star

A far-away star
entered this planet today
a stranger you say?

She came at night
her splendor to be revealed
by those who love her.

Bearing hidden gifts
to bestow upon a world
that sorely needs them.

She's a darling of
those Devas who protect her
watch your step, people.

Old Man winter chants
her name to make the snowflakes
glisten in the sun.

If you are lucky
you may meet her on your path
her presence blesses.

An Unforgettable Portrait

This man is freed from servile bands
Of hope to rise, or fear to fall:
Lord of himself, though not of lands,
And having nothing, yet hath all.

— Sir Henry Wotton

Portraying someone who turned your life upside down is not an easy task. Given the magnitude of his character, the secret to Swami Rama, learned over years of trying to figure this man out, was that unlike us, he was at home in not one, but two worlds. Side by side, as it were, he could step across the borders with ease. The more important one, the one we were struggling to discover, did not require a passport. From visits to that world, with the companionship of his Master, he drew his sustenance, his colossal vision for humanity, and his enduring encouragement for us scattered pedestrians. Although fortunate to spend nearly two decades with this gentleman at close range, I can only convey an uneven fraction of the significance of those memories.

This connoisseur of life was eagerly at ease with children and grandmothers as well as with prime ministers and royalty. Yet he was not a man to suffer fools; he could act the jester to satisfy one's curiosity, when that was all that was sought. Smiling, he sensed another replay of the old story of the pickpocket encountering a saint. But he had more in his pockets than their size, provided you stuck around.

He came on the scene during the heyday of America's shameful involvement with Vietnam. He took the pulse of the West and felt it stronger than the East's. He wanted to work with that energy. In fact, to understand it better, he grounded himself across Western culture for twenty years. The curious contrast between his formative life in his ancient cave, earlier popularized by the novelist James Hilton as Shangri-La, and his arrival on the shores of America must have tickled the mentors he left behind in the Himalayas. Americans were still celebrating the conquest of outer space. Now they were about to meet someone who would show them how to conquer inner space, man's final frontier.

Swami Rama had what might be called a holy impatience, which he did not hesitate for one second to visit upon those who came to hear him. Instead of pursuing the Hound of Heaven for himself, which he had already captured as he "fled down the labyrinthine ways," he now turned the hound loose upon his students. Utterly dismissive of mediocrity in any form, he chided, cajoled, remonstrated, cheered, and inspired his audiences as well as his true students—of which he had only a handful—to reach out beyond their best endeavors. Since he did not countenance any hint of sanctimonious, sycophant behavior in people, many students preferred to follow him at a safe, admiring distance.

Gurudev, as Swami Rama is called, was hard on those who could take his pace, but harder still on himself. When he failed, rarely, in any proposal, it was usual that someone he had counted on had quit midway. Once he told me, "I have three kinds of students. First, those who come for a blessing for themselves or their family. They are given it as often as they want it. Second, those who want to study the yoga tradition, but not too closely. I give them the best books to read and practices to do. Third, those who want to go the whole way. They take anything I give them."

When it came to human development, he handed one the ball with instructions. "Now let's see how you run with it." He never begged if there was resistance and never did he take away one's volition to refuse. Unless one threw the ball away, he would not give up on any fumbling efforts.

Occasionally, Gurudev might be a little encouraging. Once, a worldly, confident professional, accompanied by his girlfriend, came to say goodbye. The woman just happened to be someone that Swamiji had trained. The man was given the following sendoff in a stentorian manner, "If you don't marry this woman, you are doomed!" Those words were non-negotiable for the nonplussed recipient. Thankfully, that prophecy was never fulfilled.

And then there was the occasion when Swamiji received permission from some parents who had been sympathetically told by the finest physicians that their only son could not live out the year, that he might hold their sleeping seven-year-old in his arms the entire night. That fragile boy runs a corporation today.

Swami Rama's lectures glistened as a rainbow of human possibilities. He reveled in the slightest display of enthusiasm, regardless of the impediments involved. What could he do, twenty-four hours a day, to foster one's advance? It did not matter the field of endeavor or how badly one flopped before. From bankers to bakers, from candlestick makers to taxi drivers, his enthusiasm and practical wisdom was at hand for one's pending success. Titanic in his vision, yes, but he knew from personal experience that one starts from clumsiness. As long as one could muster a semblance of interest, he was there to fire it up.

Gurudev's own Master reminded him that he was a prince of the world. With that inheritance, he made us the beneficiaries. In my eyes, he did not serve anyone; he led. His service was his uncanny leadership. His whole life was an undaunted revelation of the human potential displayed before us. He was not a mannequin, then or now, to be adulated in statues and rituals; he abhorred memorials. He preferred a heart to a pedestal.

From Menninger to NASA, he loomed an inexplicable contradiction to science's less than grandiose ideas of what constituted human nature. He loved to challenge the revered notions that brought scientists grants and prestige, not so much by speculative arguments but, even better, by demonstrating personal feats that could not happen in their world view. If he engaged Carl Sagan, who asserted "I am a collection of water, calcium, and organic molecules," Swami Rama might reply, "Sorry Carl, but from what you have seen me perform, you can surmise that your narrow world is just too small for my living space."

This wandering monk wanted people not to be intimidated by life, but to taste their immortality this side of death, as he did. No one's past, as far as he was concerned, was an implacable verdict against the future. I suspect he would applaud Maria Montessori when she said, "My vision of the future is of individuals passing from one stage of independence to a higher one, by means of their own activity through their own effort of will, which constitutes the inner evolution of the individual."

Don't leave yet, Professor Sagan and fellow scientists. For your information, on November 13 of 1996, Swami Rama demonstrated his stewardship over nature once more by consciously abdicating his cancerous, molecule body. "Then," as one of his students recalled him enthusiastically saying, "I will be able do so much more with full freedom."

Are those mere words? Not for a long list of pleasantly bewildered people from around the world, students as well as strangers, who have since experienced his temporarily embodied appearances, words, and actions. What to make of all this suspicious anecdotal data? Frankly, death has no sway over Swami Rama. Matter in all its varieties, including our molecules, can change drastically, suffer decay, even go out of business. But spirit, ah, there's the rub!

So now he is more situated on that other side, back home in the precincts of the unreachable star, yet still slipping in and out at will of our terrestrial confines to remind us that we are not orphans.

One day, words rambled about that Gurudev had contracted cancer. Up to his old tricks again, I mused. Using himself as the guinea pig for this impious disease, he would casually call in the medical staff at his last hurrah, the Himalayan Institute Hospital, and scold them, during their weekly visits, for not paying sufficient attention to note carefully where and how the pathology ravaged his body. Teaching to the very end, he finally bid farewell in full consciousness to that emaciated body.

Hardly had he been cremated when the rumors spread across the oceans. Who is his successor? A few of the Americans chuckled at the prosperous prospects of a suitable replacement. From Pandit to Swami, some have tried to enforce the issue by self-proclaimed decree. Let's face it folks: pretenders, yes. Real takers, the jury awaits.

Hierarchical acknowledgement was not his style. That's why a lot of people still miss the point.

Walking at midnight with Swamiji one night, he abruptly turned to me and said, "I am leaving no successor." He wanted his versatile students to carry, not ranks and titles, but the ball! Run with the ball of yoga on the field of life as he did. Show by the conquering of those opponents of doubt, fear, defeat, and selfishness, what you are made of—as he did. Pick yourself off the floor of discouragement and boredom and rise to broader energies of commitment and accountability as he did. Trust your practice, he would relentlessly urge. Fall in love with life and prove it by your thoughts and actions. Wake up people, in this tradition each one of you is a sovereign being. Swami Rama lives, so who needs his successor?

Our job? Get busy exploring and putting to use the treasure trove of knowledge he bequeathed and shape the future from it. After all, Gurudev placed this mantle into our hands and he's standing right behind it.

The Millennium Model for Wellness in the Himalayan Mountains

In all my travels around the world, the Himalayan mountains, which have silently challenged mountaineers and trekkers for centuries, hold precedence in my mind and feelings for their auspicious power and beauty.

The past two weeks were spent living and teaching in that incomparable area, visiting ancient caves, sacred forests, and making new friends. To share some of my astonishment over the surprises that the ancient land held out to me, let me tell you about a continuing event.

Amidst this awesome region, among the rocky and scrubby foothills northwest between the towns of Rishikesh and Dehradun, walked an unusual man with a unique vision for humanity. Knowing he had only a few years to live, Swami Rama, a tall, swarthy teacher of ancient and modern skills for living, rallied his friends, benefactors, and students to join him in a culminating impossible task that matched the snowy grandeur of nature's tallest spires.

Walking in the mountains over the years, this ambassador of life, himself a physician and scientist-philosopher, felt the plight of his beloved mountain people, who had never benefited from modern medical care. He listened to his heart speak an impossible dream and announced, "I have a burning fire within me to build a great hospital which will serve people, particularly poor people." Into the unruly scorpion and cobra infested terrain of over two hundred acres, an ultra-modern hospital and educational conglomerate emerged beyond the startled expectations of the medical and scientific community of Asia.

The Swami's practical vision reached even farther. Inspired by an ancient geometrical pattern called the Sri Yantra, he designed, engineered, and became the inspecting foreman for the remaining acreage, the infrastructure of an entire city dedicated to healing humanity on all fronts. In less than the unheard-of time of five years in India, a medical, educational, and social complex was erected. It was so vast in its diverse range of care and treatments, so daring in its holistic concept to synthesize multiple traditions of medicine from allopathy and Ayurveda to acupuncture and homeopathy, that the Mayo brothers and Rockefeller medical centers would envy its magnanimity. Hundreds of apartments and homes were built for staff and resident students. Library, music hall, gardens, exhibition rooms, and a host of other buildings expanded the modern community. Rumors spread that more than human assistance was deployed in erecting the complex.

Uniquely, Swami Rama's audacious vision embraced more than the important material dimensions of his dream. He infused a holistic philosophy of life, a guiding wisdom into the curriculum and environment. Besides the body and mind, each human being possesses a creative immortal spirit. While the spirit's presence does not show up on an x-ray, its dynamism and causal impact can, nonetheless, be felt and demonstrated every day and most especially in the attitude and behavior of magnanimous individuals. Swami Rama emphasized that ideals are as real for people's metabolism as their heartbeats. For him, health and healing embrace the entire person, body, mind, and spirit. To the medical faculty he said:

> Our approach is to deal with the whole person, the totality, body, breath, senses, mind, and center of consciousness. We must learn to study ourselves on all levels, not seeking physical well-being only, but mental and spiritual well-being.

Since he grew up amidst the villages and hamlets of those mountains, the saint knew firsthand of the medical and hygienic privations of these sturdy, rustic people. Almost forgotten in India's struggling transition into the second millennium, thousands and thousands of villagers, dedicated to ancient and limited ways of caring for the sick and indigent, had rarely seen a physician, let alone been exposed to current health care methods. Women gave birth to their children in the sugar cane fields and used the knife that chopped through the stalks to sever the umbilical cords. As a result, mother and child too often become infected and died. Cooking over an open fire for years frequently affected eye maladies from smoke irritation. Childhood diseases were rampant from lack of immunization. Swami Rama devised inexpensive, handy first aid kits for pregnant mothers that included a small, sterilized razor blade and a small measure of nylon to bind the umbilical tissue; a compact clay oven with a small chimney was dispersed to the villagers' homes for cooking; and more than twenty thousand immunizations were conducted in the 450 villages, thus halting the death rate at birth.

The best of East and West are the norm at the hospital. The technological standards of Western medicine, including MRI's and CAT scans, are also available at the hospital. Patient care includes biofeedback as well as yoga therapy which educates each person into the benefits of breathing, diet changes, and gland and joint exercises. Lifestyle methods are taught based upon, and adjusted to, the natural endowment of the individual. Stress management, for example, broadened to include classes in meditation.

This amazing enterprise was recently incorporated as the Himalayan Institute Hospital Trust of Jolly Grant, India. Its unstinting mission is to develop integrated and cost-effective approaches to health care that reach out to the local population and also serve as a worldwide model for the future. Exchange programs for medical faculty are fostered along with the residential based medical and nursing schools for accredited degrees and research. Here, in an unprecedented way, a legacy of ancient wisdom combines with modern medical advances for community-oriented education and healing.

Swami Rama had spent his life rendering the impossible possible, pausing to allow the unimaginable to take a little longer. For those in doubt, all one has to do is cite the astonishing experiments conducted at the prestigious Menninger Foundation in 1970. There he turned the Newtonian world of physicists and physicians upside down, shattering forever their conventional medical paradigm that denied self-conscious communication between body and mind. In controlling his entire autonomic nervous system; stopping his heart at will; raising and lowering his blood pressure with the ease of removing a ring from his finger; generating and eliminating visible cancer cells in nanoseconds anywhere in his anatomy; and producing brain waves of sleep yet remaining fully conscious of his environment, he stunned the scientific personnel with a command of human nature hitherto unsuspected. The Swami insisted that his competency should not be unique. People simply underestimate their dignity, he remarked, and from that habitual ignorance stems most of the confusion and suffering afflicting the world today.

To commemorate the Swami's passing, an American team of his professionally-training students, of which I was a member, inaugurated the first Wellness Conference. We taught courses in the science of breath, meditation, walking and breathing, pain management, and holistic wellness, blending yoga therapy to the allopathic model.

The unconditional enthusiasm for the growth of Swami Rama's vision made me feel that here was a model of selfless service that the world needs to hear about.

Learn to See Reality

Yesterday I got an e-mail from someone I do not know. This person, Helen, lives across the Atlantic with a husband working in Dubai. She wrote me to tell a story.

About a year ago Helen was on an airplane and sitting next to her was a gentleman who was reading. After a little time the man stuck his book in the seat pocket in front of him. She glanced over and saw the words, *Perennial Psychology*, which, she could tell, was not the full title. Her estimation of the man went up a bit, however. Although she would seldom talk to anybody on a plane, especially a man, thank you, she used the title to launch conversation. The man, Matthew, pulled the book out and displayed it. Oh! She noted the unusual name and Matthew just had to tell her about the author.

He had first read the book in 1995 and was so impressed that he decided he simply must go to India. There he met Swamiji. As he narrated his story she became enthralled. When Matthew got off the plane, he handed her the book, *The Perennial Psychology of the Bhagavad Gita*.

Helen devoured the book and then noted Swamiji's autobiography, *Living with the Himalayan Masters,* listed in the back pages. She went to her bookstore to order it. The book came up on the shop computer screen and, along with it, there was another book called *Walking with a Himalayan Master.* She assumed that they were both by Swami Rama and ordered them. Little did she know!

Both books arrived at her home shortly, and when she opened the package and examined them, she thought, "Oh, that one's by an American." She put that book aside and began reading Swami Rama's book. Again she became ecstatic and thrilled; the pages answered her questions right and left. She read it more than once. Over the course of the year she had also been e-mailing the gentleman she met on the plane, Matthew, who was now in India.

Every so often Helen walked past the other book, glanced, but let it lie. After all it was written by a Yank. But after some time, that other book began to gnaw at her. About three weeks later, on a lark, she grabbed *Walking with a Himalayan Master* as she packed for a trip to Dubai. She began to read the book on the plane. Low and behold, she discovered another glimpse of Swami Rama and was completely delighted with it.

When she flew to Dubai this time, she had to catch a plane to Egypt for her husband's business and had a two-hour layover. Thinking of Matthew and past events that led her to Swami Rama, a voice behind her said, "Helen." She turned around, and guess who was standing there? Matthew. They both were convinced that this was not an accidental meeting. Of course, she began to share her new book with him. Today I'm told that Matthew will soon be sending me an e-mail. And on it goes. . . .

What's the point? When things are meant to happen they're going to happen. There are two courses in life. One is carrying on without your permission. I couldn't control the weather today, and I don't think anybody else could either. It was a bitter cold day even though it was beautifully sunny outside. Yesterday was much nicer. So here is this realm of nature, dynamically changing, oftentimes unpredictable, yet broadly consistent.

Then we each have our own private life. It's connected in various ways with our family and business and hobbies, and does not seem to have much to do with the larger dynamics of the world. Yet here were two people meeting by chance on an airplane. Somehow that book enthralled the woman and that led to something else, and that led to something else. The point is this: there is a certain order of things that is occurring that will touch our lives provided we are aware. That's the hitch. Things can sometimes go by us that were meant for us but we weren't paying attention, or we misunderstood it, and it may not come back again.

Swami Rama had a student whom I knew well. Dr. Mishra had come to America to help with the Institute when we were in Glenview, Illinois. He was a good teacher and an energetic coordinator of events. He had met Swamiji years earlier and was promised by him that he would go to America one day.

Mishra also had an impatient desire to meet Swamiji's master. So Swamiji said, "Okay, I'll ask him." Shortly he told Mishra, "You're going to meet my master."

While unknown in the West, this master yogi was unique in the annals of yoga and preferred to live a hidden life and benefit the world by his obscurity. He didn't need acclaim.

Of course Mishra, like everyone else, wanted to know when he would meet the Master, and typically with Swamiji one never got "when" out of him. He loved to catch one off guard. Swamiji was often very spontaneous, jumping up saying, "Let's go!" He never said where or when one was going to return. Why spoil it? Who needs set plans to have fun or be together? So Swamiji and Mishra ventured out for a few days, living leisurely on the banks of the Ganges River, meditating, enjoying nature, and chatting about life.

Late one night as they lay sleeping, Mishra heard a sound outside the tent so he got up and looked. As he peered out, he saw what looked like a vagabond rummaging about the supplies. Mishra yelled forcefully, "Get out of here! Beat it!" and picked up a rock to chase the intruder away. Mishra meant business. The tall, old trespasser turned and sauntered off toward the woods.

The new protector of the camp came back into the tent quite pleased with himself. That morning over breakfast, he confidently announced to Swamiji, "There was an old rag picker out here last night trying to steal our supplies, but I got rid of him."

"Oh really," Swamiji offhandedly remarked as he refilled his teacup, "that was my Master."

How do you prepare yourself so you don't miss those special chances? How do you prepare yourself so that when chances show up, you really know how to pick up the ball and run? That's where your practice comes in. The medieval scholar, Thomas Aquinas, once asserted, "Only the pure of heart can perceive reality and thus enjoy it."

There needs to be a certain purity in your mind and heart otherwise you probably won't see what's in front of you. Purity has nothing to do with sexuality. Purity means striving to be very honest with yourself, recognizing where you are, taking responsibility for what you do, and being accountable for your life. On that basis, the mind and heart perceive because you are prepared. Why? Because selfishness is missing, greed is eschewed, and there is no hidden agenda for domination and egotistical self-interest. Thus the encounter with life is wholesome and pure.

Your practice is helping you recognize how to become clearer about life. You do not want to babysit your worries, allow your hesitations permanent residence, or castigate yourself for your history, which can especially get in the way. You don't want to make yourself colorblind, seeing life only with one or two colors. Instead, why not become like the sun? Strange, without the sun's light there is no awareness of color. Yet the illumination itself remains diaphanous, unseen, while illuminating the visual beauty that hides in the shade—shining without interference or distortion.

Your person is like a sun. It's meant to illuminate all that's there as it truly exists. You are meant, not to own, but to appreciate the rainbow of life in all its purity. Following the sun is not meant to be arduous. If the latter, your approach is off. Your aim in life is something that should arise right out of your nature and that means that you have to cultivate the aspiration for a while because your habits aren't used to it—not because it's foreign to you, but because you have a lot of "stuff" that gets in the way yet. Once, in graduate school, one of my teachers spoke volumes: "Lead the student to knowledge, then get out of the way."

May I venture to insist, without being presumptuous nor superstitious, that the sages are involved in all the ruckus of our lives. My confidence in stating this proposition comes from years of observing one of their progenies at work. This is where the mystery starts. In our tradition the masterful ones take a serious interest in all the students. More, I believe, than we can comprehend. They are, in their inimitable way, influencing the order of events so that the opportunities that are meant to enter our lives actually take place. As they discern in one the growth patterns starting to mature, and they see the proclivities that are capturing one's fancy, they think, "What can we put in the path that he can't possibly miss?" They set things up so that the student can utilize his growth in awareness. Then the student walks right by. They must think, "Agh! He did it again." Without self-training we can't illuminate the rainbow—hardly any colors, definitely less fun.

So we are a challenge to the great ones much more than they are a challenge to us. They want us to thrive, they look at our aspirations. They want us to get to the freedom where they are. They won't give up on us. How can we help them come to completion?

I once asked Swami Rama, "After I get all the answers to my questions, is there more?"

He cocked his head and said to me: "My God! When you get to that level, you can have conversations with the Sages."

I replied, "I like that, Swamiji, do they still enjoy a cup of chai?" He did not say no. Someday I'll find out.

George Washington and the Himalayan Tradition

I came across an astonishing story that should have been told to me as a boy, but it never was. An American Indian Chief looked scornfully at the soldiers on the field before him. How foolish it was to fight as they did, forming their perfect battle lines out in the open, standing shoulder to shoulder in their bright red uniforms. The British soldiers trained for European warfare did not break rank even when braves fired at them from under the safe cover of the forest. The slaughter at the Monongahela River continued for two hours. By then one thousand of the fourteen hundred British troops were killed or wounded and only thirty of the French and Indian warriors firing at them were injured. Not only were the soldiers foolish but their officers were just as bad. Riding on horseback, fully exposed above the men on the ground, they made perfect targets. One by one the chief's marksmen, the braves, shot the mounted British officers until only one remained. "Quick let your aim be certain and he dies!" the Chief commanded.

The warriors, a mix of Ottawa, Huron, and Chippewa tribes leveled their rifles at the last officer on horseback. Round after round was aimed at this one man. Twice the officer's horse was shot out from under him. Twice he grabbed a horse left idle when a fellow officer had been shot. Ten, twelve, fourteen rounds had been fired by the sharp shooters, still the officer remained unhurt. The native warriors stared in disbelief. They were excellent shots. Their rifles seldom missed their mark. The Chief suddenly realized that an almighty power must be shielding this man. "Stop firing!" he commanded his braves. "This one is under the special protection of the Great Spirit." A brave standing nearby added, "I had seventeen rounds of clear shots at him. I've never missed and nothing brought him to the ground. This man was not born to be killed by a bullet."

As the firing slowed, the man, the Lieutenant Colonel, gathered the remaining troops and led them to safety. That evening as the last of the wounded were being cared for, he noticed an odd tear in his coat. It was a bullet hole. He rolled up his sleeve and looked at his arm underneath that hole. There was nothing. There was no mark on his skin. Amazed, he took off his coat and found three more in his back. The bullets had passed through the coat but had stopped before they had reached his body. The battle in Monongahela, part of the French and Indian War, was fought in 1755 near Fort Duquesne which is now the city of Pittsburgh.

Fifteen years later, in 1770, that Lieutenant Colonel returned to the same Pennsylvania woods. Word went out. The respected Indian Chief, having heard that he was in the area, traveled a long way to meet him. He sat down. They both looked face to face at each other over a counsel of fire. And then the Chief spoke directly to him:

"I am a chief and a ruler over many tribes. My influence extends to the waters of the Great Lakes and to the far Blue Mountains of Virginia. I have traveled along a weary path that I might see this young warrior of that great battle. It was on that day when the white man's blood mixed with the streams of our forests that I first beheld you. I called to my young men and said, mark you that tall and daring warrior. He is not of the Redcoat tribe. He hath an Indian's wisdom and his warriors fight as we do. Himself alone exposed. Quick, let your aim be certain and he dies. Our rifles were leveled which but for you knew not how to miss and it was all in vain. A power mightier, far more than we, shielded you. Seeing you were under the special guardianship of the Great Spirit we immediately ceased to fire at you. I am old now and shall be gathered soon to the great counsel fire of my fathers in the land of the shades. But before I go there is something that bids me to speak in the voice of prophecy to you. Listen my son, the Great Spirit protects this man and guides his destiny. He will become the chief of nations and people yet unborn will hail him as the founder of a mighty empire. I have come to pay homage to the man who is the particular favor of heaven and who can never die in battle."

His name was George Washington. Later on when he was at Valley Forge, and everything looked utterly over, a visitor stepped into his tent. He was at first not admitted by the Lieutenant outside because Washington didn't want to be disturbed, but Washington said, "Oh, let him in." And the man told him and reconfirmed everything here and told him much more. And when he left the tent he just vanished and no one knew what happened to him. So something special was happening in Washington's life. He was picked. He was selected. He was protected.

Now, you and I are entering a new year. We don't know what is held for us. We tend to be optimistic. We make our resolutions, our promises to ourselves, and many of them will be fulfilled and maybe some not. But there's also something about you that I'd like to remind you. You are also bulletproof. Not in body but in spirit. Your heart is impregnable. But you may not know that. You may not have anybody around to tell you like this Indian Chief told Washington. But you are all on a path. And because you are, that means you have been singled out.

So we're on a path, our hearts are bulletproof. Nothing can blemish them. Nothing can hurt them. Nothing can dent them. Oh, our bodies may get bounced around a little bit, but not our hearts. You, too, have a special role in life. You are not just an ordinary person. You've been selected. You didn't come on to this tradition. The tradition chose you. Washington did not know that was going to happen to him. He was picked. They selected him and they reminded him and we saw what happened. The recognition within yourself that you have this destiny needs to be occasionally brushed off and looked at so we don't forget it. Because you may have your own Valley Forges. There will be times when you say how could this be happening to me? You feel so abandoned at times. Things just turn against you through no fault of your own. Those are the moments to remember that you are special. Success is an inside job. Outer success can go, but not inner success. It stays. And you are on the path to success. You are on a path to self-discovery, which is the highest calling. You rub shoulders with the ordinary folk of the local area. They don't even know it but it doesn't matter. So you share that life as you should. Swami Rama's master once told him, "The purpose of life is not to become Divine. The purpose of life is to become human, and that's when you will discover your Divineness." So in our tradition, there is nothing, there is not a sliver of your humanness that we leave out. There is nothing to be ashamed of, there is nothing to apologize for. It's a full endorsement and beyond. And we just need to remind ourselves of that.

Interesting isn't it, how we have to live through time? You and I are in a zone, as it were. We have to move through it day after day after day. Yet there's something in you that can get above that time slot, that doesn't have to be wearied by wandering through it. That's your spirit. That's that bulletproof heart you have. And it behooves you to get in touch with it occasionally to remind yourself that you're more than your history, however glorious it may be. So never let anything in the past somehow make you feel that you're disqualified now from the future in any way. You're not. There are many stories of saints and champions who had disastrous pasts and they came out of it. We are sometimes thrown into situations, if we could have chosen, we think, "Oh boy, I don't want," but actually we did choose them. We don't always like to admit that. "Oh, how could I have made that." You did. Now let's make the best of it. You may not be perfect but you are perfectible. And that capacity is never lost, never, however you may have abused it in the past. Swami Rama used to love to remind people, "You have everything you need. You are an unfinished champion but you have everything you need." He one day said to a couple of us, "You don't need any other teacher. I've given you all the tools. Now you've got to go play with them."

This tradition in a sense goes beyond Yoga. We start you out in Yoga, you have to admit duality. It's you and me, the world and us. Then you begin to sense that maybe there's a unity. It's hard to describe. It's nebulous maybe, not that clear. We sense a kind of comradeship maybe with nature, with our family, our friends, a sense of unity. And sometimes as we're growing we tend to disdain certain aspects of reality or creation. Well, there's another part to our tradition. It requires a little ripening. And in that ripening, there's a disclosure that we are where we are meant to be. Because we all think, "Oh, if only I was born last century or when we're flying around in rocket ships visiting other planets." No, you were born here because this is the best opportunity for you to fulfill your humanness. We don't always have perfect relatives. Yet we have them. So the challenge in your heart is to become shrewd. How to work this out; how to create as best you can the kind of world you'd like to live in. You have the power of imagination, the power of intelligence, your bodily powers. You can create things, you can make things, you can do and form and shape things that will benefit not only yourself but the rest of society. To become human then is not just an individual trip, because we share that same Divineness with everybody else. If I grow, everybody else grows in some way that touches me. In an invisible but real sense, you are touching the lives of everyone you meet in some way. Don't ever underestimate that. You don't always need an oral communication. A look, a touch, a smile, the simplest things are very powerful. And so while we may not make great prophesies about you like in Washington's time, none the less the tradition in every way is attempting to bring you to their level. They are inviting you, they are beckoning you, they are putting things into your life for you to make choices about.

Three times when Theresa and I were together we've almost lost our lives. The last one was a head on crash at 65 miles per hour. Untouched. When I ran across the street to see how the other car was, it was demolished too. The man came running down to meet me and we both stared at each other. "We should be killed," he said. I said, "Yes sir." But we weren't. There was a protection that stays with you in this tradition. They don't make things hard for you. That's not what our tradition is about. Other traditions may have that but we don't. We know life is enough of a challenge.

But they do demand something. They want you to love truth. Because that's what enlightened is. To know reality as it really is and not be afraid of it. Swamiji said the last obstacle to enlightenment is to become fearless. Fearless. How could I ever achieve something like that? You are being called then to a very special vocation, each one of you in your own way. You were meant to be enlightened. You were meant to walk this globe as the freest person you know. And by your very radiance, when you're at that level one day, people will just see it coming out of you. You can't hide it.

You all know that there have been moments and maybe long periods where you didn't think things were going to work out. You thought you were just going to go down. Of course you think nobody likes you then if you're going to have all those kind of troubles. When Swamiji was attempting to build his hospital, a certain group wanted him to endorse their efforts at state sovereignty and he said, "I'm sorry. All my efforts are going to the hospital." They paid him back by bombing his helicopter hoping he was in it but he wasn't. When he was Shankaracharya, he was forced to look at life in a way that he never had to because he was living in the mountains. As he looked with the purity of his eyes, he saw a lot of imbalances there and the thought, "What can I do here?" The truth of the situation called forth in him a response. He couldn't walk away from it. He's not built that way. And so he insisted that all the women be taught all the mantras not just the men. Well some of the pundits didn't like that so they put ground glass in his food. Then he noticed that the temples, "How come the untouchables, the poorest of the poor are not allowed in there?" So the pundits once again tried to justify their actions and Swami said, "No" and he decreed all the temples are open. "Are they not God's children?" So they thanked him again by putting ground glass in his food. Four times. But he was bulletproof. When you fight for the truth and you love it, you become bulletproof in our tradition.

Don't forget that. Never be afraid. They are standing with you. They are your shield. Love the truth. That's not intellectual. It involves your whole person.

Each of you have the enormous gift within yourself to make choices. You are the freest of all beings in the hierarchy of nature. There is nobody beyond you. Your practices help you to make those choices clearer and clearer. You will resonate with the choice when it's right. You will just know even if everybody says something else. That's your path of self-discovery. It's in the making of the choices and fulfilling them. You can't think your way into self-realization. You have to do it. It's an injunctive reality. It must be performed. Not every ladder leads to the same roof top. Not every path goes the same direction. Some just spin around and around. So that's why in our tradition we want you to keep your discernment. Swamiji used to yell at people saying, "Never take anything I say on faith. Test it for yourself. Make it your own. Don't borrow it from me. Earn it by testing it out." That's what our path is all about. Because then nobody can take it from you. You've tested it. You've proved it. That's the strongest truth there is. It soon becomes self-evident to you. First you have your doubts, of course! So never lose that ability to carefully look at things. Turn them around. Then act.

So go inside, meditate and find that bulletproof heart we have that can never be defeated, never get hard.

Tradition, Philosophy, and God

Q: How does one trust the tradition when no one is at the "helm?"

A: Educated people would have no trouble honoring two Greeks, Plato and Aristotle, for their contribution to Western perennial philosophy. One day Aristotle was asked by some students why he was so critical of his former teacher of twenty years. He replied: "I love Plato, but I love truth more." Anything less would be a dishonor to your teachers. These are my sentiments exactly.

Along those lines, students need to disabuse themselves of genuflecting to any tradition. We listen, read, learn, and challenge the perennial questions about life and reality that our forebearers have cast. Whether its Plato or Shankara, or any tradition, for that matter, we enter into a dialogue, as it were, with their point of view.

Reading their works is not an exegesis on artifacts from antiquity. On the contrary, we respect these authors as if they were speaking to us here and now and thus engage their ideas by probing their reasoning and assumptions, analyzing and evaluating their conclusions, and always keeping things in the context of real life. We stay practical and down to earth with room for plausibilities. Otherwise we are not doing philosophy.

To your question: No one is at the "helm." Trust is not in allegiance to a tradition, but in one's hard-earned convictions. It's comparable to

Joseph Campbell's reply to the priest who asked him if he had faith: "No, Father, I don't need faith, I have experience."

Survey all you can, but eventually, you have to compose your own philosophy of life and defend it.

Q: In yoga we often speak of the middle path. How do you understand that?

A: No extremes, balance. Did you know that is found as an essential doctrine in the West? It just happened to a particular guy I like to read about, Aristotle. He wrote what I consider a masterpiece, *Nicomachean Ethics.* He wrote this long treatise on moral activity. For Aristotle the purpose of morality is not to be ethical. The purpose of morality is to make you happy. Just think for a moment, to be ethical in order to be happy, not to be right but in order to be happy. It doesn't mean you can't be right. But for him the purpose of ethical activity is to become happy.

Q: Vedanta's approach, apparently, is that one has to choose which one wants to reside in or pursue—the real or unreal. But who chooses, the self or non-self?

A: Over the years of reading articles and the Vedantic writings, gradually my curious fascination settled down and spontaneous questions of a commonsense variety arose. I saw that the logic in Vendantic writings resembled the way religionists proclaim their holy truth. More and more I realized that once you accept Vedanta's basic principles, the rest of what they say is plausible. Then there is the adulation, the nationalistic support, rallying around the ancient writings and myths which is done in any country. My amateur fascination waned as I saw through its failure to deal with the wonder, variety, and complexity of reality. I just got tired of it in view of the soundness of life and the richness of other traditions that honored the undeniable experiences of human intelligence. For me, Vedanta is a lingering charade turning into its own Maya, a refuge for beginning, uncritical students who are afraid to deal with reality in a commonsense manner and attracted to some Eastern esoteric doctrine that somehow makes them feel superior, along with placating an authority to make up their minds for them. It is so naive, self-deprecating, illogical. It promises that its airy abstractions can take the place of concrete, reliable, everyday reality. I challenge anyone to live daily from a Vedantic perspective and survive. Life is so precious to me that I have no patience with this evasion of human existence. Once you abandon common sense, watch out, here come the rationalizations!

Q: This whole issue of dualism and non-dualism has always been fascinating and perplexing. When one applies them to life and one's spiritual journey, it gets fuzzy.

A: You can be cognitively united to a reality and you know it since you are the experiencer. As you say, "Duality is reality" and yet simultaneously I can be united to that, which means Unity is reality too. Can we describe this paradox as "monistic dualism?"

There is the knower and that other which is to be known—dualism. When the knower knows the other, there is a unity—monism. The unity does not obliterate the other in any way.

Q: Does power give one freedom or is it through freedom that one gains power?

A: First, it seems that once we get past the impulse to get in contact with reality as a child would, there is no freedom without knowledge. In this way the more I know, the freer I can be. It seems provable in acquiring artistic and commercial skills. Yet the proclivity to know is a power, the exercise of our cognitive power, just as our senses are powers of sensation. Power and freedom seem to go together. Knowledge gives me increased power and thus more freedom to apply that knowledge which in turn amplifies my power.

Q: Is our universe real?

A: This is the classic Cartesian question. It essentially asks, how do we know that what we see around us is the real deal, and not some grand illusion perpetuated by an unseen force. More recently, the question has been reframed as the Simulation Argument. We're the products of an elaborate simulation. A deeper question to ask, therefore, is whether the civilization running the simulation is also in a simulation, a kind of supercomputer regression. This amusing stance is less a conundrum than a new version of "let's pretend." Children and politicians play that game all the time. Besides, for all you true believers in simulation-reality, just empty your pockets and sign over to me all your worldly possessions right now, and no one gets hurt. After all, what do you care, your possessions are just an illusion. For your information, my hobby is collecting illusions for a rainy day.

Matter and Nature

Q: Why engage in and explore matter?

A: Ponder for a moment: where would you be with all your powers raring to go and no objects around? It's like trying to see in a completely dark room. Most people think that freedom is a neutral state ready to go in any direction. That's not freedom—that's just being ready to experience freedom. For me, that's only the necessary beginning, meaning you have to have the potential. But unless you use it you don't even know that you have a power. Besides activating the power of freedom to apprehend life about you, you can extend your power by doing something, like inventing or planning and putting that plan into action. In the experience of being active in relationship with matter, then you discover the rest of your potential. You are a knower and a doer. I have the freedom to know something and now I can expand my freedom by doing something with what I know. Unless I realize those two dimensions of freedom, I am not actually free, just in potency to freedom. It's kind of strangely ironic for me that union is necessary. Almost like on the job training. In addition, we can affect freedom by deliberately self-training our bodily and mental powers, increasing the harmony with our nature as you say, and obviously the congruency with reality improves.

Q: How does one learn to "see things as they really are" and how does one know when one is "seeing things as they really are?"

A: In response to the first part, simply set up your attitude and determine that's what you want. And keep facing life as honestly as you can.

As for the second part, the gross level is easy: it's snowing outside; I see her dancing; the pea soup could be improved. Experience and familiarity with the subject matter enables a certain maturity in discerning what's going on, from the simple to the complex. It includes knowing in some situations that you can only grasp so much, given the facts and time.

The hard part now, is to always trust your common sense, regardless of authorities, traditions, preferences, rules, taboos, material benefits, and friendship, until and unless the facts would indicate revisions. If you start down this road less traveled in earnest, Nature will test you.

Q: The duality in my thinking comes into play when I try to decide which is my nature: the temporal or the eternal?

A: Your human nature is an embodied being, a unified composition of spirit and matter, in which the spirit animates the now living matter. The body is not a holster for the spirit but is human matter formed by the living spirit. When the spirit decides to manifest into time and space, it asserts itself as animated corporeal matter, not two laminated parts but a unified being. At the same time, to put it another way, all of the body is formed by the spirit but not all of the spirit informs the body. Rationality occurs in its body as a mode of consciousness, not the whole story. The totem of consciousness is vastly more than rationality. Your choice eventually is to stay embodied or reside as a spirit. Yet there is a fulfillment or culmination that allows one to enjoy existence exercising full powers of the spirit while in embodied form. The yoga tradition refers to this existence as a *jivamukta*. In other words, you enjoy fully your composite nature to the hilt. You flourish as a fully realized, enlightened embodied being. Or depart the body and take up residence as a pure spirit.

Q: And if I have many human lifetimes, aren't they made possible only because they are supported by the eternal life I have?

A: Yes. We choose the human scene to experience the knowledge, joys, and deficits that are found within the limits and finiteness and to be as creative as possible in the era in which we live.

Q: If my true nature is eternal, how do I find satisfaction in a temporal life and truly value it?

A: Eternality is fine, but we wanted to discover the uniqueness of finiteness. We have to learn to take it for what it's worth and appreciate it on its terms. Self-induced trouble comes when we expect more or less than the experience is meant to allow. How often we try to hurry things up in situations, like driving in crowed traffic; attempting to rush seedlings to maturity by shouting at the ground; chastising others in our mind for not acting according to our rules; etc. Duality only appears to be such. As you calmly review your intentional actions, pause and consider that the body is the expression of the spirit in its manifested form, a limitation that works through time and space but nevertheless remains an intentional expression of the spirit as it conducts itself on this planet.

Q: Yoga science talks about my current inability to remember my eternal self—my amnesia. Why would anyone leave a life of enlightenment for one of ignorance?

A: Enlightenment is your permanent nature. You have entered into an embodied form that, as it were, hides that status. You have forgotten that optimal state of being. Nevertheless, you did this not to punish yourself or just to makes things harder, but to have the full range of finite experiences along with your infinitude.

Q: Does the yogic concept of amnesia mean my goal is to become eternal and I can only "earn" that status while learning lessons in a human, temporal world?

A: Consider that it's not a matter of earning anything but simply returning to the fulfillment of your nature. As one grows in the development of virtue, including meditation and contemplation as virtues, the amnesia fades away and is replaced by expanding self-awareness. The intelligent living and union with reality brings the ever-dawning surprises of knowledge and love. This exploration of our self as a knower, lover, and doer, gradually removes the forgetfulness. As we understand the world for what it is, we can't help but become freer and more confident about ourselves. More than overcoming ignorance, it's a matter of making the right choices—without savvy, no freedom.

Q: What I think I need to remember is that I am eternal no matter which part of the duality I am occupying, a life in or a life out of a human body.

A: Could not say it better. It takes a long time to realize that temporality belongs to eternality. We are walking as eternal beings in the shoes of temporality.

Q: Is a rational way to live to simply watch the mystery unfold? Observe life in all its manifestations and see what I learn?

A: Rationality is the best discernment of life for embodied beings, since only then can consciousness work with the senses in appreciation of Nature and the cultural world. Without materiality, there is no rational appreciation of life, including oneself. Reason is our preferred mode to engage in material reality while in embodied form. It can investigate the mystery of existence, but at the same time know that it's a never-ending adventure, hence the mystery of it all. Always more truth, more good to enjoy, more creativity . . . breathless! So not just watching the world—the fine contemplative option—but also getting involved in exploring and creating your part in the dazzlement of culture. Our fulfillment is not just in knowing, but in flourishing holistically in body, mind, and spirit.

Q: I need to relax during the learning process, realizing it's only a phase of my eternal life, when I conceive of my life as many, many lifetimes. I will not try to rationally possess the meaning of life but rather admire its mystery.

A: In closing, why not combine possession and admiration: let your rational discernment be the unrestrictive impetus to grow into more truth of the meaning of life and equally draw upon its bountiful mystery for inspiration. After all, our nature is the mystery that we hound through the hills and valleys.

Q: My interest presently is regarding subjective experiences of self-realization, enlightenment, etc.—ones which St. John of the Cross said could only be captured in poems.

A: He did not have a scientific background nor was he interested in attempting to explain the phenomenon from a natural viewpoint. He was biased by his religious perspective. And every so-called mystic I have read always puts their experience into the framework of their religious beliefs. It's to be expected. It's always their deity that permits it. At the same time, their writings are censored, redacted, by the high command.

Q: If I was to have a mystical experience, everyone would question the validity of it.

A: You would be able to objectify it by the consequences in your person. These experiences change you biologically and psychologically. You are different now. And that's detectable. The problem is: what exactly is meant by mystical experience? For me, if someone can transcend the normal range of their intellectual and sensory powers and show comparable control over matter as Swami Rama did, that is mystical. A peak experience can be real and expand consciousness. While it may not approach the heights of what Swami Rama performed, it would yet qualify as a mystical experience. You are an amazing being of infinite wisdom that can enjoy immortality, invincibility, omniscience, omni-potentiality, absolute freedom, and creativity. What more do you want?

Q: Depending on one's previous indoctrination, could one justify a faith in a particular god, holistic lifestyle, etc.?

A: One of the purposes of rational scrutinizing is to pierce indoctrina-tion. One wants to get at the truth and not submit to the appealing propaganda. The whole point of growing adult is to realize that it's time to question a lot of what culture and society takes for granted. Either criticize or surrender your dignity to the highest bidder. Credit, as you say, may be allegedly given in different directions, until we carefully examine, analyze, compare, and contrast the assertions to find the evidence that justifies one's position. It is the self-evidential experience of our rationality that keeps us sane. If we forfeit our wits, then we are doomed. So we challenge so-called mystical explanations rather than taking them at face value.

Q: I may receive testimony from others, hypothesize on my own, and reflect on myths, fables, and poems which support my theory, but have no absolute proof.

A: When you learn a new truth, you expand your mind. When you demonstrate more control over your emotions, breathing, exercise, you expand your mind. The certitude comes right out of the self-action. You don't need authority figures to confirm anything. When your intuition, or skills in art, crafts, or counseling grow, you are expanding you mind. You are the culprit alone in this expansion. It's your living business to know, love, and be certain both subjectivity and objectively. Growth means expansion.

Q: Each one could verify some results and effects, but none can verify the source.

A: A psychosomatic experience is just that: it's in you. Most people talk themselves into God's visitation to them. The source of your awareness is you; it's self-evident. Your receptivity to life, your choices, your awareness, is fully within your competence, no matter how faulty. You keep yourself alive because you are the source that decides how to take care of yourself. You think the thoughts you want. It is impossible to deny these and a host more obvious truths and stay sane. I propose that there are stages of maturity in self-realization. It's a process that is going on right now. We grow into it, as it were, showing different competencies as we evolve or mature. That's just the way our nature operates even at the most mundane, pedestrian efforts at learning how to do something.

Q: Swami Rama was an enlightened one. Did his enlightenment come to fruition because of Divine Mother's grace or did he actualize his potentiality?

A: He actualized his potentiality.

Q: How does one separate emotional coloration from a true psychosomatic transformation?

A: Depending on the maturity of the individual, the emotions can be further integrated with reason, or the event can be staggering to the current emotional status of the individual and thus cause emotional imbalance, such as swooning, hallucinatory images, insistence that God visited them, etc.

Q: I have read many definitions of human nature, which is right?

A: I would start first with Nature. Let's examine what we discern about a rose, or pine tree, or spider web. Admit the objectivity of things that are easily discerned by the senses—aspects, properties, and features that regularly appear in an entity, along with the customary changes that occur with the seasons. Then come to a human being and proceed along similar lines—start with the easily identifiable aspects, characteristics that we have in common, and proceed from the broad to the subtler. This is basically a dialectical procedure where we compare and contrast, and test our ideas against the reality at hand. A biological probing is nonthreatening and fairly objective. I think we can get enough insight and facts to agree upon to have at least a general acceptance of a nature.

Implications, inferences, and connections that can be verified are not theory but facts. If I am the only one that can explain the phenomena, then it remains questionable, more like allegations. Implications can be facts or lead to new facts. For example, I take your blood pressure (fact) then you alter your breathing (fact) and now ensues a different reading of your blood pressure (fact). I conclude that this factual alteration implies that high blood pressure can be reduced to a healthy condition, which would be a new verifiable fact. Moreover, one can objectively experience (fact) the change. What Swami Rama did at Menninger can be considered both mystical experiences and objective facts, even though they were beyond the normal, ordinary, everyday competency of people. He showed new competencies that could be sufficiently proved as facts. The self-control and the effects were verifiable, repeatable, and involved definite biological alterations that could be ascertained: hence, a host of facts. At the same time, of course, he himself was factually aware of everything going on in his body-mind complex.

Q: Does one absolutely have to light one's own lamp or is grace available for assisting one?

A: The master's touch is not a depositing of something that wasn't there before. The touch, as it were, removes the blockage so that the nature matures. Now the rising and the higher can join because they are within you already. The student must still decide to use the inherent power, freed as it is now from being stuck. He has to light it himself. The forces within and above are all one complex. They exist within oneself entirely. The metaphors of rising within and descending from above are a way of showing what happens when the blockage is dissolved, a more complete integration occurs (fact).

The Quest Beyond

Heart about to fly
Long journey across the lands
Hanuman bears you.

You search in your mind
Alone sitting in silence
Divine Mother smiles.

In the crevices
Of life hides an old master
Full of surprises.

Wandering about
I will discover myself
Yoga beckons me.

My mind and my heart
Will always be there for me
I am immortal.

About the Author

Swami Jaidev Bharati (Justin O'Brien, PhD, 1932–2021) was a renaissance man: philosopher, theologian, yoga practitioner, teacher, writer, wellness expert, consultant in lifestyle management, and long-time explorer in human consciousness. In 1999 he took vows of renunciation on the banks of the Ganges River in India, becoming Swami Jaidev Bharati, "God's Victory."

Known internationally for his programs in spiritual development, wellness, aging, and leadership, his insights translate across East and West, self-care skills and scholarship, human development and organizational well-being, with an emphasis on personal spiritual growth.

Chief consultant and designer for world conferences on the future of humanity, Swami Jaidev was a gifted speaker and presenter. A well-known scholar, he was a former Professor of Theology at Loyola University Chicago; lecturer at the New School for Social Research in New York City; and Senior Research Fellow in Holistic Medicine at the University of London. He was Director of Education at the Marylebone Health Centre in England, as well as faculty and Director of Education at the Himalayan International Institute of Yoga Science and Philosophy. He was a founder and preceptor of the Institute of the Himalayan Tradition in Saint Paul, MN.

A former Catholic monk and a recognized scholar of Eastern philosophy and psychology, O'Brien studied theology under the acclaimed theologians Edward Schillebeeckx, Piet Schoonenberg, and Bernard Cooke. He held a doctoral degree in the philosophy of consciousness and a doctorandus degree in theology from Nijmegen University, The Netherlands; two master's degrees in philosophy and religious studies from Marquette University and St. Albert's College in Oakland, California; and two undergraduate degrees in the classics and philosophy from St. Albert's College and the University of Notre Dame. He was a direct disciple of the yoga saint, Sri Swami Rama of the Himalayas, having lived and studied with him for 24 years. A certified Ericksonian hypnotherapist from the American Hypnosis Training Academy, O'Brien was also certified in Neurolinguistic Programming.

His books include: *Toward a Theory of Religious Consciousness in its Reliance Upon Western Man's Understanding of Nature Ultimacy and Teleology; Superconscious Meditation; Walking with a Himalayan Master: An American's Odyssey; A Meeting of Mystic Paths: Christianity and Yoga; The Wellness Tree: The Dynamic Six-Step Program for Creating Optimal Wellness; Running and Breathing;* and *Mirrors for Men.* He was also a contributing author to *Western Spirituality; The Spiral Path; Spirituality for the Religious Educator;* and *Meditation in Christianity.* Six of his books have won national awards.

www.ingramcontent.com/pod-product-compliance
Lightning Source LLC
Chambersburg PA
CBHW020435130626
46549CB00001B/156